JULIAN BAF

Contemporary Critical Perspectives
Series Editors: Jeannette Baxter, Sebastian Groes and Sean Matthews
Consultant Editors: Dominic Head and Peter Childs

Guides in the *Contemporary Critical Perspectives* series provide companions to reading and studying major contemporary authors. Each guide includes new critical essays combining textual readings, cultural analysis and discussion of key critical and theoretical issues in a clear, accessible style. They also include a preface by a major contemporary writer, a new interview with the author, discussion of film and TV adaptation and guidance on further reading.

Titles in the series include:

J.G. Ballard **Edited by Jeannette Baxter**
Ian McEwan **Edited by Sebastian Groes**
Kazuo Ishiguro **Edited by Sebastian Groes and Sean Matthews**

JULIAN BARNES

Contemporary Critical Perspectives

Edited by
Sebastian Groes and Peter Childs

continuum

Continuum International Publishing Group
The Tower Building   80 Maiden Lane
11 York Road   Suite 704
London SE1 7NX   New York, NY 10038

www.continuumbooks.com

© Sebastian Groes, Peter Childs and contributors 2011

All rights reserved. No part of this publication may be reproduced or transmitted in any form or by any means, electronic or mechanical, including photocopying, recording, or any information storage or retrieval system, without prior permission in writing from the publishers.

British Library Cataloguing-in-Publication Data
A catalogue record for this book is available from the British Library.

ISBN: 978-1-4411-3008-2 (hardback)
      978-1-4411-5222-0 (paperback)

Library of Congress Cataloging-in-Publication Data
A catalog record for this book is available from the Library of Congress.

Typeset by Newgen Imaging Systems Pvt Ltd, Chennai, India
Printed and bound in India

Contents

Series Editors' Preface vii

Acknowledgements viii

Contributors ix

Julian Barnes: Biographical Information xi

INTRODUCTION **Julian Barnes and the Wisdom of Uncertainty** 1
*Sebastian Groes (Roehampton University) and
Peter Childs (University of Gloucestershire)*

CHAPTER ONE **The *Flâneur* and the Freeholder: Paris and
London in Julian Barnes's *Metroland*** 11
Matthew Taunton (Queen Mary, University of London)

CHAPTER TWO **Inventing a Way to the Truth: Life and Fiction in
Julian Barnes's *Flaubert's Parrot*** 24
Ryan Roberts (Lincoln Land Community College)

CHAPTER THREE **'A preference for things Gallic': Julian Barnes
and the French Connection** 37
Vanessa Guignery (École Normale Supérieure, Lyon)

CHAPTER FOUR **'An Ordinary Piece of Magic': Religion in
the Work of Julian Barnes** 51
Andrew Tate (Lancaster University)

CHAPTER FIVE **Crossing the Channel: Europe and the Three Uses
of France in Julian Barnes's *Talking It Over*** 69
Merritt Moseley (University of North Carolina Asheville)

CHAPTER SIX **The Story of Julian Barnes's *The Porcupine*:
an Epistolary ½ Chapter** 81
Dimitrina Kondeva (Obsidian Press, Bulgaria)

CHAPTER SEVEN **Julian Barnes's *England, England* and Englishness** 92
Richard Bradford (University of Ulster)

CHAPTER EIGHT **Matters of Life and Death: The Short Stories of
Julian Barnes** 103
Peter Childs (University of Gloucestershire)

CHAPTER NINE	'All Letters Quoted Are Authentic': The Past After Postmodern Fabulation in Julian Barnes's *Arthur & George* *Christine Berberich (University of Portsmouth)*	117
AFTERWORD	**Seeing and Knowing with the Eyes of Faith** *Andrew Lycett (Biographer and Critic)*	129
References		134
Index		161

Series Editors' Preface

The readership for contemporary fiction has never been greater. The explosion of reading groups and literary blogs, of university courses and school curricula, and even the apparent rude health of the literary marketplace, indicate an ever-growing appetite for new work, for writing which responds to the complex, changing and challenging times in which we live. At the same time, readers seem ever more eager to engage in conversations about their reading, to devour the review pages, to pack the sessions at literary festivals and author events. Reading is an increasingly social activity, as we seek to share and refine our experience of the book, to clarify and extend our understanding.

It is this tremendous enthusiasm for contemporary fiction to which the *Contemporary Critical Perspectives* series responds. Our ambition is to offer readers of current fiction a comprehensive critical account of each author's work, presenting original, specially commissioned analyses of all aspects of their career, from a variety of different angles and approaches, as well as directions towards further reading and research. Our brief to the contributors is to be scholarly, to draw on the latest thinking about narrative, or philosophy, or psychology, indeed whatever seemed to them most significant in drawing out the meanings and force of the texts in question, but also to focus closely on the words on the page, the stories and scenarios and forms which all of us meet first when we open a book. We insisted that these essays be accessible to that mythical beast the Common Reader, who might just as readily be spotted at the Lowdham Book Festival as in a college seminar. In this way, we hope to have presented critical assessments of our writers in such a way as to contribute something to both of those environments, and also to have done something to bring together the most important qualities of each of them.

Jeannette Baxter, Sebastian Groes and Sean Matthews

Acknowledgements

The editors and publishers would like to thank Julian Barnes for his generous support of this book, and, in particular, for his permission to let Dimitrina Kondeva use his letters and other documents for her chapter on *The Porcupine*.

This collection derives partly from the conference 'Julian Barnes and the European Tradition', which was held at Liverpool Hope University in June 2008. We would like to thank Liverpool Hope University for their generous support of the conference and the *Contemporary Critical Perspectives* series.

Special thanks are due to Andrew Lycett for kindly writing his illuminating Afterword to this volume. We are also very grateful to Dimitrina Kondeva for her extraordinary chapter on her role in the coming into being of *The Porcupine* in difficult circumstances.

The cartoon by Simon Pearsall is reproduced by kind permission of PRIVATE EYE magazine and Simon Pearsall, www.private-eye.co.uk.

We would also like to thank the series co-editors, Jeannette Baxter and Sean Matthews, and Continuum's Anna Fleming, David Avital and Colleen Coalter, for their ongoing support.

Andrew Tate is grateful to David Ashbridge for his invaluable thoughts on Barnes, and he thanks also Simon Jones, editor of *Third Way* magazine, for permission to draw on his review of *Arthur & George* from the September 2005 issue.

Sebastian Groes would like to thank his wife, José Lapré, for her support, and Peter would like to thank Stella for being there along the journey.

SG / PC
London/Cheltenham September 2010

Contributors

Christine Berberich is Senior Lecturer in English Literature at the University of Portsmouth. Her research interest focuses on Englishness and national identity. She has published on writers including Kazuo Ishiguro, Evelyn Waugh, Anthony Powell, George Orwell, and W.G. Sebald, and the monograph *The Image of the English Gentleman in 20th-Century Literature: Englishness and Nostalgia* (Ashgate, 2007).

Richard Bradford is Research Professor of English at the University of Ulster. He has published 20 books on a variety of topics including Milton, 18th Century Criticism, Russian Formalism, the History of English Metre and the Contemporary British Novel. Recently, he has concentrated on Literary Biography with his lives of Kingsley Amis, Philip Larkin and Alan Sillitoe receiving excellent reviews. His biography of Martin Amis will appear in 2011.

Peter Childs is Professor of modern English literature at the University of Gloucestershire and has published widely on twentieth-century and contemporary literature. His books include *The Twentieth Century in Poetry* (Routledge, 1999); *Contemporary Novelists: British Fiction Since 1970* (Palgrave, 2004); and *The Fiction of Ian McEwan* (Palgrave, 2005). He is contributing the chapter on 'The Contemporary Historical Novel' to the forthcoming *Cambridge History of the Novel*.

Vanessa Guignery is Professor of Contemporary English Literature and Postcolonial Literature at the École Normale Supérieure in Lyon (France). She is the author of several books and essays on the work of Julian Barnes, including *The Fiction of Julian Barnes* (Macmillan, 2006), and *Conversations with Julian Barnes* (Mississippi Press, 2009), co-edited with Ryan Roberts. *She has published* a monograph on B.S. Johnson (Sorbonne UP, 2009) as well as articles on Jeanette Winterson, David Lodge, Jonathan Coe, Alain de Botton, Michèle Roberts, Arundhati Roy and Anita Desai.

Dimitrina Kondeva is one of the two co-founders of *Obsidian Press*, established in 1992 in Sofia, Bulgaria. *The Porcupine* is the very first book of *Obsidian* which is the exclusive Bulgarian publisher of Julian Barnes, Robert Harris, John Lanchester, Pat Conroy, John Grisham, Khaled Hosseini, to mention just a few of over 120 contemporary authors on its list of publications. Dimitrina Kondeva has translated works by

Julian Barnes, H. E. Bates, Tracy Chevalier, John Updike and Nathaniel West. She has taught courses in Translation Editing and Book Publishing at Sofia University and New Bulgarian University.

Andrew Lycett is a biographer and critic. He has written the lives of several leading literary figures, including Ian Fleming, Rudyard Kipling, Dylan Thomas and Sir Arthur Conan Doyle. He is a Fellow of the Royal Society of Literature.

Merritt Moseley is Professor of Literature and NEH Distinguished Teaching Professor in the Humanities at the University of North Carolina Asheville. He is the author of books on Kingsley Amis, David Lodge, Julian Barnes and Michael Frayn and the editor of five volumes of the Dictionary of Literary Biography on British and Irish Novelists Since 1960 and Booker Prize Winners.

Ryan Roberts is a librarian at Lincoln Land Community College in Springfield, Illinois. He is co-editor with Vanessa Guignery of *Conversations with Julian Barnes* and editor of *Conversations with Ian McEwan*. In addition to maintaining Julian Barnes's official website (www.julianbarnes.com), he serves as webmaster for Ian McEwan, James Fenton, Hermione Lee, and the estate of Ian Hamilton. His most recent publication is *John Fuller & the Sycamore Press: A Bibliographic History* (Bodleian Library & Oak Knoll Press, 2010).

Andrew Tate is Senior Lecturer in English and Associate Director of the Ruskin Centre at Lancaster University. He is the author of *Douglas Coupland* (2007), *Contemporary Fiction and Christianity* (2008) and, with Arthur Bradley, co-author of *The New Atheist Novel* (2010).

Matthew Taunton is a Leverhulme Early Career Fellow in the Department of English at Queen Mary, University of London. He has research interests in English and French literature from the nineteenth century to the present, politics, and the cultural history of cities, media and film. He is author of *Fictions of the City: Class, Culture and Mass Housing in London and Paris* (Palgrave Macmillan, 2009) and numerous scholarly articles as well as journalism and book reviews. He is presently researching the response of British writers to the Russian Revolution while writing a short book on G. K. Chesterton's politics.

Julian Barnes: Biographical Information

1946	Born Julian Patrick Barnes on 19th January in Leicester England to French teachers Albert and Kaye Barnes.
1946–56	Lives in Acton, London.
1956–64	Lives in Northwood, London, and attends the City of London School
1964–68	Attends Magdalen College, Oxford University, where he studies modern languages. Teaches English for a summer at a French Catholic School in Rennes.
1969–72	Works as a lexicographer for the Oxford English Dictionary Supplement. Works on a to-date unpublished book entitled *A Literary Guide to Oxford*.
1972–74	Studies for the bar. Qualifies as a barrister, but never practises. From 1973 on, works as a freelance journalist and writes numerous book and restaurant reviews, and other pieces, many under pseudonyms.
1975	Publishes first short story in a book of ghost stories, 'A Self-Possessed Woman'.
1976–78	Works under Ian Hamilton as an editor for the *New Review* and publishes under the name Edward Pygge in the *New Review*'s 'Greek Street' column.
1977–81	Works as assistant literary editor under Martin Amis at the *New Statesman*. Serves as television critic for the *New Statesman*.
1979–82	Marries literary agent Pat Kavanagh in 1979 (d. 2008). Works as Deputy Literary Editor at *The Sunday Times*.
1980	Publishes *Metroland*, which wins Somerset Maugham award; publishes *Duffy* as Dan Kavanagh.
1981	Publishes *Fiddle City* as Dan Kavanagh.
1982	Publishes *Before She Met Me*; starts four-year stint as *Observer* television critic.
1983	Chosen by Book Marketing Council as one of the 'Best of Young British Novelists' under 40.

1984	Publishes *Flaubert's Parrot*, which is shortlisted for the Booker prize.
1985	Publishes *Putting the Boot in* as Dan Kavanagh. Geoffrey Faber memorial prize for *Flaubert's Parrot*.
1986	Publishes *Staring at the Sun*. Wins E M Forster award in USA and Prix Médicis in France for *Flaubert's Parrot*.
1987	Publishes *Going to the Dogs* as Dan Kavanagh. Wins Gutenberg Prize in France.
1988	Made Chevalier of the Order of Arts and Letters in France. Translates Volker Kriegel's book *The Truth about Dogs*.
1989	Publishes *A History of the World in 10½ Chapters*.
1990	London correspondent for *The New Yorker* for next five years.
1991	Publishes *Talking It Over*.
1992	Publishes *The Porcupine*. Wins Prix Femina in France for *Talking It Over*.
1993	Wins Shakespeare Prize in Hamburg.
1995	Publishes *Letters from London, 1990–95*. Made Officer of the Order of Arts and Letters in France. Teaches creative writing at Johns Hopkins in Baltimore, USA.
1996	Publishes *Cross Channel*. French-language film of *Talking It Over* appears with the title *Love, etc.*, Dir. Marion Vernoux.
1997	Film of *Metroland* appears, Dir. Philip Saville.
1998	Publishes *England, England*, which is shortlisted for Booker prize.
2000	Publishes *Love, etc.*
2002	Publishes *Something to Declare* and English translation on Alphone Daudet's *In the Land of Pain*.
2003	Publishes a collection of essays about cooking, *The Pedant in the Kitchen*.
2005	Publishes *Arthur & George*, which is shortlisted for Booker prize.
2008	Publishes *Nothing To Be Frightened Of*.
2010	David Edgar's adaptation of *Arthur & George* staged in Birmingham. Publication announced of Barnes's forthcoming book of short stories entitled *Pulse*.

INTRODUCTION

Julian Barnes and the Wisdom of Uncertainty

SEBASTIAN GROES AND PETER CHILDS

Julian Barnes is perhaps the most versatile and idiosyncratic author of an astoundingly talented generation of writers, and he is also intensely prolific and at home in many genres. Over the past three decades, Barnes has written ten novels, three collections of essays, numerous pieces of journalism and reviews, three collections of short stories, and a memoir. In the 1980s, Barnes also penned four intriguing detective novels, collected in *The Duffy Omnibus* (1991), written under the pseudonym Dan Kavanagh. Barnes is additionally a sharp and refined critic and reviewer, perhaps one of the finest thinkers of his generation, whose interests include politics, sports, nature, food, the arts and literature, and 'difficult' or taboo subjects such as death, religion and adultery. Barnes's writing includes some of the work that is central to our canon of contemporary fiction, such as *Flaubert's Parrot* (1984), *A History of*

the World in 10½ Chapters (1989), *England, England* (1998) and *Arthur & George* (2005). His work has been adapted as well. *Talking it Over* (1991) was made into a French film by Marion Vernoux called *Love, etc.* (1996), Adrian Hodges turned *Metroland* (1980) into a screenplay for Philip Saville's *Metroland* (1997) and after Valerija Cokan and Boris Cavazza turned *Talking it Over* into a Slovene play in 2007, David Edgar adapted *Arthur & George* (2005) for the Birmingham stage in 2010.

In the satirical magazine *Private Eye*, a cartoon shows Barnes working on an early draft of *Flaubert's Parrot*, called *Flaubert's Dead Parrot*. The cartoonist Simon Pearsall may have intended to mock 'the parrot guy' for having become synonymous with the novel, but by putting Barnes in the *First Drafts* series he was closer to the truth about this masterpiece than he could know. In Chapter Two of this volume of critical work, Ryan Roberts traces the development of Barnes's novel, showing by means of thorough archival research at the Harry Ransom Center, Texas, how the novel's concern with the relationship between life and art emerged from real-life experience. With a Braithwaithian sense of pursuit, Roberts takes us on an inspirational journey that illuminates our understanding of *Flaubert's Parrot*, while also complicating and deepening it. Not only does it show how Barnes's project turns a quest for an author into a work of art, it also demonstrates the necessary transfigurative processes that an author needs to employ to transform his *own* experiences into literature. It is the novel form that can achieve such a feat successfully, as Roberts notes: 'Fiction offers the possibility to create symbols, metaphors, and multiple layers of meaning not easily represented in journalism or that too often are disregarded in real life'.

We can deduce from Pearsall's cartoon that, like Monty Python in relation to their parrot sketch, Julian Barnes has become wedded in many people's minds to one novel. *Flaubert's Parrot* has thus become an albatross of sorts – in her chapter Vanessa Guignery calls Barnes 'condemned to parrotry' – in the sense that its success cancelled out its original criticism of our current celebrity-obsessed age that is interested in the author and not the text itself. The novel has also created an unhappy yet persistent conflation of Barnes with postmodernism, which for various reasons is a reductive commonplace. Witty animal comparisons notwithstanding – Mira Stout famously labelled Barnes 'the chameleon of British letters' (Stout 1992: 29) – many critics have pigeon-holed the author based solely on readings of a select group of novels. This underestimates the impact of Barnes's work within recent literary history: his work was not postmodernist upon its arrival, but nevertheless became central to *shaping* the moment of British high postmodernism in the 1980s. Barnes's work gave a clear sense of the ideas that are key to the period's intellectual history in self-scrutinizing metafiction that challenges established readings of the past and conventional social categories, and, perhaps most importantly, exhibits an interest in the intellectual significance and subversive potential of generic hybridity and serious play. Barnes has, for instance, also been making his mark as a translator of two works, Volker Kriegel's humorous cartoons depicting *The Truth about Dogs* (1988) and Alphonse Daudet's illness notebook *In the Land of Pain* (2002). These provide a sign of his genuine interest in working across geographical and linguistic borders, and of his commitment to continental literature, most clearly expressed in his detailed, scholarly essays on European writers. Sweeping statements about Barnes the postmodernist also misrepresent the subtleties and complexity of the author's achievement. Frederick Holmes, for instance, remarks that Barnes's fiction 'displays a self-reflexive, postmodernist scepticism regarding any truth claims' (Holmes 2009: 12), but to portray Barnes primarily as a relativist would do insufficient justice to the seriousness and intellectual intensity of the writer's engagement with the world beyond the subjective self.

This volume is an attempt to revalue Barnes's work, and to resituate his *oeuvre* beyond the limits of postmodern trickery by placing his writings in various traditions and new critical contexts, such as the various European cultural traditions (Taunton, Guignery, and Moseley), the new historical novel (Berberich), the 'genetic' approach to the creative process (Roberts and Kondeva) and the productive tension between the renewed interest in religion and the school of militant atheism spearheaded by Richard Dawkins (Tate and Childs). Like that of all the finest intellectual and artistic minds, Barnes's work is defined by a curiosity that often evades clear categorization.

Some of the finest critics working on contemporary fiction have pointed this out. Dominic Head suggests that, although *Flaubert's Parrot* makes the point that finding the author is essentially a useless undertaking, paradoxically the novel 'remains a celebration of Flaubert the writer as personality' (Head 2006: 16). As Vanessa Guignery notes, Peter Childs questions the postmodernist stigma when noting that 'Barnes is sometimes considered a postmodernist writer because his fiction rarely either conforms to the model of the realist novel or concerns itself with a scrutiny of consciousness in the manner of modernist writing' (Guignery 2006: 1; Childs 2005: 86). Richard Bradford also identifies a general laziness in the approach many critics take to Barnes's writing, noting of *England, England,* for instance, that it the novel is laxly 'treated as a work of satire, its targets abidingly self-selecting and open for ridicule'. For Bradford, the novel is more delicate and ambivalent than such readings suggest because Barnes draws us, perhaps against our better judgement, 'toward the possibility that there might just be something, albeit wonderfully intangible, that touches a genuine emotion . . . . a sense of belonging' to the memory of a lost England. Vanessa Guignery also resists the temptation to file Barnes away under postmodernism. In her chapter, she traces the evolution of Barnes's profound and long-standing engagement with French literary traditions, particularly writers of the nineteenth century. Beyond the better-known examples of

Flaubert, Charles Baudelaire, Paul Verlaine and Arthur Rimbaud, she introduces us, for instance, to Barnes's interest in eighteenth-century moralist Nicolas Chamfort (1741–1794) and Jules Renard's *Journal* (1887–1910). Subtly and expertly, Guignery shows that Barnes's interest in France and French literature does not simply involve a static monolithic body of writers, but follows a fascinating trajectory that traces the changing tastes and interest of the evolving writer.

Barnes's passion for the Continent, and France in particular, is one of the worst-kept secrets in recent literary history. This French connection is one of the things that sets Barnes apart from many of his contemporaries, who often turn to the dominant cultural power of the U.S. In this volume, Merritt Moseley gives us an American point of view on an author unconditionally committed to the European literary tradition. Moseley wittily claims Barnes as 'a mid-Channel author' whose cross-generic skills are matched by his interest in geographic displacement. For Barnes, France represents difference, the Other, but 'France is a synecdoche for Europe' also. In his chapter, Moseley proceeds to trace three different levels of representation in *Talking it Over*: France as symbol of cultural sophistication; as a place of refuge; and as a country associated with Eros. The latter interest again sets Barnes apart from other authors of his generation: whereas for many (male) writers love, carnality and sexuality are the well-trodden topoï of the classics, for Barnes they are topics that deserve renewed and often humorous investigation.

Another way in which this volume re-values Barnes's work is by carefully examining the evolution of a sustained engagement with history across his *oeuvre*. This re-examination also takes place by historicizing the novels themselves. Matthew Taunton revisits Barnes's first novel, *Metroland*, by exploring the faultline across the representation of cultural and temperamental tension between metropolitan London and urbane Paris. Taunton investigates Barnes's tale of two cities by analyzing the novel's juxtaposition of the stifling London suburbs to Paris as the exciting home to the *flâneur*, a place of limitless sexual, social and political freedom. The novel is a dramatization of widespread disenchantment with the utopian politics of the 1960s but also demonstrates a dialogic cultural and literary relationship between the past and the present. Taunton also historicizes Barnes's work, concluding that '*Metroland* is a product of its historical moment, a time when the utopian impulses of the 1960s and early 1970s had run aground. . . . and *Metroland* seems thoroughly aware that it is situated at a time of profound cultural and political change'. For Taunton, the novel additionally anticipates the climate of Thatcher's Britain, which Barnes was to criticize directly in his non-fiction.

In a special, epistolary contribution, Barnes's Bulgarian translator, Dimitrina Kondeva chronicles her collaboration with Barnes during the writing and publication of Barnes's satirical exploration of Cold War

INTRODUCTION 5

totalitarianism, *The Porcupine*. Kondeva and Barnes engaged in an intensive exchange of letters and faxes – here recaptured in a facsimile reproduction of a number of examples – in which Kondeva supplied Barnes with facts about life in Bulgaria. In a striking passage from his letters to Kondeva we already find an intimation that Barnes's conception of history goes beyond the sweeping relativist accounts of postmodernism:

> So while I'm initially tempted to say something like 'You will probably recognize bits of your recent history but all this really takes place in the country of my and your mind', this would a) not pacify literalist readers, who will complain about reality being betrayed; and b) <u>be completely obvious and therefore</u> irritating to intelligent people who know what a novel is and how it differs from a newspaper report. I wouldn't want to sound either defensive or patronising.

The lived experience, and trauma, of a Central European nation is not reducible to a purely textual experience, although Barnes is unable to explore his fascination for people 'living in interesting times' without acknowledging that our understanding of the world is to a large extent determined by the fictions and fantasies that shape our subjective (and often mediatized) perception. Kondeva's and Taunton's politicized reading of Barnes's work gives us another perspective on the writing, once again underlining Barnes's commitment to capturing, and ability to penetrate, the contemporary. In a 1994 piece on Tony Blair, Barnes himself presents us with an acute linguistic analysis that sees through the spin-filled years of New Labour that would commence three years later: He notes that the young 'Blair's theme song . . . consists not so much of sound-bites as word-bites, and his speech would not be greatly betrayed by simply playing the highlighted words in the order he used them' (Barnes 1995: 334).

The insights that Kondeva's piece on *The Porcupine* gives us in many ways adumbrates the later 'turn' towards more historical fidelity and factuality in Barnes's *Arthur & George*. Christine Berberich notes that *Arthur & George* forms a deliberate and important turning point within Barnes's *oeuvre* as the author moves from the earlier historical metafiction of *Flaubert's Parrot* and *A History of the World in 10½ Chapters* to what Richard Bradford describes as a 'new historical novel' (Bradford 2007: 95). By teasing out Barnes's detailed historical research for the novel in relationship to the fictional, imaginative and, inevitably, speculative components, Berberich argues that '*Arthur & George* offers something new, an ingenious combination of realism and post-modern historiography'. Perhaps provocatively, Berberich argues that 'fact and fiction converge and intermingle in a way that makes it difficult, or maybe even irrelevant, for the reader to see the fine dividing line'. Ultimately, she argues, it is the reader of Barnes's generic hybrid who is asked 'to critically assess all narrative and take nothing for granted', which again underscores Barnes's interest in challenging the intellectual ground beneath our feet.

While in England Barnes is often viewed as a Francophile, in France he is valued for being a quintessentially English writer. This is nowhere more apparent than in his novel that features both a French post-situationist Baudrillardian intellectual and a list of the 50 quintessences of Englishness: *England, England*. Another novel that toys with postmodernist sensibilities, it is most explicitly a study of the invention of tradition, as Richard Bradford's essays discusses in this volume. Barnes's second Booker-shortlisted novel is also situated in the literary tradition of the English pageant play. Arguably in acknowledgement of the fact that a 'pageant' is a play on wheels, the word originally meaning the movable scaffolding on which the play was performed, Barnes presents England as pageant, wheeled on to the Isle of Wight to tell its story on a miniature stage. Barnes's millennial novel starts and ends with mis-remembered bucolic history lessons, the Agricultural Show of Martha's childhood, and the imitation pastoral Anglia of her adulthood, but its twentieth-century intertexts are, for example, E. M. Forster's *Abinger Pageant* (1934) and *England's Pleasant Land* (1940), or John Cowper Powys's *A Glastonbury Romance* (1932) and Virginia Woolf's *Between the Acts* (1941): attempts by the great English writers in the first half of the century to explore community and national identity through the simulacrum of the pageant-play. Here, as in *Letters from London*, *Arthur & George*, *Before She Met Me*, *Staring at the Sun*, and countless other texts, Barnes shows an abiding interest in the past currents converging on Englishness and its contemporary currency in his lifetime.

Another idea that has become associated with Barnes is that he is an experimental author, a term most writers would consider synonymous with failure. In his study of the writer, Holmes talks of Barnes as a 'cosmopolitan, intellectually and culturally sophisticated fictional experimenter' (Holmes 2009: 12), and Barnes himself has stated that 'In order to write, you have to convince yourself that it's a new departure for you and not only a new departure for you but for the entire history of the novel' (Stout 1992: 68). Barnes's interest in experimentation with form has given us some of the most challenging and insightful work in contemporary fiction, but this self-imposed rule of constant innovation is also a guiding principle for the entire *oeuvre*. Paradoxically, with every new work, Barnes is seeking continuity in *change*.

This interest in experimentalism is not necessarily postmodern, but it is certainly the influence of the Continent and its invention of one of the greatest cultural forms of art – the novel – that have had a major impact upon the formation of Barnes's thinking about writing. Cervantes is particularly important for Barnes because he is at the start of an intellectual, and perhaps more importantly, temperamental, line of writers that includes Samuel Richardson (1689–1761), Laurence Sterne

(1713–1768), Honoré de Balzac (1799–1650), Flaubert, Leo Tolstoy (1828–1910), Marcel Proust (1817–1922), Franz Kafka (1883–1924), James Joyce (1882–1941), Thomas Mann (1875–1955), Robert Musil (1880–1942) and Hermann Broch (1886–1951). For another contemporary writer working in the European tradition, Milan Kundera, this wide-ranging and disparate group of writers 'saw, felt, grasped the *terminal paradoxes* of the Modern Era' (Kundera 1999: 11). Barnes's work also suggests that we are tolerant but also know that the liberal tradition makes us passive; that we have a desire to believe in God but fear the mysteries of life and death; that we are selfish and cannot accept the fact that we are limited beings; that we have faith in progress and the power of rationality, but are haunted by the darker, regressive aspects of human nature; we are fascinated by sex, but terrified of the sexual imagination and continue to embrace taboos as a form of self-protection; we believe in social equality but are afraid of an underworld of social outcasts and immigrants; we are afraid of our bodies and, above all, we fear the ultimate taboo, death. We are an accident of evolution, but like to think that man is at the heart of the universe.

It is this heritage of paradox that is particularly strong in Barnes's writing: feeding on 'the big Perhaps', challenging ideologies with the novel as a form of intellectual enquiry and not as a moral position, the latter being a Leavisite tendency we find in many writers of the English tradition of writing. Yet it is also a reason why Barnes became interested in writing about the ambiguities of the Communist totalitarian systems and the Cold War period. Kondeva notes that Barnes 'is interested in individuals' "inner voices" and their own truths rather than the ultimate Truth. *The Porcupine* is a complex novel about the guilt of the accused and the accusers, the ideological fanaticism and the dangers of being trapped in dogma. It deals with the personal interpretations of recent events'.

Matthew Pateman states: 'Barnes's novels are all searching for ways of knowing the world, each other; they all have characters who are striving for some way of finding meaning in an increasingly depoliticized, secularized, localized, and depth-less world' (Pateman 2002: 2). Another characteristic of his writing is that Barnes never goes for the obvious: when it comes to his novelistic engagement with the totalitarian Communist regimes during the Cold War, he does not go to divided Berlin or to Stalin's Siberian slave camps, but to Communist Bulgaria. It is this contrariness which undermines any totalizing or totalitarian understanding of the world that reduces its richness and complexity, its ambiguities and contradictions. Again Kundera provides an illuminating insight here: 'To take, with Cervantes, the world as ambiguity, to be obliged to face not a single absolute truth but a welter of contradictory truths . . . , to have as one's only certainty the *wisdom of uncertainty*, requires no less courage' (Kundera 1999: 6). This kind of wisdom is under pressure in a modern technocracy increasingly rationalized and interspersed with technology.

The wisdom of uncertainty seems a more adequate way of describing the speculative, inquisitive and subversive qualities of Barnes's work than self-reflexive scepticism.

Peter Childs's chapter also demonstrates that Barnes's ability to write across genres is a part of his exploitation of doubt as a productive force. His gift for the short story form is evident, as Childs shows, in three remarkable collections: *Cross Channel* (1996), *The Lemon Table* (2004) and *Pulse* (2011). Childs traces some of the linkages and commonalities in the later two volumes, illustrating Barnes's range but also his careful planning of story sequences that display continuity in variety as well as change. The thematic focus lies on the author's sardonic take on how ageing confronts us with thoughts of the 'Big D' – death – and with the thoughts of those who write about the afterlife, immortality and oblivion. In Barnes's universe, there are two deaths; the death of youth, and the death of old age, and the author concludes, soberly, that death is merely a necessity: 'death happens to us for no other reason than because the universe happens to us', Childs notes as Barnes's stoical stance.

Barnes's 'memoir', *Nothing To Be Frightened Of*, continues to present us with his own struggles with death in the light of religion, and it sits well with the return of religion at the beginning of the twenty-first century. Barnes contributes a subtle vision to what can often seem a divisive debate between atheist hardliners and rationalists such as Richard Dawkins and Ian McEwan. In interview he has said: 'As a writer, I would see we made up the Bible as a very good novel which then got corrupted by power systems. It's a wonderful story in the great tradition of Hollywood, a great tragedy with a happy ending. It's not such a good story when you die and don't go to heaven' (Davis 2008: 18).

Andrew Tate, one of the authors of *The New Atheist Novel* (2010), explores Barnes's sustained engagement with questions of religion and spirituality through his extensive body of work. Tate situates Barnes within a largely secular culture of contemporary British fiction and notes that he is part of practitioners who are 'at least tacitly hostile to the truth-claims of theistic religions'. In Barnes's words to a clergyman: '"I'm afraid I'm a happy atheist"' (Barnes 2009: 17). Yet, Tate carefully unstitches this position by showing that Barnes's *oeuvre*, rather than representing a wholly secularized society or English empiricism, 'is frequently energized by a sensation of wonder, mystery'. Just as Bradford shows that the loss of a particular England does not leave Barnes cold, Tate shows that the waning of a religious sensibility is a cause for mourning while it becomes the task of literature to take upon itself religion's role to express the ineffable. Tate also shows, again, that it is a mixture of curiosity and doubt that is the creative dynamo behind Barnes's authorship.

In response to Berberich and Tate, Arthur Conan Doyle's biographer Andrew Lycett gives us his perspective on the work of Barnes, and

Barnes's fictional account of the relationship between Conan Doyle and George Edalji in *Arthur & George* in particular. Discussing Barnes's interest in the nature of knowledge and spirituality, Lycett agrees with the readings that Berberich and Tate give of the tension in Barnes's work between knowledge and spirituality. Lycett shows us some minor flaws in the extensive research of Barnes, to the extent that he doubted this was a fictional work of art: 'Back in 2005 I remember wondering if, given its palpable use of factual information, *Arthur & George* should have been entered for the Man Booker Prize for Fiction at all'. However, what ultimately becomes evident in the biographer's tale is admiration for the ways in which the novelist creates an amalgam of fact and fiction that illuminated the life of Conan Doyle in a new, and, more importantly, truthful way.

What Lycett suggests, in a way, is that we should read Barnes's fictional work as a biography of its author. Each of Barnes's works is like the description of biography as the fishing net in *Flaubert's Parrot*. In that novel, Geoffrey Braithwaite explains that biography is considered a string of words designed to encompass the subject just as a fishing net is a web of string in which to catch fish; but, a net can logically be thought a collection of holes tied together, and so can a biography (Barnes 1984: 38). Similarly, the gaps in *Flaubert's Parrot* are what intrigue the writer and the reader. There are so many missing pieces that Braithwaite's life becomes as elusive for us as Flaubert, or his parrot, is for him. Similarly, *A History of the World in 10½ Chapters* presents itself disingenuously as a net to capture history but stands as a string of partial stories that tie together a novel composed of twice-told tales, except these retellings are tangential to their originals and not copies. They sit seriously but subversively, like Tom Stoppard's *Rosencrantz and Guildenstern are Dead* (1966) or Jean Rhys's *Wide Sargasso Sea* (1966), teasing at our recognition and their own echoes of each other as well as numerous intertexts, historical, mythical, anecdotal, philosophical and fictional. For its part, *England, England* rests on the missing jigsaw piece at the heart of Martha's map of Britain. The story of the relationships in *Talking it Over* and *Love, etc.* will not be found in the testimonies of Oliver, Gillian and Stuart, but in the gaps between them: the holes in the narrative that are occasionally filled by a chorus of voices, from Gillian's mother to Stuart's ex-wife, but mostly lie empty. The lacunae of *Metroland*, as with many of Barnes's novels, are the long silent years in between the three sections of the narrative, while in *Before She Met Me* it is everything that Graham does not know, and can only imagine, that torments him. *The Porcupine* is Barnes's most sustained analysis of political turmoil and protest striating an obscured background of half-truths, self-deceptions, unspoken facts, and insincere protestations, while the unanswered and unresolved meanings of life and death suffuse all Barnes's work from *Staring at the Sun* to *The Lemon Table*, from *Nothing To Be Frightened Of* to *Pulse*.

Arthur & George makes still more explicit this fascination with the fissures and omissions of narrative. Another biographical novel, it foregrounds the search for clues, for truths, for answers in amongst the false memories, circumstantial evidence, virulent rumour and concealed prejudice. Arthur thus focuses explicitly on what is missing between the 'persecutions': 'the first runs from 1892 to the very beginning of 1896. It is intense and increasing. All of a sudden it stops. Nothing happens for seven years. Then it starts up again, and the first horse is ripped. February 1903. Why the gap . . . ?' (Barnes 2005: 229). This stretches even beyond the realms of evidence and forensic investigation as Arthur is also 'playing detective' for The Society for Psychical Research. He concludes that sometimes 'the unknown and the marvellous press upon us from all sides; they loom in fluctuating shapes, warning us of the limitations of what we call matter' (Barnes 2005: 223).

At the start of the twenty-first century, the evolution of the novel, and fiction in general, will continue to be shaped by Barnes's influence on our contemporary culture. Barnes finishes *Nothing To Be Frightened Of* with a sober reflection, which is simultaneously a promising one: 'So, that's the view from here, now, from what, if I'm lucky, if my parents are any sort of guide, might be three-quarters of the way through my life' (Barnes 2008: 249). As we have noted, the material of Barnes's novels exists as much in the interstices of the text and the often unexpressed doubts of the characters: the aporetic disjunctions that open up to reveal more truth than the facts. This sits well with his abiding concern with testing the boundaries of the novel form, turning its bagginess into an opportunity for exploration, ignoring generic definitions and espousing the mongrelization of fiction that issues in newness. This underlines once more why Barnes is perhaps the most idiosyncratic and innovative of contemporary British authors; a writer who with each fictional departure does not just make it new for himself 'but for the entire history of the novel'.

CHAPTER ONE

The *Flâneur* and the Freeholder: Paris and London in Julian Barnes's *Metroland*

MATTHEW TAUNTON

> **Chapter Summary:** *Metroland*'s depiction of London and Paris engages with the characteristic literary associations that have accrued to the two cities. The London suburbs are initially seen as stiflingly conventional, while Paris is home to the *flâneur,* a place of limitless sexual, social and political freedom. The narrator comes to celebrate Metroland, and the comforts of family and home it provides. His suburban marriage is a challenge to those sexual revolutionaries and Parisian intellectuals who held up promiscuity as a panacea. The novel dramatizes a widespread disenchantment with the utopian politics of the 1960s, but also suggests that suburban contentment is tied up with political quietism, and, perhaps, the rising tide of Thatcherite conservatism.

To the young Christopher and Toni – two precocious adolescents in Julian Barnes's first novel *Metroland* (1980) who are growing up in a London suburb – the condition of rootlessness is alluring and Romantic, the very essence of their rebellion against the petty-bourgeois mores of suburbia:

> Toni and I prided ourselves on being rootless. We also aspired to a future condition of rootlessness, and saw no contradiction in the two states of mind; or in the fact that we each lived with our parents, who were, for that matter, the freeholders of our respective homes. (Barnes 1990: 29)

This tension between the competing appeals of a grounded, homely existence and a more exotically cosmopolitan life is played out between the twin poles of suburban London and Paris. The dichotomy is informed by the traditions of literary representation that pertain to each city. Chris and Toni grow up in Metroland, a suburban area to the northwest of London, served by the western stretch of the Metropolitan Line, a place associated with the comforts of home ownership, family, and conformity: as Toni contemptuously puts it, 'wife, baby, reliable job, mortgage, *flower* garden' (Barnes 1990: 202). Paris, on the other hand, appears infused with the excitement and erotic thrill of the metropolis, a place where the anonymity of the *flâneur* prevails and one can exist as Chris and Toni aspire to do, *'sans racines'* (Barnes 1990: 29): without roots. The three-part structure of the novel takes the action from Metroland to Paris and back, an arc that reflects the narrator's progression from the subversiveness of youth to the suburban contentment implied in 'praising the central heating' (Barnes 1990: 212). There is also a distinct historical progression: Paris in the 1960s stands for free love, transgression and unlimited sexual freedom; the London suburbs in the late 1970s for marriage and the nuclear family.

Metroland is a debut novel, and it shows: a laboured text, dense with literary allusions, it sets up a rather schematic dialectic, opposing London and Paris, conformity and rebellion, Chris and Toni. Its representations of Paris and London therefore have little to do with a detailed, realist depiction of the two cities. Rather, the novel focuses our attention on the literary traditions and cultural associations of these two capitals, using a web of intertextual references to imbue the two locations with rich significance.

The young Chris's and Toni's desire to escape their roots is in one sense a reflex reaction against the suburban environment in which they live and which they view with a 'raucous cynicism' (Barnes 1990: 9). But this aspiration also fundamentally looks towards France, and to Paris in particular, as suggested by the fact that the vocabulary of the boys' rebellion is amply stocked with French phrases. Chris and Toni live by two transgressive mottos: *'écraser l'infame'* (Barnes 1990: 9) – 'crush the infamous one', the call to insurrection against church and convention with which Voltaire signed his letters – and *'épater la bourgeoisie'* (Barnes 1990: 9), the injunction to 'shock the bourgeoisie' that was the rallying cry for later generations of Parisian poets and rebels. The boys take their inspiration from art and literature, and are drawn above all to the French writers most closely associated with the rebellion against bourgeois morality:

> we cared for [French] literature largely for its combativeness. French writers were always fighting one another – defending and purifying the language, ousting slang words, writing prescriptive dictionaries, getting arrested, being prosecuted for obscenity, being aggressively Parnassian, scrabbling for seats in the Académie, intriguing for literary prizes, getting exiled. (Barnes 1990: 10)

The heroic figure of the rebel-writer in exile – so crucial to the self-image of modernist writers from Joyce to Gertrude Stein – is, as Chris and Toni notice, indebted to the French writers of the nineteenth century. These writers are a constant presence in his work, and if *Metroland* is not quite an exercise in postmodernist metafiction like *Flaubert's*

Parrot (1984) or *A History of the World in 10½ Chapters* (1989), it is certainly highly self-conscious about its use of the literary canon and is peppered with references to Rimbaud (Barnes 1990: 119), Gautier (Barnes 1990: 59), Zola (Barnes 1990: 38) and Mallarmé (Barnes 1990: 211). Perhaps the most important inspiration for the young Chris and Toni is the poet Charles Baudelaire. Chris's precocious fascination with Baudelaire leads his brother to refer to him mockingly as 'Chris Baudelaire' (Barnes 1990: 70), and later on, after breaking up with his first serious girlfriend – the French Annick – he writes a series of prose poems which he calls *Spleenters* (Barnes 1990: 150), the title alluding to Baudelaire's posthumous collection of prose poems, *Le Spleen de Paris* (1869). This infatuation is pertinent because Baudelaire is not just a poet – he represents a distinctive and influential attitude to modern life and above all to the modern city.

For Baudelaire, modern life was a rootless affair, summed up in his essay 'The Painter of Modern Life' (1863) as 'the ephemeral, the fugitive, the contingent' (Baudelaire 1995: 12). Baudelaire's poems and prose sketches sought to capture the fleeting and elusive experiences of the city and so to escape from the *ennui* of contemporary bourgeois existence. It is easy to see why he might become the model for precocious adolescents like Chris and Toni, and why the recently dumped Chris, wandering the streets of Paris, models his poetic outpourings on those of Baudelaire. With a hint of self-satire, he pretentiously describes *Spleenters* as a set of 'urban allegories, sardonic character-sketches, elusive verse, and passages of straight descriptions, which gradually built up into a portrait of a city, a man, and – who could say? – perhaps a bit more' (Barnes 1990: 150). This description is redolent of Walter Benjamin's seminal work on Baudelaire, which saw the endlessly mobile *flâneur* as a central figure in his poetry, which could, in turn, help us to understand the vital modernity of the nineteenth-century metropolis (Benjamin 2006: *passim*). The *flâneur* becomes a key figure for Chris and Toni and is integral to their idea of the 'Constructive Loaf':

> It was Toni who first put forward the concept of the Constructive Loaf. Our time, he argued, was spent being either compulsorily crammed with knowledge, or compulsorily diverted. His theory was that by lounging around in a suitably *insouciant* fashion, but keeping an eye open all the time, you could really catch life on the hip – you could harvest all the *aperçus* of the *flâneur*. (Barnes 1990: 24)

The humour and energy that makes the first section of *Metroland* so enjoyable derives largely from the boys' attempts to be *flâneurs*. This is enhanced by the fact that the narrator – the grown-up Chris, now himself the epitome of petty-bourgeois, suburban contentment – is at a level of ironic remove from his youthful escapades. The highfalutin theories that the boys took so seriously – including the Constructive Loaf – are now viewed with a wry scepticism.

Much of the irony stems from the basic incongruity of seeking to apply the Baudelarian street philosophy of metropolitan Paris to the relatively unglamorous milieu of London and its suburbs in the early 1960s.

> Toni and I were strolling along Oxford Street, trying to look like *flâneurs*. That wasn't as easy as it might sound. For a start, you usually needed a *quai* or, at the very least, a *boulevard*; and, however much we might be able to imitate the aimlessness of the *flânerie* itself we always felt that we hadn't quite mastered what happened at each end of the stroll. In Paris, you would be leaving behind some rumpled couch in a *chambre particulière*; over here, we had just left Tottenham Court Road Underground station and were heading for Bond Street. (Barnes 1990: 11)

The syllables of 'Tottenham Court Road' seem here to lack the poetic sonorities of the *'chambre particulière'*: it is as if London – notwithstanding T.S. Eliot's attempt to import the Parisian sensibility of Baudelaireian street poetry in *The Waste Land* (1922) – is inherently a more prosaic city. Contrary to a literary critical tendency to see *flânerie* in the London novel, notably in Rachel Bowlby's *Virginia Woolf: Feminist Destinations* (1988) and Deborah Parsons's *Streetwalking the Metropolis* (2000), Barnes's novel suggests that the *flâneur* is incongruous with London. Indeed, there are fundamental differences of urban geography that make London less well adapted to *flânerie*. Central to Benjamin's argument is the idea that Haussmann's rationalising, geometric rebuilding of Paris in the nineteenth century opened up the *boulevards* for the *flâneur*. London has tended to grow horizontally in an organic and piecemeal way so that, with the possible exception of John Nash's Regent Street (itself modelled on Napoleon's Rue de Rivoli (Frampton 1992: 23)), its thoroughfares lack the theatrical grandeur of the Parisian *boulevards* and tend to lead quickly into anonymous thoroughfares or mazy residential suburban streets. It is only in Paris, on his first date with Annick, that Chris feels that he has really mastered the art: 'We flâned (we really did) our way to a bar, knocked off a couple of drinks, and I walked her to a bus stop' (Barnes 1990: 106). Nevertheless, the Anglicisation of the word is clumsy and inelegant: the fact that there is no translation for the term hints at the cultural differences between the English and French attitudes to urban life.

Flânerie is even less suited to an extensive network of commuter dormitories such as the London suburbs. Barnes's depiction of Metroland evokes a tradition of representation that is firmly associated with the London suburbs and the lower-middle class suburban commuter. The *flâneur* is without roots, moving freely through the boulevards, while the suburban – like Chris and his parents before him – is a freeholder, fixed to his semi-detached cell with a mortgage and a family to support, and locked into routine work. In Paris, the task of the poet was to celebrate and identify with the *flâneur*, while in London, writers competed to pour coruscating scorn on the figure of the suburban clerk. In *The Intellectuals and the Masses* (1992), John Carey has catalogued a wide variety of hostile reactions to suburbia in the literary intelligentsia, from poets and novelists like E. M. Forster, Graham Greene and T. S. Eliot to social commentators like C. F. G. Masterman and T. W. H. Crosland (Carey 1992: 46–70). Metroland plays into this tradition, juxtaposing the self-confidence of a knowing metropolitan artistic culture against the supposed philistinism and social conservatism of the suburbs. The view of the suburban middle class as suffering from *'le syphilis de l'âme'* (Barnes 1990: 163) [syphilis of the soul] is given voice by the two boys and by the adult Toni. As Chris matures and settles down in Metroland, he begins to defend the suburban lifestyle from the criticisms to which it has been subjected.

So *Metroland* fits into – but also questions and subverts – a well-established tradition of representation of the London suburbs. One of the ways that it does so is through its engagement with a more specific discourse around Metroland in particular, an area that has autobiographical significance for Barnes, who lived there from 1957 to 1964, commuting to school, like Christopher, on the tube (Guignery 2006: 8). Barnes has written elsewhere that Metroland is 'a bogus place, a concept dreamed up by an expanding railway network in partnership with property developers' (Barnes 1997: 38), and in the novel, his description of the historical development of this particular string of suburbs is similarly unfavourable:

> As the Metropolitan Railway had pushed westward in the 1880s, a thin corridor of land was opened up with no geographical or ideological unity: you lived there because it was an area easy to get out of. The name Metroland – adopted during the First World War both by estate agents and the railway itself – gave the string of rural suburbs a spurious integrity. (Barnes 1990: 31)

Here is a place without any intrinsic 'unity' or 'integrity', a place whose main selling point is the ease with which its inhabitants can escape it.

The old man that Chris meets on the train in Part I articulates a curiously nostalgic view of the Metropolitan Railway, reflecting wistfully on its earlier days and excoriating its more recent decline: 'Used to be a great line. Used to have . . . ambitions' (Barnes 1990: 33). This 'rickety old fugger' (Barnes 1990: 34) is nostalgic for the time when there were grand plans for the Metropolitan:

> Fifty miles from Verney Junction to Baker Street; what a line. Can you imagine – they were planning to join up with Northampton and Birmingham.

> Have a great link through from Yorkshire and Lancashire, through Quainton Road, through London, joining up with the old South Eastern, then through a Channel Tunnel to the Continent. What a line. (Barnes 1990: 35)

The Victorian faith in technology and progress is celebrated: 'Don't sneer at the Victorians, lad' (Barnes 1990: 36), the old man admonishes, a reaction that evokes a post-Imperial Britain in decline.

Barnes's 'rickety old fugger' insists on a distinction between the charm of the old and the corruption of the new and is openly contemptuous of what he sees as the more recent, cynical branding of the area as 'Metroland':

> 'Metroland? That nonsense.' He turned his attention to me again. 'That was the beginning of the end. No, that was much later, some time during the war before Hitler's. That was all to please the estate agents. Make it sound cosy. Cosy homes for cosy heroes. Twenty-five minutes from Baker Street and a pension at the end of the line,' he said unexpectedly. 'Made it what it is now, a bourgeois dormitory.' (Barnes 1990: 37)

The fate of the Metropolitan line mirrors Chris's development over the course of the novel, starting with grand cosmopolitan ambitions and ending in a state of benign, cosy contentment. The line that was to link Britain to the continent ended up becoming synonymous with the most parochial of English tastes and values. When, after this tirade, the 'rickety old fugger' freely admits to being a bourgeois himself, the young Chris is puzzled by the apparent contradiction: 'Hey. Christ. You can't say that. It's not allowed. Look at yourself. I can call *you* bourgeois. ... You can't call yourself it' (Barnes 1990: 37). For the young Chris, the word 'bourgeois' is just an insult; yet as an adult, he learns to come to terms with a similar contradiction, to live the comfortable life of the suburban bourgeois while remaining – to some extent – ironically detached from it.

Barnes's novel asks what the political implications of this are. As I argued in *Fictions of the City* (2009), the suburban middle classes are often seen as 'politically conservative and fiercely hostile to socialism' (Taunton 2009: 86), certainly by the narrator of George Orwell's scathing satire on suburban life, *Coming Up for Air* (1939). If Chris loosely fits this mold, it is more that he is willing to accept the status quo than that he has an overt ideological commitment to the tenets of conservatism. The novel explores this partly through an engagement with the contrasting associations of suburban London and Paris. The literary and aesthetic rebellion by Parisian writers, artists and intellectuals against the culture and values of the establishment has been discussed above, but Paris has also always been the centre of political rebellion, with revolutions in 1789, 1848 and 1870. It is highly significant that Barnes places Chris in Paris in May 1968, at the time of student protests, strikes and massive political upheaval. Guy Debord and the Situationist International, an influential intellectual force from the mid-fifties, took the *flâneur* in a more political direction by means of the concept of the *'dérive'* (Debord 2006: 77), as described by Debord in 'Theory of the Dérive', a kind of urban drift. Yet Chris fails to become involved in the student protests, the street fighting, the general strike and everything else – remaining practically oblivious to it: 'I was there, all through May, through the burning of the Bourse, the occupation of the Odéon, the Billancourt lock-in, the rumours of tanks roaring back through the night from Germany. But I didn't actually see anything' (Barnes 1990: 86). Chris's juvenile rebellion against the bourgeois conventionality of his suburban upbringing does not translate into political activism in adulthood, even at the one time and place in post-war history when the claims of politics were almost impossible to ignore. This was not a case of a few student demonstrations – the whole of France was virtually brought to a standstill for several weeks (Ross 2002: 4). The bourgeoisie had suffered something more than an *épat*, and for a short while its lasting hegemony seemed (however deceptively) to be in doubt.

Chris's experiences of May 1968 suggest a disjuncture between the consciousness of the protagonist and the grand political struggles of his time. Chris increasingly adapts himself to his environment, and accepts his role as a contented suburbanite. Toni insists that the individual is free to choose his own path and is quick to upbraid Chris for his political apathy: 'What about the strikes?' (Barnes 1990: 109), he writes, in response to a letter filled with romantic reminiscences about Annick. Toni is a kind of existentialist, and from this perspective Chris is in 'bad faith', as defined by the Parisian philosopher Jean-Paul Sartre in *Being and Nothingness* (1943), a condition whereby we trick ourselves into believing that our actions are not freely chosen, but constrained by our environment or other factors.

The divergence between the two friends' responses to May 1968 brings their differences to the surface, and the political disagreement proves to be a lasting one. The adult Toni spends his days 'Trying to get the local Labour fascists to haul ass' (Barnes 1990: 173): it is clear that for him, juvenile rebellion has developed into political commitment. When Chris suggests that Toni has become more political, he responds that his politics have simply moved to the Left, concluding that '[m]an is never not political' (Barnes 1990: 174). Toni's criticisms of Chris's lifestyle thus imply that his apparent political detachment amounts to conservatism. Chris's fleeting analysis of the crisis of 1968 – offhandedly delivered in letters whose main subject was Annick – tends to support this view: 'the students were too stupid to understand their courses, became mentally frustrated, and because of the lack of sports facilities had taken to fighting the riot police' (Barnes 1990: 87). This view is both conservative and naïve and it is telling in terms of Barnes's later fiction that in his debut novel, it is the crisis of 1968 that provides the context for an exploration of the disjuncture between history and subject. The failure of 1968 is often seen as a point of origin for a postmodern literary sensibility and this is enacted by Barnes's oeuvre. *Metroland*'s ironic self-consciousness about the difficulties of taking a determinate political position on the events of 1968 – or even of accessing them – develops in *Flaubert's Parrot* (1984) into a high postmodernist attitude which would see 'historical truth' as completely inaccessible, lost somewhere between competing subjective accounts.

The relationship between London and Paris in *Metroland*, then, is a part of the same dialectic which is played out in the relationship between Chris and Toni. Chris has now achieved middle-class contentment, whilst Toni leads a bohemian life as a struggling writer and political activist, cohabiting in a non-exclusive 'modern arrangement' (Barnes 1990: 178) with his girlfriend Kally. There are fundamental differences in the ways in which the two old friends live, but there are also differences of style: Chris's 'crew-neck sweater, corduroy trousers and Hush Puppies' are set off comically against Toni's 'couture jeans' and 'ingeniously rumpled shirt' (Barnes 1990: 172). Toni is deliberately brash and rude – still, perhaps, trying to *épat le bourgeois* – while Chris, increasingly assimilated into the suburban middle classes and starting to live by their code, finds Toni's behaviour 'a bit embarrassing' (Barnes 1990: 172). Chris's newfound politeness is a marker of his acceptance into the genteel petty-bourgeois world of the suburb, while Toni's 'grammar and vocabulary had taken on a more demotic cast' (Barnes 1990: 172), an affectation which is meant to signal his political allegiance with the working class.

The most important tension is between Chris's abandonment of the ideals he held in adolescence, and Toni's determination to stick to them. The values that Toni clings to are of dubious validity, but Chris's position is a purely pragmatic compromise. The ending of the novel leaves us poised between an acceptance of the mantle of middle-class respectability, and the persistence of a youthful but still vibrant political and aesthetic idealism. This polarity is complicated by the problem of perspective, arising from the fact that it is Chris, and not Toni, who narrates the story. From Chris's point of view, it is difficult to think of Toni as anything but immature and pretentious. We are, to an extent, encouraged to identify with the narrative voice, which notably lacks the absurd grandiloquence normally associated with suburban satire, like that that of Charles Pooter, the protagonist of George and Weedon Grossmith's *The Diary of a Nobody* (1892). Chris is measured and realistic, and the case that he makes for the benefits of a quiet and conventional suburban life is, if not compelling, then at least plausible. After an affectionate description of marital sex, for example, Barnes writes:

> I think these must be the happiest times of my life. People say that happiness is boring; not for me. They also say that all happy people are happy in the

same way. Who cares; in any case, at times like this I'm hardly interested in arguing the toss. (Barnes 1990: 161)

It is clear from this passage not only that Chris's happiness is real, but that the usual truisms of anti-suburban critique – 'happiness is boring', 'all happy people are happy in the same way' – have themselves become clichés. The two options that Barnes gives us to choose from – the idealism of Toni who sticks to his childhood values and the down-to-earth pragmatism of the suburban Chris – do not start out on an equal footing. As John Carey argues, the adjective 'suburban' has accrued overwhelmingly pejorative connotations, 'combining topographical with intellectual disdain' (Carey 1992: 53). Barnes's novel ends poised between two seemingly equal alternatives, but in order to achieve this ambiguity it has had to rehabilitate the suburban from a position where it has tended to be viewed with unbridled contempt. This balanced ending throws into doubt a widespread literary orthodoxy that celebrates the metropolitan *flâneur* at the expense of the suburban freeholder. Paradoxically, it is Toni whose opinions have become predictable and clichéd at the end of the novel and it is Chris – by embracing his suburban surroundings – who can claim an *épat*. Conventionality has itself become a subversive condition.

Chris enjoys this paradox, and lives his suburban life self-consciously, accepting inconsistency and irony. He notes that 'I'm surprised at how well camouflaged I seem' (Barnes 1990: 159), as if he were an undercover agent merely posing as a bourgeois. Barnes playfully juxtaposes the conformity of Chris's appearance with the elements of his inner life that retain an allegiance to Parisian modernity: 'as I track the lawn mower carefully across our sloping stretch of grass, rev, slow, brake, turn and rev again, making sure to overlap the previous stripe, don't think I can't still quote you Mallarmé' (Barnes 1990: 211). While droll, this also touches on a central Barnesian concern: is one's path through life a matter of free choice, or do history, culture and chance play a determining role? This is summed up at the end of Part I where the adolescent Chris is described as 'a creature part willing, part consenting, part being chosen' (Barnes 1990: 82). If for Toni this is merely bad faith, for Chris, learning to live with this kind of contradiction is part of the process of becoming an adult: 'It's certainly ironic to be back in Metroland. As a boy, what would I have called it: le syphilis de l'âme, or something like that, I dare say. But isn't it part of growing up being able to ride irony without being thrown?' (Barnes 1990: 163). In adolescence, Barnes's novel suggests, it is possible to see these things through a simplifying Manichean lens, as a battle between the forces of stale conformity and a vital and energetic rebellion. Toni, in a sense, still operates in these terms, while Chris and his wife Marion have embraced a more complicated and contradictory reality where idealism is replaced by ironic acceptance, but also – more optimistically – the progress and new experiences that go with starting a family.

If politics is one of the key areas on which the adult Chris and Toni disagree, then another important battleground is the traditional institutions of marriage and the nuclear family, which are ideological cornerstones of the suburban life into which Chris has now settled.

The contrast between Chris's two main love interests in the novel – Annick and Marion – is important here, and the difference between them is again explored in relation to the different characteristic associations of Paris and of the London suburbs. Chris's first encounter with Annick is in a Parisian café where she is casually reading Lawrence Durrell's *Mountolive* (Barnes 1990: 99–100). She is exotic, intense, intellectual and beautiful: their dates are spent discussing the latest Bresson film (Barnes 1990: 106), and their arguments turn around such questions as who has read the most Rimbaud (Barnes 1990: 119–20). The affair, certainly as Chris describes it, evokes a stereotypical idea about love in Paris, as Toni is quick to point out in a letter: 'You do realise, I hope, that Spring is not officially over yet, that you are in Paris, and that if I catch you anywhere near completing the cliché you can count on my lasting contempt' (Barnes 1990: 109). Chris has expectations that this affair will follow the prescribed literary precedents and achieve his goal of 'fusing all the art and the history with what I might soon, with luck, be calling the life' (Barnes 1990: 108). There are suggestions that this is not happening, and when it comes to sex the virginal Chris has to acknowledge that reading '*Lady C*' – D. H. Lawrence's *Lady Chatterley's Lover* (1928) – was not necessarily the best preparation for the *boudoir*: 'Practical stuff, I began to discover, really was different from written stuff' (Barnes 1990: 114).

There is a sense, then, in which the privileging of art over life that had characterized the first part of the novel begins to unravel as Chris gains experience of love. Annick differs from literary stereotypes in important respects, but Marion proves to be still less predictable. As Kate Flint puts it, 'central to the suburban dream was the vision of the nuclear family, with a wife who is seen to obtain her fulfilment through passive acceptance of her material good fortune' (Flint 1986: 117). Yet Barnes's portrayal of Marion tends to subvert the image of the suburban woman as a chaste, wifely and ultimately dull figure. To be sure, she is 'sensible, intelligent, pretty' (Barnes 1990: 169) rather than exotic, beautiful and emotional, and from the beginning she asks Chris grown-up questions about what he intends to do with his life (Barnes 1990: 133). This intelligence and attention to practical detail are not predictable and dull – on the contrary, Marion constantly surprises Chris with her unconventional insight and wit.

Here lies one of the failings of Philip Saville's film adaptation of *Metroland* (1997): Emily Watson's Marion is prim, snippy and censorious. In this version of the story, Chris is having a midlife crisis and instead of defending his lifestyle, he starts to believe what Toni tells him, and to desire an escape from his stifling marriage. It is hard not to sympathize with him as Marion nags, and then at the end of the film Chris (somewhat implausibly, given what has gone before) is finally convinced by Marion that after all he has everything he wants and that Toni is not only immature but profoundly jealous of both his marriage and his mortgage. The irony and ambiguity which leaves the ending of the novel delicately poised is less convincing in the film.

The debate around the institution of marriage is again presented though a clash of opinion between the two old friends. Toni feels 'unable on principle to attend' Chris and Marion's wedding and the letter in which he declines the invitation includes 'a carefully argued case against marriage' (Barnes 1990: 165). As he explains during an argument in Chris's garden, Toni takes the view that the ethical basis of marital monogamy amounts to nothing more than 'soiled old Judaeo-Christian rubbish topped up with Victorian wankers' sex-hatred' (Barnes 1990: 178–79). Toni's critique of marriage has a long heritage in nineteenth-century socialism from Fourier to Engels. But the more immediate context for his disaffection with marriage is the sexual revolution, the widespread questioning of sexual morality that was associated with the decade in which Chris and Toni came of age, the 1960s. Although Chris undergoes a sexual revolution of his own in Paris, May 1968, losing his virginity to Annick, the wider cultural changes that have come to be associated with that date passed him by, as Barnes makes abundantly clear. Chris's affair with Annick leads him to question his belief in the subversive power of sex, a belief which starts to take on the complexion of an adolescent prejudice. In bed, after sex, Chris reflects on the fact that he is maturing, and considers the ways in which his attitudes are changing: 'Pre-marital sex – a triple-épat, a double écras at school – suddenly didn't feel as if it had anything to do with the bourgeoisie' (Barnes 1990: 121). Chris tries to apply the insights of '*Lady C*' in the bedroom, and dismisses the missionary position (no doubt because of its association with 'Victorian wankers' sex-hatred') but the narrator parenthetically concedes that 'nowadays I reckon that the missionaries knew a thing or two' (Barnes 1990: 114). Perhaps the warning of the 'rickety old fugger' on the train – 'Don't sneer at the Victorians lad' (Barnes 1990: 36) – has been heeded. Yet it would be foolish to assume that *Metroland* returns its protagonist to suburbia in order to reassert Victorian pieties about sex and marriage.

Marion is far from being an evangelical and idealistic believer in marriage, listing a number of prosaic motivations that may lie behind it: 'Opportunity, meal ticket, desire for children, . . . fear of ageing, possessiveness. I don't know, I think it often comes from a reluctance to admit that you've never in your life loved hard enough to end up married' (Barnes 1990: 137). For her, getting married is not a passive acceptance of the status quo, but a considered choice. Her knowing attitude towards infidelity surprises Chris when it emerges after he confesses to an unconsummated flirtation at a party: 'It's alright, Chris.

You didn't go into marriage expecting a virgin and I didn't go in expecting a flagrantly faithful husband. Don't think I can't imagine what it's like to be sexually bored' (Barnes 1990: 196). Marion admits to having had a brief affair, a fact that shocks Chris, but one that he accepts. Chris's defence of marriage, then, is not some pious reassertion of the virtue of marital monogamy, even if the bland acceptance of adultery is itself something of a suburban cliché.

Through the course of the 1970s (and into the 1980s) the initial burst of 1960s optimism when writers and intellectuals celebrated the tearing down of Victorian sexual shibboleths was on the wane. Georg Frankl's *The Failure of the Sexual Revolution* (1974) was indicative: he argued that the transgression of existing rules and taboos – primarily expressed through promiscuity – was a means that had come to be viewed as an end in itself. For Frankl, the true end of sexual liberation – 'the fulfilment of man's primary urges, his freedom to love and be acknowledged as a whole person' (Frankl 1974: 173) – had been cast aside. In *Metroland*, Chris makes a very similar case during his argument in the garden with Toni:

> I don't believe in this new orthodoxy. It used to be, don't screw around because you'll be unhappy and catch VD and give it to your wife and have mad children, like in Strindberg or Ibsen or whoever it was. Now it's screw around otherwise you'll become a bore and won't meet new people and will eventually become impotent with everyone except your wife (Barnes 1990: 180).

Chris recognizes that nineteenth-century sexual morality was in part a defence against sexually transmitted diseases, a risk drastically reduced in the post-war period by antibiotics 'which appeared to remove the major risks from sexual promiscuity' (Hobsbawm 1994: 270). The availability of the birth control pill gave further credence to the idea of sex without consequences. Yet, as Chris seems to imply, the sexual revolution – beloved by metropolitan intellectuals – quickly became an empty creed that blandly celebrated promiscuity. Toni is a caricature of the Parisian type of metropolitan intellectual who thinks that sexual fulfilment rises in direct proportion to number of partners, claiming that 'I can barely think of a woman I *don't* want to fuck' (Barnes 1990: 89). Chris is more characteristically suburban, believing that even without the scaffolding of Judaeo-Christian morality, marriage remains meaningful: 'I'm not Jewish, I don't go to church, I don't wank – I merely love my wife' (Barnes 1990: 179). This may not constitute a weighty and idealistic justification of the institution of marriage, but it is – less ambitiously perhaps – an affirmation of the fulfilment that can be found in a lasting relationship.

Metroland is a product of its historical moment, a time when the utopian impulses of the 1960s and early 1970s had run aground. The young Chris's and Toni's discussion of the 'Sexy Sixties' prompts them comically to postulate a theory of history – described as 'Sex, Austerity, War, Austerity' (Barnes 1990: 55) – premised on the idea of a cyclical progression of decades. Barnes is writing in the knowledge that the 1970s had been a decade of economic and social instability and *Metroland* seems thoroughly aware that it is situated at a time of profound cultural and political change, at a point when a 'lengthy period of centrist and moderately social-democratic rule ended' (Hobsbawm 1994: 248). Margaret Thatcher became Leader of the Opposition in 1975 and was elected Prime Minister in 1979 (the year before *Metroland* was published) with a mandate to dismantle the Keynesian mixed economy that had prevailed since the war. The final section of *Metroland* anticipates the atmosphere of Thatcher's Britain. Like Toni's and Chris's friendship, the country was polarized along ideological lines. A naïve and idealistic Left struggled for credibility as the trade union movement suffered a series of defeats, and the Conservative party gleefully embraced free-market capitalism with the complicity of the property-owning, suburban middle class. Thatcherism's infamous motto, 'there is no alternative' seems to hang in the air at the end of the novel, even if it was yet to become the battle cry of the monetarist right (Evans 2004: 46). Toni has only his leftist idealism to offer and his protest against the status quo seems merely adolescent. The novel suggests, uneasily, that we have no choice but to lower our ambitions for ourselves and for humankind, and to live out our lives as small people enjoying essentially private pleasures.

Metroland is a book about transgression, and it questions the assumption that there is any inherent value in breaking the conventions of suburban bourgeois morals and manners, in the épat. Transgression, in this novel, is a false idol. But what, Barnes asks, is the alternative? Chris's political apathy effectively equals an acceptance of the status quo, and opens the door to Thatcherism. The victory of the freeholder over the *flâneur* may have its compensations, and Chris is able to articulate some of them. Yet the problem highlighted by the novel's ending is that once the childish and ineffective gesture of the épat has been discarded, there may be nothing left but political quietism.

CHAPTER TWO

Inventing a Way to the Truth: Life and Fiction in Julian Barnes's *Flaubert's Parrot*

RYAN ROBERTS

Chapter Summary: Julian Barnes's novel *Flaubert's Parrot* now serves as the embodiment of the author's growing concern with the relationship between life and fiction. Examining the novel's formation, its origins in Barnes's journalism and short fiction, and changes in manuscript drafts provides insights into the depth and complexity of Barnes's exploration of the differences between biography and fiction and the distinctions he makes between author and narrator. Analyzing these foundational texts and the writing process that Barnes employed to develop the novel reveals how each works to create a fictional text that resonates with greater truth than the factual episodes on which it is based.

In September 1981, Julian Barnes traveled to Normandy to visit sites associated with Gustave Flaubert in Rouen. He stood beneath Flaubert's statue in the Place des Carmes, examined exhibits at the Flaubert Museum at the Hôtel Dieu, and stopped to see the small pavilion which served as the last remnant of Flaubert's house at Croisset. The museum at the Hôtel Dieu contained examples of antiquated medical equipment, some artifacts left by the Flaubert family, and, as Barnes noted in his travel journal, 'the bright green, perky-eyed parrot which was lent to [Flaubert] when he was writing *Un coeur simple*' (Barnes 2005: 30). A few days later, while surveying Flaubert memorabilia at Croisset, Barnes spotted a second parrot, and his notebook similarly reflects the excitement of his discovery.

Barnes did not immediately recognize the incident's potential to evolve into a fictional narrative, though he later identified it as 'the moment at which the novel [*Flaubert's Parrot*] began' (Barnes 2005: 30). While he was intrigued by his find, he told Vanessa Guignery in an interview that he was unsure whether it was much more than 'an interesting coincidence, a provocative ambiguity' (Guignery 2002: 258). He later recalled, 'It had clearly made an impression, but of what sort – and with what consequences, if any? Was this just a Curious Fact? Half of an anecdote? A small article for an academic journal? I didn't know, nor did I really ask' (Barnes 2005: 30).

Barnes's subsequent creation of the narrative surrounding his discovery of the two parrots underwent several textual revisions before becoming the foundation of *Flaubert's Parrot* (1983), a novel that now serves as the embodiment of Barnes's growing concern with the relationship between life and fiction. Examining the novel's formation, including its origins in Barnes's journalism and changes in manuscript drafts now housed at the Harry Ransom Center, reveals how Barnes uses the text to explore this relationship, specifically as it relates to the differences between reality and fiction and the distinctions between author and narrator.

'Art Is Not a *Brassière*': On Biography and Fiction

Barnes addresses the counterpoints of life and fiction throughout *Flaubert's Parrot*, but of special interest are those passages that originated in his writings *prior* to the novel's publication in 1984. Each instance reveals insights into how Barnes viewed the distinctions between life and fiction and helps to clarify his views on the unique ability of literature or art to portray truth more effectively than traditional forms of life writing.

On August 18, 1983, Barnes published a lengthy essay titled 'Flaubert and Rouen' (1983a) which recounts key events in Flaubert's life and discusses his writing style, friendships, and dislike for the bourgeois. The text reads like a sampler from *Flaubert's Parrot*, with numerous passages echoing lines found later in the novel. While Barnes recounts the plot and themes of Flaubert's *Un coeur simple* (1877) in the article, he does not mention his discovery of the two parrots that were vying for authenticity as the model used for the story. The essay remains purely factual and does not hint at any information of an autobiographical nature.

Instead, Barnes draws upon his personal discovery of the multiple parrots to form the basis of a short story, which he titled 'Flaubert's Parrot' and published in the *London Review of Books* the same week as his non-fiction essay (Barnes 1983b). The story would eventually become the first chapter of a novel, with Barnes later reflecting, 'I wrote a version – quite a close version, I think, of the first chapter – as a story, as a separate story. But it was clearly a fiction, a piece of fiction' (Guignery 2002: 258).

When Barnes noted the first parrot from the Hôtel Dieu in his notebook, the details were merely informative. The passage recounts the colour of the feathers and the short story for which the parrot was used as a model. Braithwaite's fictionalized discovery of the bird at the Hôtel Dieu, however, imbues the bird with far greater significance: 'I gazed at the bird, and to my surprise felt ardently in touch with this writer who disdainfully forbade posterity to take any personal interest in him' (Barnes 1984: 16). Braithwaite's encounter with the second parrot at Croisset remains much closer to Barnes's journal entry, which notes:

> Then, crouched on top of one of the display cabinets, what did we see but Another Parrot. Also bright green, also, according to the gardienne & also a label hung on its perch, the authentic parrot borrowed by GF when he wrote UCS!! I ask the gardienne if I can take it down & photograph it. She concurs, even suggests I take off the glass case. I do, & it strikes me as slightly less authentic than the other one: mainly because it seems benign, & F wrote of how irritating the other one was to have on his desk. As I am looking for somewhere to photograph it, the sun comes out – this on a cloudy, grouchy, rainy morning – & slants across a display cabinet. I put it there & take 2 sunlit photos; then, as I pick the parrot up to replace it, the sun goes in. It felt like a benign intervention by GF – signalling thanks for my presence, or indicating that this was indeed the true parrot. (Barnes 2005: 30)

The passage in *Flaubert's Parrot* is much shorter, but the central elements still exist:

> Then I saw it. Crouched on top of a high cupboard was another parrot. Also bright green. Also, according to both the *gardienne* and the label on its perch, the very parrot which Flaubert had borrowed from the Museum of Rouen for the writing of *Un coeur simple*. I asked permission to take the second Loulou down, set him carefully on the corner of a display cabinet, and removed his glass dome. (Barnes 1984: 21)

Although Braithwaite grants significance to the first parrot, he views the second with scepticism and as a symbol for the inaccessibility of an author: 'The writer's voice – what makes you think it can be located that easily? Such was the rebuke offered by the second parrot' (Barnes 1984: 22).

In discussing these passages years later, Barnes acknowledges he had altered the real and fictional reactions to the parrots. He consciously 'shifted the inner narrative of the parrot encounters: the first makes the reader-pursuer feel warmly close to the writer-hero, while the second acts as a rebuking reply – Ha, don't be so sentimental, don't think you can get in touch with the artist as easily as that' (Barnes 2005: 30). The manipulation of his real experience allowed Barnes to create a fictional, but far more symbolic encounter that helps establish the foundation for one of the novel's central themes – the inaccessibility of the past and the unreliability of historical artifacts.

More subtle origins of passages from the novel can be found in Barnes's short fiction and journalism from the early 1980s, and each instance provides insights into how Barnes perceives the distinctions between life and fiction. At times, such distinctions are discussed in terms of 'truth and art', 'factual and fantasy', or 'biography and fiction', but the central dilemma between life and fiction remains constant and provides Barnes the opportunity to more fully develop the novel's themes.

The first example of an influence of a prior text on *Flaubert's Parrot* reveals Barnes's attempt to address the relationship between truth and art. In his short story 'One of a Kind' (1982), an exiled Romanian writer named Marian Tiriac recounts the artistic and political environment he left behind decades earlier. He remembers, 'I was getting into disfavour by now. Too despairing, they said of me. The few scraps of work I offered to publish were held to be insufficiently uplifting to the human spirit. Uplifting . . . ha. As if writing were a brassière and the human spirit were a pair of bosoms' (Barnes 1982b: 23). Braithwaite echoes this passage in 'The Case Against', a chapter formed from a series of 15 complaints about Flaubert that Braithwaite defends in turn. The final lines of the chapter outline the narrator's argument against the claim that Flaubert 'didn't believe Art had a social purpose': 'Do not imagine that Art is something which is designed to give gentle uplift and self-confidence. Art is not a *brassière*. At least, not in the English sense. But do not forget that *brassière* is the French for life-jacket' (Barnes 1984: 136).

The similarities between these passages go beyond the *brassière* metaphor. In each instance, Barnes uses the image to comment on art's relationship to truth and literature's (or an author's) ability to impact the human spirit. The relationship between art and truth forms one of the novel's primary themes. The *brassière* metaphor speaks to Barnes's views on the ability of art or, in his case, literature, to resonate this greater truth. Braithwaite's suggestion, 'Do you want art to be a healer? Send for the AMBULANCE GEORGE SAND. Do you want art to tell the truth? Send for the AMBULANCE FLAUBERT' (Barnes 1984: 136), echoes Barnes's personal view that literature is 'the best way of telling the truth; it's a process of producing grand, beautiful, well-ordered lies that tell more truth than any assemblage of facts' (Guppy 2001: 57).

Such an 'assemblage of facts' underpins much of *Flaubert's Parrot* and leads to a second example of how the novel confronts the interconnections between life and fiction. In the chapter 'Emma Bovary's Eyes', Braithwaite comments on the unreliability of facts and questions whether factual discrepancies really matter within a fictional text. In the process of developing his argument, Braithwaite provides numerous examples of textual errors by well-known authors in his defence of Flaubert:

> Yevtushenko, for example, apparently made a howler in one of his poems about the American nightingale. Pushkin was quite wrong about the sort of military dress worn at balls. John Wain was wrong about the Hiroshima pilot. Nabokov was wrong – rather surprising, this – about the phonetics of

the name Lolita. There were other examples: Coleridge, Yeats and Browning were some of those caught out not knowing a hawk from a handsaw, or not even knowing what a handsaw was in the first place. (Barnes 1984: 76)

Braithwaite continues his discussion by mentioning additional errors by William Golding in *Lord of the Flies* (1954) and in Tennyson's 'The Charge of the Light Brigade' (1854). His knowledge of the errors committed by such well-known and respected authors would be surprising had he not already informed the reader that these examples originated from a lecture he once attended 'some years ago at the Cheltenham Literary Festival' (Barnes 1984: 76). The lecturer was Professor Christopher Ricks, who Braithwaite thought gave 'a very shiny performance. His bald head was shiny; his black shoes were shiny; and his lecture was very shiny indeed. Its theme was Mistakes in Literature and Whether They Matter' (Barnes 1984: 76).

Barnes also attended Ricks's lecture at the Cheltenham Literary Festival and reported on his experiences for *The New Statesman* in October 1976. In his article, he recounts much of what Braithwaite remembers, including the same 'shiny' or 'well-polished' imagery associated with the lecturer:

> As if the writer's lot hadn't enough discomforts, the Festival had laid on Christopher Ricks, who reprimanded various authors for getting their facts wrong. In a dazzling bustle of wit, the Prof put the well-polished boot into Yevtushenko (wrong about American nightingales), Nabokov (wrong about the phonetics of the name Lolita), Pushkin (wrong about military dress at balls), John Wain (wrong about the Hiroshima pilot), Coleridge, Yeats, Browning, Tennyson, Hugh Scanlon and William Golding (wrong about optics in *Lord of the Flies*: Piggy's specs were for myopia, and so couldn't have been used as burning glasses). There was, of course, a positive side to the argument – that irony and fantasy become unusable if the factual side of literature is unreliable. (Barnes 1976: 492)

The importance of the similarities between Barnes's reported experiences and Braithwaite's rests in what Barnes identifies as the 'positive side' of the lecture. As Braithwaite explains, '[Professor Ricks's] argument was that if the factual side of literature becomes unreliable, then ploys such as irony and fantasy become much harder to use. If you don't know what's true, or what's meant to be true, then the value of what isn't true, or isn't meant to be true, becomes diminished' (Barnes 1984: 77). Barnes purposefully references the historical event of the Cheltenham Festival and provides details of the exact examples mentioned in Professor Ricks's lecture in order to establish the fictional scene as 'true'. Barnes creates this 'true' scenario in which his fictional world and narrator exist and, as a result, helps to establish Braithwaite's 'value' and credibility. Braithwaite bridges the line between these worlds, adding an additional dimension to the novel's underlying theme of the connections between life and fiction.

Barnes draws upon two additional non-fiction publications in order to question the nature of biography and its reliance on detritus to illuminate truths about a person's life. Throughout *Flaubert's Parrot*, Barnes gives special attention to Jean-Paul Sartre and his voluminous biography of Flaubert, *L'Idiot de la famille: Gustave Flaubert de 1821 à 1857* (1971). Sartre's name appears 13 times in the novel, including once as a main entry in Chapter 12, 'Braithwaite's Dictionary of Accepted Ideas': 'Jean-Paul Sartre: Spent ten years writing *L'Idiot de la famille* when he could have been writing Maoist tracts. A highbrow Louise Colet, constantly pestering Gustave, who wanted only to be left alone. Conclude: 'It is better to waste your old age than to do nothing at all with it'' (Barnes 1984: 155). Much of Braithwaite's information about Sartre echoes sentiments first expressed in Barnes's lengthy book review of Sartre's *The Family Idiot: Gustave Flaubert, 1821–1857* published in the *London Review of Books* in June 1982 (Barnes 1982a).

Examining Barnes's review for similarities with the novel uncovers two points of particular interest to his approach to biography and truth, two issues central to his creation of *Flaubert's Parrot*. In the first instance, Barnes questions the very nature of biography by claiming, 'The traditional, academic approach to biography – the search for documentation, the sifting of evidence, the balancing of contradictory opinions, the cautious hypothesis, the modestly tentative conclusion – has run itself into the ground; the method has calcified' (Barnes 1982a: 22). He reiterates this position in interviews conducted after the novel's publication, explaining, 'I don't think I'm capable of writing a straight biography. I lack the patience, and the capacity for constant checking. There's a tumulus of opinions that gradually grows over a dead writer, and I see no good reason for adding to it. I looked for a way of approaching Flaubert obliquely – of sinking the shaft in at a different angle' (Walsh 1984: 20). Sartre's biography of Flaubert served as an example to Barnes of just how ineffective traditional biographical approaches have become in recording the truths about a life.

The trouble, of course, was finding a more appropriate alternative, something that would approximate biography while still holding true to Flaubert's axiom that 'Style is a function of theme. Style is not imposed on subject-matter, but arises from it. Style is truth to thought' (Barnes 1984: 88). Once again, the seeds of Barnes's approach are found in his review of Sartre: 'Of course, to say that swathes of *L'Idiot* are fiction is not to deny them the possibility of truth' (Barnes 1982a: 22). By making such a claim, Barnes is clearly stating his belief that fiction and truth can coexist and, more importantly, that a work of fiction has the power to *function* as truth.

This perspective serves as opposition to the view that biography seeks truth in real life, in the 'relics' left by an author, in what Braithwaite calls the 'image, the face, the signature; the 93 per cent copper statue and the Nadar photograph; the scrap of clothing and the lock of hair' (Barnes 1984: 12). As Braithwaite wonders at the beginning of the novel – 'Do we think the leavings of a life contain some ancillary truth?' (Barnes 1984: 12). Through such questioning, we are led to conclude that fiction may indeed serve as an alternative to the traditional approaches of biography or life writing.

Supplementing these discussions, Braithwaite refers to a story about Robert Louis Stevenson as his primary example of how seeking author 'relics' undermines the quest for truth about an author's life. The story appears at the beginning of the first chapter as Braithwaite recalls, 'When Robert Louis Stevenson died, his business-minded Scottish nanny quietly began selling hair which she claimed to have cut from the writer's head forty years earlier. The believers, the seekers, the pursuers bought enough of it to stuff a sofa' (Barnes 1984: 12). Barnes first mentions this story, though in slightly longer form, in the lead to a television review he wrote for the *New Statesman* in April 1980. In both instances, the essential story and its punch line remained the same – '[T]here was enough of Stevenson's hair in circulation to stuff a pouffe' (i.e. a padded stool) (Barnes 1980b: 561). The story of Stevenson's hair raises questions about the reliability of tangible remains from an author's life (or anyone's life, for that matter). The story suggests that much of what is discovered or claimed as 'true' about a life may, in fact, be misleading or blatantly false.

Barnes begins the novel with the story of Stevenson's nanny as a way of foreshadowing Braithwaite's search for and uncertain identification of the true parrot that perched on Flaubert's desk while he wrote his famous short story. Barnes references the story once again in his essay, 'The Follies of Writer Worship' (1985), but this time concluded 'there is enough Stevenson hair around to open a wig-shop' (Barnes 1985: 16). The essay ran in the *New York Times Book Review* and served as prepublicity for the American edition of *Flaubert's Parrot* by focusing on the questions raised by Braithwaite in the novel's opening chapter: 'Why does the writing make us chase the writer? Why can't we leave well alone? Why aren't the books enough?' (Barnes 1984: 12). Barnes expands upon this in the essay by discussing examples of author worship within his own life, including Flaubert, a writer he 'had idolized unswervingly for 20 years or so' (Barnes 1985: 16). He eventually concludes, 'You may feel "close" to a writer when you walk round his house and examine a lock of his hair, but the only time you are truly close is when [you] are reading words on the page. This is the only pure act; the rest – from fandom to Festschrift – is dilution, marginality, betrayal – the higher sentimentality. Biography is only sophisticated hair-collecting' (Barnes 1985: 16).

Barnes continues to struggle with the problematic nature of biography throughout the essay. While he wishes to chronicle Flaubert's life, he evidentially feels uncomfortable assuming the role of biographer. He senses there are 'other things wrong with the biographical form, especially when applied to someone as long dead and as long famous as Flaubert' (Barnes 1985: 16). He questions the rationale of traditional biographical methods and believes new biographers were:

> forever condemned to that dutiful trudge in the footsteps of [their] predecessors, reinterpreting here, questioning there, being a little more judicious, being fair. I wanted to write about Flaubert, though in quite what form I didn't as yet know. All I knew was that I didn't want to be fair or judicious; I wanted the process, and the result, to be somehow more active, more aggressive. (Barnes 1985: 16)

Throughout *Flaubert's Parrot*, Barnes turns to his previously published fiction and non-fiction for images and metaphors that influenced and supported his scepticism of biography. He determines that fiction possesses the ability to resonate some greater truth, that Sartre proves the ineffectiveness of the biographical form, and that fiction serves as an appropriate alternative given the propensity for author remains or 'relics' to mislead or misinform the traditional biographer.

'Dear Dr. Barnes': The Intersection of Author and Narrator

Barnes addresses the tension between life and fiction within *Flaubert's Parrot* through his development of his central narrator Geoffrey Braithwaite and, more specifically, the means by which Barnes attempted to separate his personal experiences as a writer from those shared with the novel's narrator. To better comprehend this matter, it is important to understand the special relationship shared by Barnes the author and Braithwaite the narrator and fictional author of *Flaubert's Parrot*.

Julian Barnes clearly loves Flaubert. He has written dozens of essays, reviews, and fictional pieces about Flaubert both prior to and since the publication of *Flaubert's Parrot*. He has published literary criticism, as seen in his perceptive study of Justin, a minor character in *Madame Bovary*, as well as appraisals of several collections of Flaubert's letters, numerous Flaubert-related biographies, the film adaptation of *Madame Bovary*, and details about his search for *The Temptation of St. Anthony*, a painting said to have served as the inspiration for Flaubert's novel of the same name.

As a result of his continued focus on Flaubert, Barnes keeps open the possibility that readers may confuse him with Geoffrey Braithwaite. Indeed, Barnes refers to this tendency in his short story 'Knowing French', which consists of a series of letters the story suggests he received during the mid-1980s from an elderly woman in an old folkery home.

Sylvia, having read *Flaubert's Parrot*, writes to the author and addresses her first letter to 'Dr. Barnes'. Her second letter gently chastises him: 'Now why did you say you were a doctor in your sixties when you obviously can't be more than forty? Come now!' (Barnes 2004: 161) Sylvia's confusion should not be viewed simply as a result of her old age. Barnes includes her question as a way of acknowledging that he is well aware readers frequently confuse him with Braithwaite.

While some critics have commented on the relationship between the author and narrator of *Flaubert's Parrot*, few have investigated the depth and complexity of Barnes's exploration of the matter. Literary studies of the novel tend to focus on other postmodern aspects, such as intertextuality, historiographic metafiction, multiplicity of form or texts, and the novel's approach to the intersections of history and art. Those studies that consider the novel's postmodern concerns with narration typically only analyse the ways in which Braithwaite the narrator interacts with the historical facts and stories surrounding Flaubert. They attempt to reconcile the factual, biographical form of the text and its concern with Flaubert with the fictional, autobiographical form of Braithwaite's hesitant confessions about his relationship with his wife and, ultimately, her death.

When critics *do* note the similarities between the author and narrator within the novel, the discussion centres primarily on their shared fascination with Flaubert and elements of writing style. Matthew Pateman has written about the trouble that reviewers and readers often have distinguishing between Geoffrey Braithwaite the narrator and Julian Barnes the author, concluding, 'The indeterminacy of [Braithwaite's] position within the text has led many critics to elide him as narrator with Barnes as author' (Pateman 1998: 38). Merritt Moseley agrees with this claim when he notes that Barnes, 'as a student of foreign languages at Oxford' was 'more likely than Geoffrey Braithwaite . . . to have heard Dr Enid Starkie lecture' (Moseley 1997: 83). Mélanie Joseph-Vilain distinguishes between Barnes and Braithwaite, but suggests Barnes 'allows doubt to subsist, so that ontological tension is created between the author and the narrator, and therefore between reality and the fictional world' (Joseph-Vilain 2001: 184). In a more recent critique of the novel, Keith Wilson pushes this viewpoint even further, suggesting, 'Braithwaite's characterization is skimpy, his literary interests and rhetorical style sufficiently close to Barnes's own to enforce an involuntary bridging of the notional divide between author and narrator' (Wilson 2006: 362).

What all of these appraisals fail to address is how Barnes's creation of a central narrator through which to express the events of the story was essential to his development of the text *as fiction*. Barnes has commented on this process in several interviews, most recently stating, '[A]s soon as I had the sort of person who, in my stead, would be able to write passionately about these two parrots – so someone rather pedantic, rather obsessed, ready to draw the fullest meanings out of the smallest coincidence or ambiguity – I began to have Geoffrey Braithwaite with me' (Guignery 2002: 258). The claims of an author regarding his intentions can only be trusted so far, of course, but Barnes's manuscripts of the novel, including the initial drafts of the chapter 'Flaubert's Parrot' and a key passage from 'Emma Bovary's Eyes', reveal his clear intentions to separate himself from the text and to invent a defined fictional narrator.

The Julian Barnes Archive at the Harry Ransom Center contains several manuscript drafts of the novel's opening chapter. These drafts can be placed in chronological order according to changes in draft titles and by tracing Barnes's handwritten notes, additions, and/or corrections to the text between draft typescripts. Of the numerous changes made to the text throughout this process, the most notable occur in relation to Barnes's development of Braithwaite's defining characteristics.

The first draft shows Barnes attempting to clarify the boundaries of his character by providing details about Braithwaite's profession and his interest in literature or, more specifically, Flaubert. Braithwaite quickly attempts to characterize himself by claiming, 'I'm a doctor by profession, and on and off, for some twenty years now, I've been a Flaubert buff'. Surprisingly, Braithwaite also reveals himself to be a writer:

> I'm a bit of a writer myself. I suppose you can always call yourself that, even if you haven't published anything for nearly thirty years. Just a couple of novels, back in the Fifties; then – what? – marriage and the care of children intervened. Supervened, rather. I don't regret it, not at all, there are far too many books published anyway, and mine weren't that good – and I'm sure you should try and concentrate on doing one thing well. Flaubert would have agreed. (Barnes 1983–4b)

The fact that Barnes describes Braithwaite as, essentially, an older version of himself reveals how he struggled to fictionalize the discovery of the parrots in his initial draft. At this point, Braithwaite is not just a writer but a published novelist. Barnes provides his narrator with a history of creating stories, characters, and setting in order, perhaps, to explain how a retired doctor could write so eloquently about Flaubert. Braithwaite's history as a novelist in this early draft also aligns him with Flaubert and provides Barnes an opportunity for comparisons between their lives. 'I chose a fictional narrator', Barnes said in an interview shortly after publication, 'precisely because I could invent a life for him against which to bounce the facts of Flaubert's own' (Walsh 1984: 20).

Barnes repeats the passage with only a slight revision in a second draft, but in the third draft he removes the reference to Braithwaite as a novelist while retaining his status as a writer. He crosses out the lines 'I'm a bit of a writer myself. I suppose you can still call yourself that, even if you haven't published anything for thirty years. Just a couple of novels' and replaces them with the hand-written phrase, 'I published a couple of books myself' (Barnes 1983–4c: 2). This shift may seem slight, but it changes the focus of Braithwaite's character. He no longer specifically writes fiction, just 'books'. As a result, his past professional life centers more strongly on his role as physician.

The remaining drafts further distance Barnes from his narrator by completing Braithwaite's shift from a writer to physician: 'I thought of writing books myself once; had the ideas, even made some notes. But, well, I was a doctor, and I had a wife and children. You can only do one thing well: Flaubert knew that' (Barnes 1983–4d: 3). Note here that Braithwaite no longer has a publishing history at all. He has only *thought* of writing books. He is simply a doctor, husband, and father. Such characteristics define him as a person and narrator while allowing for far greater associations between his experiences and, not Flaubert the author, but, rather, those of Charles Bovary.

Similarly, comparing the chapter 'Emma Bovary's Eyes' with an early draft titled 'Eyes of Blue' provides an example of Barnes's playfulness as an author and how he purposefully removed direct references to himself from the final text. As mentioned above, in this chapter Braithwaite discusses authorial errors in literature and provides a lengthy list of such mistakes in the works of well-known authors. He cites the following example to illustrate his point:

> I read the other day a well-praised first novel in which the narrator – who is both sexually inexperienced and an amateur of French literature – comically rehearses to himself the best way to kiss a girl without being rebuffed: 'With a slow, sensual, irresistible strength, draw her gradually towards you while gazing into her eyes as if you had just been given a copy of the first, suppressed edition of *Madame Bovary*'. (Barnes 1984: 78)

Of the numerous corrections made to this passage during its draft stage, one change in particular stands out. Between the lines and just following the phrase 'a highly praised first novel,' Barnes typed the words 'called *Metroland*' (Barnes 1983–4a). That the words were typed suggests he inserted them at the time he wrote the first draft, prior to editing the text by hand. The words were subsequently crossed out by Barnes, but his initial impulse was to identify himself within the reference.

Keeping the novel unidentified allows for a greater association between the narrator and the reader. Failing to identify the novel does not alter the essential meaning or usefulness of *Metroland* as an example, but for those readers who identify the source from past exposure to Barnes's early novels or for those who hunt down the allusion, the reference creates a sly and meaningful inside joke about the invisibility of the author within the work. Such a reader is immediately aligned with

Braithwaite's own search for meaning and cross-references in Flaubert's work and, as such, is provided a unique glimpse into Braithwaite's nature and character.

Barnes's allusion to *Metroland* also serves to establish Braithwaite as a legitimate literary critic. Braithwaite explains the significance of the error related to *Madame Bovary*:

> The novel, as I should have thought was tolerably well known, first appeared serially in the *Revue de Paris*; then came the prosecution for obscenity; and only after the acquittal was the work published in book form. I expect the young novelist (it seems unfair to give his name) was thinking of the 'first, suppressed edition' of *Les Fleurs du mal*. No doubt he'll get it right in time for his second edition; if there is one. (Barnes 1984: 78)

When asked about this passage and the authorial error it criticizes, Barnes answers, 'I suppose I thought it was rather cute to leave it in' (Guignery and Roberts 2009: 170). Outside the realm of fiction, the only way Barnes could have corrected his mistake would be to follow Braithwaite's advice to change the text in future printings. He chose instead to remain true to Braithwaite's characterization, and *Metroland* retains the error in all subsequent editions and translations.

Despite some critics' claims of similarities between author and narrator in *Flaubert's Parrot*, Barnes's alterations to Braithwaite's character in the passages above reveals his clear intention to distinguish himself from his narrator. The removal of Braithwaite's experience as a novelist and more concerted focus on his history as a doctor supports Barnes's fictionalization of his personal experiences related to the parrots. As Barnes clarified in an interview about the novel, 'Life, one chapter says, just isn't like books. It's less easy to understand than it is to understand a novel – because the life that's being so conveniently dealt with is always someone else's' (Walsh 1984: 20). Barnes seeks meaning in his personal experiences by giving ownership of his narrative to Braithwaite. He transforms his discovery of Flaubert's parrots into fiction in order to reflect one of the major themes of the novel – that fiction is closer to truth than reality.

'I Tried to Be as Truthful About Him as I Could': A Conclusion

Barnes believes, as did Flaubert, in the invisibility of the author within the work. While critics have disagreed about the level of success he has had in removing himself from his novels, and in particular *Flaubert's Parrot*, the fact remains that Barnes does attempt to create a fictional narrative and fully developed character in Geoffrey Braithwaite. He wanted to create homage to Flaubert but wanted to do so in a new and unique way. Barnes chose to create a work of fiction instead of a traditional biography, because he felt the traditional forms of life writing had become stagnant, that 'the method [had] calcified' (Barnes 1982a: 22).

Barnes's experiments with form create a text with more universal appeal and with a greater ability to resonate the underlying truths of Flaubert's life. 'I didn't fictionalize Flaubert', Barnes claims. 'I tried to be as truthful about him as I could' (Guppy 2001: 69). By remaining truthful about Flaubert, Barnes frees himself to employ and, at times, undermine traditional texts and narrative forms.

Similarly, Barnes elaborates and expands upon his previously published journalism in the process of writing *Flaubert's Parrot* because he thinks journalism is sometimes too much rooted in reality. Fiction offers the possibility to create symbols, metaphors, and multiple layers of meaning not easily represented in journalism or that too often are disregarded in real life. When asked why he prefers fiction over other literary forms, such as essays or journalism, Barnes replied:

> Well, to be honest I think I tell less truth when I write journalism than when I write fiction. I practise both those media, and I enjoy both, but, to put it crudely, when you are writing journalism your task is to simplify the world and render it comprehensible in one reading; whereas when you are writing fiction your task is to reflect the fullest complications of the world, to say things that are not as straight-forward as might be understood from reading my journalism and to produce something that you hope will reveal further layers of truth on a second reading. (Guppy 2001: 58)

As readers, we understand the life span of a piece of journalism is short-lived. The reviews and essays Barnes wrote about Flaubert prior to the publication of *Flaubert's Parrot* served their immediate function and have been, more or less, forgotten. By integrating some of the same information and observations into a work of fiction, however, Barnes created a work of art with lasting effect. That is the true success of *Flaubert's Parrot* – that Barnes took a non-fictional story destined for the ephemera pages of a literary journal or newspaper and, by scrutinizing and experimenting with the interplay of life and fiction, fashioned a novel that resonates with greater truth than the factual episodes on which it is based.

CHAPTER THREE

'A preference for things Gallic': Julian Barnes and the French Connection

VANESSA GUIGNERY

Chapter Summary: This chapter explores Julian Barnes's relationship with French culture and literature in his fiction and non-fiction, and seeks to delineate the contours of the traditions within which he situates himself and explore the ways in which he revisits and assesses the French legacy from a British viewpoint. Although frequently labelled 'postmodernist', Julian Barnes is nevertheless often drawn back to the literature of the nineteenth century and to French masters of realism and modernism. His admiration for the French literary canon leads him to engage a fertile exchange with the past while at the same time creating his own original voice.

In *Flaubert's Parrot*, the narrator, driving off the boat at Newhaven, imagines answering the customs officer's 'Have you anything to declare?', with 'Yes, I'd like to declare a small case of French flu, a dangerous fondness for Flaubert, a childish delight in French road-signs, and a love of the light as you look north' (Barnes 1985: 115–16). If Julian Barnes claims to be a European, his relationship with France which he calls his 'second country' (Barnes 2002a: xiii), and to French culture more specifically, is both intimate and passionate. Barnes presents himself as 'an English Francophile' (Barnes 1995: 320) and willingly admits: '[France] is my other country. There is something about it – its history, its landscape – that obviously sparks my imagination' (Swanson 1996). His work – more particularly *Metroland* (1980), *Flaubert's Parrot* (1984), *Talking It Over* (1991), *Cross Channel* (1996), *Love, etc.* (2001), *Something to Declare* (2002) and *Nothing To Be Frightened Of* (2008), but also his various essays, reviews and notebooks which form part of his archives held by the Harry Ransom Humanities Center at the University of Texas in Austin – is teeming with references or allusions to French culture, their presence justified by the topics and contexts of these books, as well as by the personality of their fictional characters. Beyond the thematic level, a more literary approach to the various connections between Julian Barnes and France can help to delineate the contours of the traditions within which the writer situates himself and explore the ways in which he revisits and assesses the French legacy from a British viewpoint. These numerous links with a foreign culture raise questions as to the contemporary writer's relationship to the literary past and his own search for originality. How does Barnes address his fascination and admiration for Flaubert and other French nineteenth-century writers? Are his works so full of respect and devotion that they are bound to retell, repeat so as to celebrate? Are his books a homage, a eulogy, a commemoration and an imitation, or does he use the postmodernist strategies of irony, subversion and deconstruction? Can a writer be both respectful towards the past and original in his own creation? Do the extensive French references in his work suggest that the literary space is saturated, exhausted, condemned to parrotry, or does the British writer manage to break free from the French literature of the past to give vent to an original voice? Finally, is Barnes's fascination for French nineteenth-century literature the sign of a dissatisfaction with the present state of British contemporary fiction, and could it be related to the nostalgic mode that some critics have associated with postmodernism and more particularly with the neo-Victorian (Gutleben 2001: 199)? In order to probe these issues, I will first provide a rapid overview of the French cultural and literary traditions which attract Julian Barnes and I will then examine how the writer deals with this legacy of a foreign past.

A Fondness for Provincial France

Julian Barnes's interest in France was undoubtedly sparked by the fact that both his parents were French teachers and that from 1959 on, the family spent their summer holidays driving through various regions of provincial France, holidays which, however, were 'filled with anxiety' for the teenager (Barnes 2002a: xii). In 1966–67, Barnes taught English at a Catholic school in Rennes, and was initiated into Francophone popular culture through singers such as Jacques Brel and Georges Brassens whom he valued for their individualism and non-conformity (Barnes 2002a: 19–33). Barnes then studied modern languages (French and Russian) at Magdalen College, Oxford, but as he remarks in the introduction to *Something to Declare*, his fondness for France really started when he was in his thirties:

> . . . in the long silent quarrel and *faux* existentialism of late adolescence, I took against my parents' values and therefore against their love of France. At university I gave up languages for philosophy, found myself ill-equipped

for it, and returned reluctantly to French.... It was only in my mid-thirties that I started seeing France again with non-filial, non-academic eyes. (Barnes 2002a: xii)

It is thus only at this period that the author developed a passion for France, which he shares with his older brother, Jonathan Barnes, who owns a house in the Creuse, a step the younger brother has always declined to take and which encouraged him to travel regularly through different regions of France on holiday, exploring the Ardèche, the Drôme, the Cantal, enjoying long walks in the countryside or the mountains, savouring local food and wine of which Barnes is a distinguished connoisseur. The France Julian Barnes likes is the one his parents preferred: 'provincial, villagey, under-populated', 'a France of the regions rather than the centre'. He is not drawn to 'Paris or the larger cities or some yelping exhibitionist beach, but to quiet working villages with rusting café tables, lunchtime torpor, pollarded plane-trees, the dusty thud of boules and an all-purpose *épicerie*' (Barnes 2002a: xiii, xiv, xiii). Because Barnes's fiction and essays are very often marked by an affectionate tenderness towards French items and people, some critics have accused him of sentimental idealism and nostalgia in his portrayal of France. However the author acknowledges his partiality: 'My view of France has been acquired from literature, from holidays, from living amongst you for only one year; it is necessarily partial' (Barnes 2006b: 5.1). Moreover, Barnes argues that you choose a second country to find antitheses to your own and your judgment is 'seldom fair or precise' (Barnes 1996: 207) because you 'project, perhaps, your romanticism and idealism' (Swanson 1996) onto this other country, and also, one may add, onto its culture and literature.

The Combativeness of French Literature

Together with the lifestyle, French culture and literature are decisive factors in explaining Barnes's Francophilia. In 1996, the writer euphemistically told an interviewer: 'it's a literature I know well', adding: 'A lot of my intellectual points of reference are French rather than English' (Swanson 1996). This web of references is apparent in Barnes's fiction and non-fiction alike, and points to the French tradition that attracts his characters and himself. In *Metroland*, whose first part is, as Barnes conceded, autobiographical in 'spirit' and 'topography' if not in its 'incidents' (Hayman 2009: 3), the literary erudition and affected rebellion of the two teenagers, Christopher and Toni, impel them to idealize French poets from the second half of the nineteenth century, including Gérard de Nerval, Théophile Gautier, Charles Baudelaire, Paul Verlaine and Arthur Rimbaud. The narrator remarks early in the book that what particularly appealed to him and his friend as teenagers was the rebelliousness of French authors:

> ... we cared for its literature largely for its combativeness. French writers were always fighting one another – defending and purifying the language, ousting slang words, writing prescriptive dictionaries, getting arrested, being prosecuted for obscenity, being aggressively Parnassian, scrabbling for seats in the Académie, intriguing for literary prizes, getting exiled. The idea of the sophisticated tough attracted us greatly. (Barnes 1990: 16)

The two adolescents are thus drawn to a subversive and combative literature, a literature of opposition, resistance, and dissidence, which quarrels with tradition in order to try and create something new. Julian Barnes admits for his part that, contrary to his heroes, he didn't want to be a rebel: 'Perhaps I *wasn't* rebellious enough. Or maybe I was saving it all for the novel' (Stout 1992: 29). However, in the introduction to *Something to Declare*, he confesses that the France he values is 'contrarian in spirit' (Barnes 2002a: xiv), and just as for his characters, he admits that 'there was an element of cultural snobbery in [his] initial preference for things Gallic'. He explains that snobbery in terms that echo those of *Metroland's* narrator: 'their Romantics seemed more romantic than ours, their Decadents more decadent, their Moderns more modern' (Barnes 2002a: xii–xiii).

This 'preference for things Gallic' also applies to cinema. In *Something to Declare*, Julian Barnes celebrates the *nouvelle vague* film director François Truffaut whose film *Jules et Jim* (1962) is revisited with postmodernist irony both in *Metroland* (Barnes 1990: 112) and in *Talking It Over* (Barnes 1992: 22–24). If Barnes's homage to Truffaut is oblique and whimsical in his fiction, maybe in the vein of postmodernist ironical practices, in his review of the director's correspondence, the writer is much more open about his admiration for Truffaut, which he contrasts with his impatience with Jean-Luc Godard. What he values in particular in Truffaut is his revolt against *le cinéma de papa*, traditional cinema, and the term 'revolt', which Barnes uses, deliberately reminds the reader of the rebelliousness of French literature valued by *Metroland*'s teenagers.

In this very 'literary novel' (Hayman 2009: 3), Christopher's and Toni's admiration for French culture goes beyond literature and cinema to include language as well. The narrator remarks: 'We were, you may have guessed, mostly doing French. We cared for its language because its sounds were plosive and precise' (Barnes 1990: 16), characteristics which could be related to the combativeness of French literature that fascinates the two teenagers. Moreover, the use of French words or expressions and the bilingual puns enable Christopher and Toni to cultivate their marginality while further exposing their pedantry. They thus sometimes mix French words with literary references as in their mottoes: '*écraser l'infâme*' and '*épater la bourgeoisie*' (Barnes 1990: 15), two expressions which are never translated throughout the novel and are respectively borrowed from Voltaire and Charles Baudelaire. The teenagers then create their own idiolect or language when they Anglicize the French verbs in sentences such as 'How about écrasing someone?' (Barnes 1990: 17) or 'Think I épated him much?' (Barnes 1990: 18). They also deliberately ostracize their fellow pupils when making monolingual puns in French which only they understand. These forays into French can certainly be seen as playful, amusing and clever but they also epitomize the teenagers' premature sophistication, cynicism and self-absorbed snobbery. Moreover, Christopher's attachment to all that is French may be the sign of his impatience with Britain and his need to create an identity for himself that would not be strictly English. The adolescents' appropriation of French specificities partly finds an echo in Barnes's own approach to his Francophilia which he attempts to define in *Something to Declare*: 'Knowing a second country means choosing what you want from it, finding antitheses to your normal, English, urban life' (Barnes 2002a: xiii). In *Metroland*, Christopher cultivates a form of rootlessness and can only look up to Toni whose parents are Polish Jews. Thus, the boy's adoption of French culture, literature and language is a way for him to approach the assumed class of rootless people. According to Merritt Moseley, in *Metroland*, 'France is an idea, as well as a style, a language, a pose, an image of the right sort of life, and a rebuke to Metroland' (Moseley 1997: 30).

The French Essayistic Tradition

The two boys in *Metroland* will later find an heir in *Talking It Over* and *Love, etc.* in the character of Oliver who is most memorable and entertaining for his erudition, flamboyance, wit and his tendency to 'scatter *bons mots* like sunflower seeds' (Barnes 1992: 239). However, Oliver's literary quotes, allusions and references are more often British than French, whereas Gillian's mother, a Frenchwoman, regularly quotes French eighteenth-century moralist Chamfort, and especially his maxims and reflections on love. In 2003, in his review of a new translation of Chamfort's reflections, Barnes pointed to the fondness of French people for such 'little books of wisdom' while the British viewed them with some suspicion, judging them 'lordly, snobbish' or 'merely flash' (Barnes 2003b: 34). The author's own essayistic inclination, both in his fiction and non-fiction, may partly find its source in a French moralist such as Chamfort whom he finds 'engaging, human, modern', 'various, contradictory, but always stimulating' (Barnes 2003b: 34). Barnes may also have drawn inspiration from the methods of the sixteenth-century essayist Montaigne whom he greatly admires and whose learned pages on death he respectfully quotes or refers to in *Nothing To Be Frightened*

Of, describing them as 'stoical, bookish, anecdotal, epigrammatic and consoling' (Barnes 2008: 39).

Barnes has repeatedly demonstrated his great talent as an essayist in his reflections about art, history, memory and death throughout his novels, in his disquisition on love in the 'Parenthesis' of *A History of the World in 10½ Chapters*, but also in his three volumes of essays, the many uncollected pieces published in newspapers and magazines, his introductions and prefaces, and of course, in *Nothing To Be Frightened Of*. In that respect, the British writer situates himself within a rather ancient French (but also, more broadly, European) tradition of the essay as a type of writing which is – somehow paradoxically – simultaneously personal and abstract, intimate and metaphysical. But Barnes also manages to be very modern in that his meditations engage with the contemporary world and his images belong to the late twentieth century. This is the case for instance in *Nothing To Be Frightened Of* when he ponders modern death in hospitals, surrounded by the latest but also most impersonal technology. In this book, Julian Barnes seems to find his own place within that hybrid essayistic tradition by including anecdotes drawn from his private life – some of them jaunty and even hilarious, others melancholy and poignant – which he mixes with serious philosophical reflections, delightful epigrams and quotes from great novelists, musicians and thinkers. The result is partly a personal though cagey family memoir and partly an intimate conversation with Barnes's literary predecessors whom he considers his second family, affectionately calling them 'non-blood relatives' (Barnes 2008: 46, 195): 'Such artists – such dead artists – are my daily companions, but also my ancestors. They are my true bloodline . . . The descent may not be direct, or provable . . . but I claim it nonetheless' (Barnes 2008: 38). Through this original form of beyond-the-grave conversation, Julian Barnes proves that the literature of the past is very much alive to him: 'I think of the writers who speak to me as my coevals. Or not as my coevals, but as my elders and betters. I don't think of them as being as dead as other people' (Herbert 2008).

A Portrait of the Artist as a Reader

If one compares the writers favoured by Julian Barnes's fictional characters and those the author himself admires, the overlap quickly becomes obvious. Some 15 years after *Metroland*, in the short story 'Gnossienne' from *Cross Channel*, the writer Clements, an alter ego for Julian Barnes, makes a list of the French authors he is loyal to, and the names are familiar to the Barnes reader: Montaigne, Voltaire, Flaubert, Mauriac, Camus (Barnes 1996: 127). These names recur in the memoir *Nothing To Be Frightened Of* where the writer offers quotations from and stories about Montaigne, Flaubert, Renard, Zola, Daudet, the Goncourts, Stendhal,

Camus. One may perceive an evolution in the characters' references, which mirrors the writer's own progress. In an interview in 1986, Julian Barnes said that while he was at university he liked Baudelaire, Verlaine, Rimbaud, Gide, Camus, Sartre, i.e. the rather rebellious writers praised by *Metroland*'s teenagers. He added that in his forties, he preferred Voltaire, Montaigne, Mauriac, Tournier (Salgas 1986: 13), i.e. the ones favoured by his more mature and sedate characters, thus suggesting some degree of change in the author's preferences and confirming the fact that intertextuality can be an efficient tool of characterisation. Moreover, from *Metroland* to *Nothing To Be Frightened Of*, one may discern an evolution from a fondness for rebellion associated with the impetuosity of the young, to a keenness on insolence which may be a more mature attitude. In an essay about Michel Houellebecq whom Barnes refers to as 'the most potentially weighty French novelist to emerge since Tournier', Barnes explains that what strikes him about Houellebecq is his literary insolence which he traces back to Voltaire and La Rochefoucauld, and defines as a tendency to 'systematically affront all our current habits of living, and treat our presumptions of mind as the delusions of the cretinous' (Barnes 2003a). Part of Barnes's own work could be qualified as insolent, the best example being the first chapter of *A History of the World in 10½ Chapters*, where the narrator – a woodworm – satirizes certain assumptions which turn out to match what Barnes sees as the targets of literary insolence, i.e. 'a purposeful God, a benevolent and orderly universe, human altruism, the existence of free will' (Barnes 2003a).

It is needless to say that the French connection asserts itself fully in Barnes's masterpiece, *Flaubert's Parrot*, which celebrates the French master and exposes Barnes's fondness for the work of this distinguished writer. This deep attachment to Flaubert is also confirmed by numerous essays and reviews on the hermit of Croisset, some of which are collected in *Something to Declare*, and by his latest book, *Nothing To Be Frightened Of*, in which Flaubert is regularly evoked and quoted. To Kingsley Amis's provocative and exasperated remark, 'I wish he'd shut up about Flaubert', Barnes jokingly replied: 'Not Shutting Up About Flaubert . . . remains a necessary pleasure' (Barnes 2002a: xiv). Thus, even in his most recent essay on Guy de Maupassant, he cannot help starting by reminding the reader of the connection between the two writers and by quoting one of Flaubert's letters at long length (Barnes 2009: 25).

In 2001, Barnes undertook to translate into English Alphonse Daudet's *La Doulou* (1930; *In the Land of Pain*), a notebook Daudet kept of his bouts of pain in the terminal stages of syphilis from which he suffered most from the early 1880s until his death in 1897. This decision to make Daudet's notebook known to the British public and to do the translation himself certainly confirms Barnes's interest in and intimate relationship with French literature and language. Barnes first read the book when he was researching *Flaubert's Parrot*, and was struck by its 'honesty and its directness and its lack of either sentimentality or self-dramatisation' (Wild 2009: 96). In a letter to Professor Peter Bayley, he described the book as 'a work of great truth, precision and bravery' (Barnes 2006b: 4.3), and a few years later, he praised it for 'the exact glance, the exact word, the refusal either to aggrandize or to trivialize death' (Barnes 2008: 97). These characteristics may also be found in Barnes's own work and more particularly *Nothing To Be Frightened Of* whose main subject is also death and dying. What is interesting about Daudet is that Barnes was attracted to this rather obscure and almost forgotten set of dying notes, rather than the lighter and comic part of Daudet's work, such as *Letters From My Windmill* (1880) and *Tartarin de Tarascon* (1872), which are set in a sunny and agreeable if partial Provence. Barnes's archives in Austin reveal that he devoted himself very seriously to the task of translation and edition. In particular, he wrote several letters to try and trace the original and unedited manuscript, and had in mind to publish the first complete French edition of the book. In terms of language proper, while working on the translation, Barnes sent very precise queries to friends and scholars to make sure he perfectly understood all the nuances of the French hypotext in which some sentences are extremely cryptic, even to the French reader. While translating the book, the writer felt 'a strong sense of service': 'I felt that it was my duty to represent this man as closely as possible in tone and weight of words to what he wrote' (Wilde 2009: 97).

Barnes's choice of a nineteenth-century French writer and of Daudet's book in particular makes even more sense after the publication of *Nothing To Be Frightened Of* where Barnes proposes an answer to the question he asked in the introduction to *In the Land of Pain*: 'How is it best to write about illness, and dying, and death?' (Barnes 2002b: v). In this latest memoir, Julian Barnes's cool and dispassionate tone recalls Daudet's own detachment, lack of self-pity and calm and steady gaze on acute suffering. To flesh out his arguments, Barnes draws again from nineteenth-century French literature, quoting from Flaubert's correspondence, but also from Jules Renard's *Journal* which he kept from 1887 until his death in 1910. The British writer draws particular attention to Renard's talent at 'compression, annotation, pointillism' (Barnes 2008: 48), his 'intense precision' in his description of the natural and human world, and his deep understanding of 'the nature and function of irony' (Barnes 2008: 49), all traits that could equally be applied to Barnes's own work. There thus seems to be a genuine kinship between the twentieth-century writer and the melancholy Renard who share the same first name (Jules, Julian) and whose parents bear similarities: Barnes presents Renard's parents as 'an extreme, theatrical version' of his own (Barnes 2008: 159). As was the case for Daudet, Barnes chooses the less-obvious and less-known work by Renard, the *Journal*, rather than his famous and more expected novel, *Poil de Carotte* (1894), a bitterly ironical account of his own childhood. Barnes thereby confirms his fondness for French writers' diaries and letters, those of Flaubert, Renard but also Sand, Baudelaire, Mallarmé and the Goncourts which Barnes reviewed for various newspapers, valuing for example the Goncourts' journal for being 'an intimate, gossipy, catty, candid panorama of French social and artistic life from 1852 . . . to 1896' (Barnes 2006b: 5.1). This inclination towards journals and correspondences may be partly explained by the fact that they are fascinating documents not only about the life and work of its authors, but also about the literary and cultural context of the time.

There is thus a coherent circulation of writers and texts in Julian Barnes's work, the cultural period he is constantly drawn back to being 'roughly 1850–1925, from the culmination of Realism to the fission of Modernism' (Barnes 2002a: xiv). This is also the period Barnes covers when he devotes essays to French painters such as Gustave Courbet, Edouard Manet, Edgar Degas, Odilon Redon, Pierre Bonnard, Édouard Vuillard and Henri Matisse. Such an attachment to this particular French tradition may seem unexpected for a writer who is frequently labelled 'postmodernist' and whose metafictional strategies are often interpreted in the light of former eighteenth-century experiments, such as Laurence Sterne's *Tristram Shandy* – which Barnes confesses he has never read (Barnes 2000: 114) – or the novels by Henry Fielding and René Diderot. This should certainly draw the reader's attention to the sometimes misleading aspect of labels and to the fact that writers cannot be placed in neat little boxes for the convenience of critics. Like most writers, Julian Barnes is reluctant to be reduced to a specific school, and the variety of his production proves that his work is profoundly dialogic in the Bakhtinian sense, mixing several traditions and voices while aiming for originality. One may wonder however whether the weight of the French literary tradition is not sometimes too onerous for the contemporary British writer, and the palimpsestic dimension of many of Barnes's works raises questions as to the originality of any work of art and the way in which a twenty-first century author can deal with the legacy of the past.

Negotiating the Literary Past

Julian Barnes has often been labelled a postmodernist writer, especially because of the extensive formal experimentation of *Flaubert's Parrot*. The prefix 'post' in its historicized meaning demands to be probed in relation to the literary past as Barnes comes not only after modernism but also after realism, and more generally after canonical literature. This leads one to wonder what an erudite and Francophile author *can* write in the wake of such great novelists as Flaubert or such great essayists as Montaigne, and how he can situate himself in the present when the past tradition he calls upon is so overwhelming. Barnes is aware of the risk that the literary legacy may prove too much to handle: 'There's bound to be a certain burden of the past, a certain oppressiveness of great writing' (Freiburg 2009: 38). This is more true when one is imbued with massive admiration or enthusiasm for a great artist whose work strikes one as perfect and who could therefore condemn all future writers to silence. Barnes's position in relation to Flaubert is daring and ambitious as, instead of sidestepping the master or using the common postmodernist devices of irony or subversion, he takes up the challenge to deal with the Flaubertian inheritance directly, by making Flaubert the central figure of his most accomplished novel and his literary essays, systematically eulogizing his work.

As T. S. Eliot remarked in 'Tradition and the Individual Talent' (1919), any writer needs to take the literary past into account: 'the historical sense compels a man to write not merely with his own generation in his bones, but with a feeling that the whole of the literature of Europe from Homer and within it the whole of the literature of his own country has a simultaneous existence' (Eliot 1920: 49). The whole of literature can of course be considered as a huge palimpsest with layer upon layer of intertexts, but the way intertextuality is used and perceived has evolved in recent times. In the second half of the twentieth century, in the context of postmodernism and the death of the author, the romantic concept of originality and the exaltation of the autonomous creative imagination have become obsolete. As Frederic Jameson sternly explains, the demise of the subject as viewed by modernity as a single individual generating his own vision of the world, means the end of individual style, 'in the sense of the unique and the personal, the end of the distinctive individual brushstroke' (Jameson 1984: 64). This is replaced by a nostalgic polyphony of voices and styles from the past which Jameson deplores: 'with the collapse of the high-modernist ideology of style – what is as unique and unmistakable as your own fingerprints . . . – the producers of culture have nowhere to turn but to the past: the imitation of dead styles, speech through all the masks and voices stored up in the imaginary museum of a now global culture' (Jameson 1984: 65).

It is certainly true that in contemporary fiction, 'telling has become compulsorily belated, inextricably bound up with retelling, in all its idioms: reworking, translation, adaptation, displacement, imitation, forgery, plagiarism, parody, pastiche' (Connor 1996: 166). One needs only think of the great success in recent years of the neo-Victorian, but also of biographical novels based on the lives of famous writers. In Barnes's *Metroland*, the narrator dryly refers to 'trading on resonances' as 'that most twentieth-century of techniques' (Barnes 1990: 126). In *England, England*, the French twenty-first-century intellectual continuously refers to Guy Debord for his concept of a society of spectacle, and to Jean Baudrillard for the notion of simulacrum, and he remarks: 'in our intertextual world . . . there is no such thing as a reference-free zone' (Barnes 1998: 53).

If one takes the example of *Flaubert's Parrot*, the book reads like a vibrant and original homage to the French writer, in which Flaubertian intertextuality is so extensive and Braithwaite has so fully incarnated and impersonated Flaubert's voice that sometimes the narrator's own voice seems to disappear beneath or behind that of Flaubert. Chapters such as 'The Flaubert Bestiary' and 'Examination Paper' almost take the form of a collage of quotations from Flaubert's correspondence so that Braithwaite's role seems limited to that of a compiler or a parrot, Flaubert's parrot. The third chronology of Flaubert's life is a great achievement in confusion as some readers believed it was a pastiche of Flaubert's style (Bouillaguet 1996: 54), while it is entirely composed of quotations from Flaubert's correspondence in the form of metaphors and comparisons, thus forming an original autobiography. This strategy of collage might be a nod of homage to the end of *Bouvard et Pécuchet* by Flaubert, where the two copyists attain serenity by simply copying. But Braithwaite's activity is not restricted to copy as he is also imitating Flaubert. 'Braithwaite's Dictionary of Accepted Ideas' in particular reveals the scope of the narrator's ventriloquism as the chapter consists of a parody and a stylistic pastiche of Flaubert's *Dictionary of Accepted Ideas*. The deliberate confusion of voices throughout the novel seems to suggest that the notion of paternity or author-ity has been seriously shaken and that the words themselves are more important than the identity of the writer.

A pessimistic view on this issue may consist in thinking that works of the past exert such a huge influence on the present that all innovation is impossible, that the literary space is now saturated and that all writers are condemned to repetition, stammering, retelling. They can only imitate what has been done before, and thus the notion of originality is truly exhausted. Is this then what contemporary novelists are condemned to? Is there no way out other than that of repetition and replication? Tristram Shandy was already pondering that subject in the eighteenth century: 'Shall we for ever make new books, as apothecaries make new mixtures, by pouring only out of one vessel into another? Are we for ever to be twisting, and untwisting the same rope? For ever in the same track – or ever at the same pace?' (Sterne 1985: 339).

One could certainly take a more positive view on the subject and suggest that it is possible to take the past into account and appropriate it in a dialogic way which would not be mere parrotry or submission. Barnes certainly does not consider himself as a victim of the famous 'anxiety of influence' developed by Harold Bloom (Bloom 1973). In an essay in 2000, he confidently asserted: 'I am uninfluenced by anybody' (Barnes 2000: 114). Talking about Flaubert more specifically, he says that '[i]t's not a question of direct influence, or tempted emulation . . . it's a question of feeling that someone sympathetic has been there before you, has seen it all, and is squinting down at you – benevolently, you hope' (Barnes 1983: 14). In 2001, he asserted:

> I always deny any influence on me whenever it is proposed. It's obvious when reading *Flaubert's Parrot* and other things that I've written that I regard Flaubert . . . as an iconic figure, as the writers' writer, the saint and martyr of literature as Tournier refers to him. But when it comes down to actual stylistic influence – I'm a British writer in the twenty-first century, Flaubert is a nineteenth century Frenchman – I simply don't see it on a word to word level. I agree with many of his positions on writing, on art . . . But I don't think I've ever been praised as a Flaubertian stylist. (Guignery 2001: 123)

Julian Barnes's relation to Flaubert is indeed one of admiration, respect and fascination but he is certainly not trying to imitate the master, since this would be anachronistic. So *Flaubert's Parrot* does not read as a submissive and repetitive text, but is an act of genuine and original creation in which Barnes respectfully celebrates Flaubert but also evinces his great talents as novelist and stylist. He tactfully handles grief and emotion, culminating in the highly moving chapter called 'Pure Story'. He creates a convincing Louise Colet and his great achievement consists in rendering an unheard and unsung voice palpable. The metaphors are finely developed and well related to twentieth-century reality, while the style is precise, elegant and has a specific Barnesian touch to it. A reviewer praised the book for performing 'a couple of literary marriages straight out of critics' dreams: he's written a modernist text with a nineteenth-century heart, a French novel with English lucidity and tact' (Rafferty 1985: 22). Indeed, Barnes parodies the story of *Madame Bovary* through the fictive couple of the Braithwaites, but he brings a new light to it by transferring it to England and to the late twentieth century. The linguistic shift from French to English is also meaningful in that it suggests a different conception of the world. In 2006, for the one hundred fiftieth anniversary of *Madame Bovary*, Barnes wrote a different ending to Flaubert's novel called 'The Rebuke' in which Emma, the first person narrator, does not kill herself and, looking back, gives her own version of her story (Barnes 2006a). The voice Barnes conjures up in this text is extremely original, modern, intimate, drawing the reader into an affectionate complicity which is quite different from the type of narration developed by Flaubert in his novel. Barnes explained in an interview that he had to take a diverging path: 'it was more of a tribute to Flaubert that I didn't try and modify an existing episode from the book, but that I did something subversive. If I had tried to fill in a little gap in the book or something and try to narrate it Flaubertianly, I expect I would have failed' (Guignery and Roberts 2009: 172). In his translation of Daudet's *In the Land of Pain*, Barnes also seems to set up a dialogic exchange across centuries, across countries and across languages, as he is intent on being very faithful to Daudet in the translation but he also asserts his presence in the illuminating introduction and footnotes. Barnes remarks: 'I want the reader to hear Daudet's voice as clearly as possible in the text, and then hear my voice, helping to explain what his voice is saying, in the notes' (Wilde 2009: 97). This intertwining of voices is furthered by the fact that, as Hermione Lee suggested in one of her letters to the writer, for all the faithfulness of Julian Barnes's translation, one may imperceptibly feel the writer's own personal style: his translation 'sounds uncannily like [him]. It's very eloquent & elegant without being mannered' (Barnes 2006b: 4.3).

Barnes's work in general thus seems to oscillate between repetition and difference, between the awareness of past literature and a desire to go beyond and make something new and hybrid. The writer is in no way constrained by the heritage of French literature or by past conventions, but manages on the contrary to create a voice of his own and a form of his own. In *A Poetics of Postmodernism* (1988), Linda Hutcheon remarks that '[intertextuality] can both thematically and formally reinforce the text's message *or* it can ironically undercut any pretensions to borrowed authority or legitimacy' (Hutcheon 1988: 138). Barnes can be scathing towards a few French writers such as, for example, Jean-Paul Sartre, whose biography of Flaubert, *The Family Idiot* (1971), he disparagingly refers to in *Flaubert's Parrot*, and about which he wrote a ferocious review, describing the book as 'a puzzling and frustrating book, needlessly difficult to read, shuffling between dogma and perceptiveness', a passage which was deleted in the later version published in *Something to Declare* (Barnes 1982; Barnes 2002a: 158–70). But apart from a few examples such as this one, Barnes's intertextual approach is on the whole benign. Unlike some of his postmodernist or post-colonial contemporaries, Barnes's acknowledgement of a literary debt is neither brutal nor subversive, but rather smooth, cathartic and celebratory, even if his celebration does not exclude irony, nor lead to an excess of crepuscular nostalgia or morbid melancholy. As far as Flaubert is concerned, Barnes does not contest or subvert the master's works but he conjures them up, commemorates them and liberates some space to let his own voice resonate.

Conclusion: 'Knit Your Own Stuff'

This survey of Julian Barnes's connections with the French literary past sought to delineate the contours of a continuous, fertile and amiable dialogue with nineteenth-century literature, which may be related to the polyphonic dimension of postmodernism but not with its more subversive stance nor with the nostalgic tendency with which this aesthetic movement has sometimes been associated. Through his appropriation of certain specific texts, Barnes manages to 'replenish' the literature of the past (Barth 1980), to give it a second life. This is more particularly true for Alphonse Daudet and Jules Renard, two writers who are no longer frequently read in France, or only for a limited part of their work. In the introduction to *In the Land of Pain*, Barnes presents Daudet as 'a substantially forgotten writer nowadays' (Barnes 2002b: vi), and his translation of Daudet's notes on dying has certainly helped to put him under the spotlight again, if only temporarily. In 2007, a new edition of *La Doulou* was published in France with Barnes's own preface, notes and postscript. Despite his admiration for his distinguished ancestors, Barnes is far from being trapped in the French literary past, far from being reduced to silence by overwhelming ancestry. His choice of writers such as Flaubert, Daudet and Renard with whom one feels his kinship, might actually be a way to express his fascination for them, to claim a cultural identity which is linked to the French literary canon, but also to suggest his own obsession for originality. The motto 'everything has been said' does not condemn any literary project but may actually incite one to write in order to silence or challenge this certainty that all is said, and find new ways of saying what has already been said. Staring at the literary past as Julian Barnes but also Peter Ackroyd and A.S. Byatt do is a way of accepting its weight so as to appropriate it and also free oneself from it. As Barnes said in an interview, '[o]ne part of your brain knows that you are writing in a literary and social continuum and that what you write is dependent on the fiction that has gone before. But in order to inhabit the novel that you're writing and make it live, you have to think of it as something completely special' (Porter 1995: 6). You may identify your literary parents and grandparents, but, in order to create something new, it is necessary to put them behind in a process which simultaneously entails acknowledgement and challenge. Barnes thus views 'the exemplary and companionable novelists of the past' as 'both your masters and your fellow-students; sometimes they daunt, sometimes they encourage. But their true influence is to say, simply and repeatedly, across the years: Go thou and do otherwise' (Barnes 2000: 115), or, as the narrator of *Flaubert's Parrot* more prosaically suggests: 'Knit Your Own Stuff' (Barnes 1985: 99), which is what Barnes has repeatedly and so skilfully achieved.

CHAPTER FOUR

'An Ordinary Piece of Magic': Religion in the Work of Julian Barnes

ANDREW TATE

> **Chapter Summary:** Julian Barnes has engaged with religious ideas and motifs in the novels *Staring at the Sun* (1986), *A History of the World in 10½ Chapters* (1989), and *Arthur & George* (2005), as well as in his memoir *Nothing to Be Frightened Of* (2008). A discussion of the attitudes apparent in those texts, this chapter observes that while Barnes writes out of the secular sensibilities of the present his work is frequently energized by a sensation of wonder and mystery such that the loss of the 'beautiful lie' or 'supreme fiction' of religion is for him a cause for grief similar to that felt at the close of a great novel.

Can God be found in the pages of a Julian Barnes novel? Does this agnostic man of letters, polite iconoclast and heir to great literary sceptics such as Gustave Flaubert, have anything to say to theologically minded readers? The prevailing view of contemporary British fiction is that it is an emphatically secular form and that most of its practitioners, including Julian Barnes, are at least tacitly hostile to the truth-claims of theistic religions. If Anglophone realist writing has a faith-centred perspective, notes Terry Eagleton, its instinct is to keep quiet about such matters and to be 'as nervous of religious debate as a pub landlord' (Eagleton 2005: 3). For other critics, religion is less a matter of potential public embarrassment than an increasing irrelevance, both to lived reality and literature. Dominic Head, for example, has observed that 'the fact of a predominantly secular society is really a "given" for novelists in the entire post-war period' (Head 2002: 18) and, indeed, the decline of institutional Christianity, in particular, is one of the central social narratives of late twentieth-century British history. 'If a core reality survives for Britons', argues Callum Brown, a leading proponent of secularization theory, 'it is certainly no longer Christian' (Brown 2001: 193). It would be easy to read Barnes as typifying a wholly irreligious, soundly materialist tradition in postmodern thought; his work embodies values that might be described as secular, ethical, humanist and liberal. For James Wood, the author represents a strand of peculiarly English empiricism, whose 'fiction is beguiling because it is confident about the known and jauntily undaunted about the unknown' (1999: 264).

Unlike many of his nineteenth-century literary forebears, Barnes had no religious faith to lose; his family's recent spiritual history, is, the writer himself notes, one 'of attenuated belief combined with brisk irreligion' (Barnes 2009: 12). In a wry description of an encounter with a college chaplain during his early undergraduate days at Oxford, Barnes recalls warning the clergyman: '"I'm afraid I'm a happy atheist"' (Barnes 2009: 17). Yet this not-quite-oxymoronic statement, combining insouciance and apologetic anxiety, is a subtle clue to a richer engagement with religious questions, sacred texts and the possibility of faith than might be immediately obvious. Barnes's work does not easily fit into the category of 'New Atheist novel' that is sometimes used to describe the work of his peers such as Martin Amis and Ian McEwan, for whom 'the novel apparently stands for everything – free speech, individuality, rationality and even a secular experience of the transcendental . . . that religion seeks to overthrow' (Bradley and Tate 2010: 11). The 'God question' persists across his oeuvre in a way that might seem surprising for a novelist who, superficially, seems reconciled to a godless worldview. Barnes is a writer with a keenly sceptical sensibility, one whose novels limn a world of contingency, trauma and absurdity. This chapter will trace Barnes's engagement with religious ideas and motifs in the novels *Staring at the Sun* (1986), *A History of the World in 10½ Chapters* (1989), *Arthur & George* (2005) and the memoir *Nothing To Be Frightened Of* (2008).

Screaming at the Sky: 'Ordinary Miracles' in *Staring at the Sun*

Paradise – of a distinctly earthly kind – makes an early appearance in Barnes's fourth novel (part ironic *Bildungsroman*, part novel of ideas), a narrative that finds everyday experience charged with miraculous possibility. Jean Serjeant – whose long, unremarkable life we follow from the 1920s to 2021 – recalls accompanying her roguish, enigmatic Uncle Leslie to the golf course, a place he affectionately names 'the Old Green Heaven' (Barnes 1987: 7). In Jean's fragmented, occasionally sepia-tinged memory, this unlikely suburban Eden is a space of mischief and mild subversion. On one occasion Leslie, a man who combines playful and sinister qualities – he has a charming penchant for nifty tricks with cigarette ash but is also given to muttering glib, anti-Semitic sentiments – suggests that he and his niece 'have a good old scream' which concludes with the pair falling to the ground, in breathless, fatigued ecstasy, staring '[h]alf-way to heaven' at 'the quiet sky' (Barnes

1987: 9–10). This ritualized, cathartic act, a kind of wordless prayer, brings together the novel's defining, elemental sky motif and a concern with displaced spirituality. Close to a century after a half-remembered, breathless game of her childhood, the ninety-something Jean reflects that she was never 'encouraged to pray' and, indeed, her religious training was limited to hazily remembered scripture lessons (Barnes 1987: 147–48). She also suspects that her (now middle-aged) son's sudden turn to mystical questions is simply another way of 'screaming at the sky . . . roaring at the empty heavens, knowing that however much noise you made, nobody up there would hear you' (Barnes 1987: 157). The absence of religion is a powerful presence in the narrative: one of Barnes's implicit arguments is that the decline of orthodox sacred traditions ironically perpetuates rather than diminishes a yearning for spiritual consolation.

Staring at the Sun might reasonably (if less elegantly) have been titled *Screaming at the Sky*: like an agnostic, twentieth-century equivalent of the Jewish book of praises (known in English as the Psalms), Barnes's text addresses anxieties about God, death and the afterlife. However, where the psalmists petitioned a deity they believed would hear their prayers, this novel focuses on less spiritually confident characters, men and women who are neither conventionally religious nor entirely content with rational unbelief. Barnes presents a world in which the vast, unknowable, empty sky, once a symbol of God-filled eternity, has become a signifier of mystery and the limits of human knowledge.

The title is derived from the novel's prologue which narrates an incident in the life of Sergeant-Pilot Tommy Prosser, later billeted with Jean and her family during the war. 'On a calm, black night in June 1941', Prosser, a World War II British Airman returning from a poaching raid over Northern France, witnesses the sun rising, not once but twice: 'an ordinary miracle he would never forget' (Barnes 1987: 1–2). The double sunset – either an ocular accident or a product of the speed of new war-driven technologies – frames the novel's representation of the search for meaning in a life that human beings know will end in death. The paradoxical 'ordinary miracle', combining the mundane and the magical, becomes something of a litany in the novel: the usually taciturn pilot (nicknamed 'Sun-Up' Prosser by his sceptical colleagues) shares the story with Jean who thinks of it in moments of personal crisis, including a richly poignant passage in which she is shown how to fit a female contraceptive before her marriage (Barnes 1987: 52). The term 'ordinary miracle' is used for a third time to describe Jean's unexpected pregnancy, conceived at the end of a long (and largely joyless) married life. Gregory is presented as a solitary blessing from a relationship rooted in abusive, patriarchal notions of authority (Barnes 1987: 79).

Flight is the narrative's key metaphor for transcendence – or, at least, the longed-for possibility of transcendence, a desire to escape the overwhelming fact of gravity. 'Sun-Up' Prosser's account of the double sunset, witnessed from the cockpit of a machine designed to kill, blends reverence with the ordinary horrors of war. He stresses that the event is unique but rates it as less important than his desire to return to combat: '"What I *miss* . . . is killing Germans"' (Barnes 1987: 26). This blurring of the miraculous – a violation of the natural (or rational) order – with bloodlust is a disturbing reminder that humanity is not always ennobled by its encounters with the numinous. Although Prosser's visionary experience is distinctive, he reveals that other airmen tell similarly logic-defying tales. One pilot believed that he saw a mountain rising from the ocean; another witnessed a motorcyclist riding across the waves (Barnes 1987: 31). For readers who have even the vaguest familiarity with the Christian gospels, this law-of-physics defying image recalls the story of Jesus walking on water, an act that terrified his disciples, who initially believed they had seen a ghost (Matthew 14. 25). Indeed, Jean, whose religious background is vague and unfocused, giggles as she makes a comparison between the mirage of an ocean-going motorcyclist and one of the most famous miracles performed by the son of God. Significantly, however, this irreverent attitude inspires a sharp response from Prosser ('"don't blaspheme in front of those who are going to get it"' [Barnes 1987: 31]), despite his apparent lack of faith. Prosser's superstitious antipathy for such a gently irreligious quip accentuates a connection between flight and fear of, and fascination with, death sustained throughout the novel.

Barnes's reluctant visionary, who confesses that he has been 'grounded' after losing his nerve, stands in a twentieth-century literary tradition of aviators contemplating their own mortality and echoes, in particular, the speaker of W. B. Yeats's 'An Irish Airman Foresees His Own Death' (1919): 'I know that I shall meet my fate/Somewhere among the clouds above' (ll. 1–2). Prosser, reminiscent of Yeats's fatalist flyer, confides that he could imagine seeking his own death in the skies ('When I've had enough' [Barnes 1987: 30]) by allowing the plane to soar way above its flight path. Forty years later, Jean meets the pilot's widow and discovers that 'Sun-Up' Prosser's 'last flight', one that ended in death rather than contented retirement, fulfilled his earlier dream of climbing towards an unreachable sun. While the authorities are uncertain about what caused this terminal ascent, Jean, who decades ago listened to her friend's secret longing to die amid the clouds, alone imagines the 'gathering cold . . . The gradual invasion of contentment, then of joy' (Barnes 1987: 105–6). Jean's private reflections on Prosser's death are, again, resonant of Yeats's uncannily calm airman who knows that '[a] lonely impulse of delight/Drove to this tumult in the skies' (ll. 11–12). Both texts register the belief that flight defies rational understandings of human limit. Tommy Prosser is not only emblematic of the many military pilots who died in two world wars, but his death also re-works the myth of Icarus, the daring son of Daedalus who flew too close to the sun. The novel suggests that twentieth-century flight technology, ostensibly the product of a rational, disenchanted worldview, still has near-mythic resonance in the contemporary imagination. Gregory, Jean's rather solipsistic son, thinks of flight as a product of faith: 'The pilot at the end of the runway believes in flight. It's not just a question of knowledge, of understanding aerodynamics; it's also a question of belief' (Barnes 1987: 108).

Although air travel typifies a secular aspiration to transcendence, it also provides Gregory with a vivid analogy for eternal punishment. Where Prosser was elated at the escapist possibilities of flight, Jean's son is viscerally terrified by the prospect of airborne death. Gregory has little faith in Christian visions of heaven but his imagination is haunted by secular equivalents of the torments of hell: the whiff of kerosene on a trip to the airport triggers images of 'charred flesh' and the sound of the engines becomes 'only the pure voice of hysteria': 'Now there was no hell, fear was known to be finite, and the engineers had taken over . . . they had created the most infernal conditions in which to die' (Barnes 1987: 94). Death in the skies, for Gregory, emblematizes the fact that the modern way of dying lacks all sense of scale or significance. In the Christian tradition, apocalyptic visions are frequently violent but they also anticipate renewal, rebirth and the hope of resurrection. Gregory's terror, by contrast, constitutes a form of mock apocalypse – a terrifying end surrounded by soft furnishings – in which death is inconsequential (Barnes 1987: 96–97).

The concept of the 'good' death haunts Gregory to the point of near obsession. Gregory is not simply a thanatophobe, a person with an excessive fear of death; rather, he is anxious that the manner of a person's demise might undermine the integrity of life itself and wonders if it is 'an illusion to believe that there had been good deaths – brave, stoical, consoling, affectionate deaths – in the past?' (Barnes 1987: 134) At one level, the book confronts senescence in a curiously carefree manner, particularly compared with Barnes's later representations of old age (see, in particular, *The Lemon Table* (2004)). Jean's parents, for example, die and disappear from the narrative without registering shock or upset and she lives to an exceptional old age. But the pathos of Uncle Leslie's final days gives particular focus to Gregory's fears: this enigmatic, mischievous figure exudes a comic dignity despite his reputation for cowardice (Barnes 1987: 129). In this sequence, Barnes pastiches the kind of exemplary deathbed tableaux that are such a familiar part of nineteenth-century realist fiction (see, for example, the death of Little Nell in Dickens's *The Old Curiosity Shop* (1840–41). The 'old villain', however, surrounded by contraband clutter and the detritus of a wayward life rather than attended by devoted family or priest, experiences no last-minute religious conversion and retains an odd, persuasive charisma. Although Barnes resists facile sentiment, Leslie's death (one of 'courage, even grace') is an improbably sanguine moment in a novel that is frequently sceptical about the human capacity to acknowledge mortality (Barnes 1987: 134).

If Barnes's characters find belief in an afterlife to be impossible, this does not weaken their resolve to find meaning in life itself. Jean is an unlikely pilgrim who seems to have little appetite for the numinous but she also resists rational formulations of the sacred. 'One cathedral', she reflects, 'is worth a hundred theologians capable of proving the existence of God by logic' (Barnes 1987: 98). In the liberated but restless years after her unhappy marriage and (happier) late motherhood, Jean becomes a solitary traveller, touring the world in search of meaning. This peripatetic phase, in which Jean seeks to encounter the seven great wonders of the world, yield a solitary (and abundantly ambiguous) experience of the sublime. The Grand Canyon, Nevada, a 'place beyond words, beyond human noise, beyond interpretation' moves a reticent, apprehensive woman to reassess her instinctive materialism (Barnes 1987: 98). However, the Canyon does not precipitate a leap of faith but, instead, stuns Jean 'into uncertainty' (Barnes 1987: 98). Nature, she reflects, provides 'miracles' but reason resists such possibilities (Barnes 1987: 99).

The novel registers a certain disappointment with the decline of orthodox spirituality: religion has become, like everything else, democratic, consensus bound and mundane. The intimations of immortality that surprise Jean at the Grand Canyon are dissipated by the pattern of quotidian life. However, in Barnes's novel, visionary experiences are possible for those who have no religious convictions. Jean's encounter with silent mystery is closer in spirit to the anti-epiphanies narrated by James Joyce in *Dubliners* (1914) than to a Romantic-pantheistic moment of revelation. Although she recognizes that '[t]he mind longs for certainty', Jean is content to exist in a state of doubt, what John Keats named '*negative capability*' (1987: 98; Wu 1998: 1019). Jean senses that her inability either to believe or to wholeheartedly discard the supernatural implies the lack of a fully formed spiritual sensibility:

> It was said that one of the worst tragedies of the spirit was to be born with a religious sense into a world where belief was no longer possible. Was it an equal tragedy to be born without a religious sense into a world where belief was possible? (Barnes 1987: 99)

Jean's sense of the tragic echoes the prologue to George Eliot's *Middlemarch* (1871–72) which compares the life of the reforming sixteenth-century holy woman, Saint Theresa, with the spiritual struggles of its own nineteenth-century protagonist, Dorothea Brooke. Eliot's heroine is born into a world inimical to her spiritual quest; Jean, by contrast, finds herself incapable of experiencing the world with a vividly religious consciousness. Her anxious son is closer in spirit to Dorothea and the third section of the novel, prefaced with a quotation from Søren Kierkegaard (1813–55) ('Immortality is no learned question'), addresses religious belief rather more urgently than in its early stages via Gregory's escalating theological quest (Barnes 1987: 137).

Significantly, the final section of the novel leaps forward into the (then) near future of the early twenty-first century and to the advent of a publicly funded General Purposes Computer. The GPC is the closest that the novel can muster to the voice of God. What now appears to be a rather clunky piece of technology, anticipates the God-like status of search engines such as Google; it also reflects humanity's capacity for making God in its own image. Inevitably, the technology anticipated in 1986 appears quaint from a perspective that outstrips the futuristic landscape projected by the novel. One innovation, pioneered in the narrative's version of 2008, is an 'information category' known as TAT ('The Absolute Truth') which allows enquirers to ask questions about God, death and the afterlife (Barnes 1987: 146). Gregory's frustration with the fuzzy ambiguities and quasi-mystical nostrums of TAT embodies a longing for absolute truth in unmediated and (possibly) unfair terms: 'Why had everything become democratic? Why was everyone coddled with fair-mindedness? Gregory longed to be cuffed with certainty' (Barnes 1987: 179).

The final section of *Staring at the Sun* parallels some of the debates and motifs of John Updike's *Roger's Version* – also published in 1986 – regarding the burden of humanity's religious impulses and the impossibility of proving, one way or the other, the existence of God. In Updike's novel, Roger Lambert – a neo-orthodox theologian, tenured in an Ivy League Divinity School – is confronted by an Evangelical graduate determined that he can prove God's existence with new information technology. Gregory, like Updike's academic, is frustrated by technology but discovers a different category of religious experience. Where Jean is reconciled, not unhappily, to quiet but convinced atheism ('We live beneath a bombers' moon, with just enough light to see that nobody else is there'), her son, perhaps equally ambiguously, lands on the side of faith (Barnes 1987: 191). Gregory resists rationalist theism – the idea of God as the 'trick-cyclist . . . the master magician, the great prestidigitator who juggled the planets like glistening balls and hadn't dropped one yet' (Barnes 1987: 188). Instead, he takes a line that echoes the troubled faith of Kierkegaard and the neo-orthodoxy of Karl Barth: Gregory wants neither 'explanations' nor 'conditions' and merely believes – in a non-dogmatic mode – simply 'because it was true' (Barnes 1987: 188).

The final image of the novel, the last incident of Jean's life, is one of qualified transcendence, as the near-centenarian is joined by her son in a trip that mimics Tommy Prosser's final flight. Cocooned in the plane's cabin, she stares at the sun and ambiguously smiles at 'this post-mortal phosphorescence'. For Jean, ultimately '[t]he sky is the limit' but the novel itself remains open to the possibility of something beyond the clouds (Barnes 1987:193, 195).

'Everything *Is* Connected': *A History of the World in 10½ Chapters*

Where *Staring at the Sun* gazes at the sky, *A History of the World in 10½ Chapters* takes to the oceans. Barnes's short-story cycle continually returns to narratives of aquatic peril: from a playful re-writing of the biblical account of the flood to the twentieth-century tale of a born-again astronaut determined to find Noah's Ark via emblematically and thematically linked stories of terrorism, shipwreck, ship-bound political exile and post-apocalyptic survival at sea, water is this ambitious novel's element. 'We are all lost at sea, washed between hope and despair, hailing something that may never come to rescue us', reflects Barnes in one story (Barnes 1990: 137). God is frequently 'hailed' by his dramatis personae but the novel is doubtful that rescue by a divine source is imminent. Like *Staring at the Sun*, this pithy chronicle of human endeavour and catastrophe engages with issues of faith, justice and the redemption. However, in *10½ Chapters*, Barnes shifts his theological emphasis from abstract, philosophical questions regarding the existence of God to specific aspects of the Judeo-Christian grand narrative. The novel begins with a fable inspired by Genesis, the first book of the Bible, and ends with a dream vision of the afterlife, in what might be read as a sceptical re-writing of its last book, Revelation. Bookending a sequence of stories that explores the 'apparent chaos of history', as Matthew Pateman has observed, 'within the rigidly teleological structure' of the biblical narrative is a useful framework for examining the purpose and limits of storytelling and its religious value (Pateman 2002: 45).

'It wasn't a nature reserve, that Ark of ours; at times it was more like a prison ship', claims the mysterious narrator of 'The Stowaway' (Barnes 1990: 4). In Jewish and Christian tradition, the story of the flood (Genesis 6–8), emphasizes rescue and redemption as well as divine judgement but Barnes's opening short story embodies an attitude of irreverence towards such authorized histories. Noah, according to the titular interloper, was 'a monster, a puffed-up patriarch who spent half his day grovelling to his God and the other half taking it out on us' (Barnes 1990: 12). 'The Stowaway' not only critiques orthodox theological perspectives on scripture, it also plays with sentimental, 'nursery versions in painted wood' of life on the ark (Barnes 1990: 3). The reality is dirty, dangerous and altogether more Darwinian: not all species survive the voyage and humanity is figured as the most rapacious predator of all.

That Barnes's witty and voluble opening narrator is finally revealed to be a woodworm accentuates the novel's desire to give voice to the outsider. The absurd, defamiliarizing twist of an articulate larva reminds us that canonical versions of history are normally delivered by those in power: the woodworm, a despised species, typifies the position of the outcast, the figure whose viewpoint is rarely heard. The separation of animals into categories of 'clean' and 'unclean', for example, directly derived from the Genesis account, is not represented as a signifier of holiness but as evidence of bigotry (Barnes 1990: 10). In Barnes's novel, the apparently random hierarchy that Noah enforces on the animal kingdom ('Why should the camel and the rabbit be given second-class status?') foreshadows the most wicked events of the twentieth century and, specifically, acts of persecution and genocide (Barnes 1990: 11). Descendants of the woodworm work their way through Barnes's fractured, skewed history: in 'The Wars of Religion' – an apparently fantastical tale, in fact based on historical record, of sixteenth-century ecclesiastical courts convened to judge animals – woodworm are condemned and cast out of the church for destroying the Bishop of Besançon's chair and casting the cleric 'down into the darkness of imbecility' (Barnes 1990: 79). This comic image of authority dethroned is an example of what Barnes's woodworm narrator names 'the outcast's laugh' (Barnes 1990: 11). This laughter is both cathartic and ironic and constitutes a mode of resistance against all manner of authoritarian and oppressive acts.

A motif of division – the chosen from the damned, the clean from the unclean – is woven into this history of the world. The narrative is particularly concerned by the ways in which humanity creates scapegoats or sacrificial victims. For example, Kath, the traumatized (and possibly delusional) woman who partially narrates 'The Survivor', asks 'Why are we always punishing animals? . . . we've been punishing animals from the beginning, haven't we? Killing them and torturing them and throwing our guilt on to them?' (Barnes 1990: 87). In Chapter Two, 'The Visitors', a story inspired by the hijack of the Achille Lauro in 1985, tourists on board a luxury cruise ship are classified by anti-Zionist hijackers according to nationality; similarly, in 'Shipwreck' – an exploration of a nineteenth-century maritime disaster remembered, chiefly, because of Géricault's painting, *The Raft of Medusa* (1819) – Barnes observes that the 'healthy were separated from the unhealthy like the clean from the unclean' as a prelude to sacrificing the sick (Barnes 1990: 121). This chapter also makes a chilling allusion to the Holocaust as Barnes imagines an alternative version of the painting in which the shipwreck victims have '[s]hrivelled flesh, suppurating wounds, Belsen cheeks' (Barnes 1990: 136). Each of these examples – prison ships, scapegoats, racial classification, emaciated bodies – can all be read as references to Hitler's 'final solution'. These allusions coalesce in the last of 'Three Simple Stories' narrated in Chapter Seven: another historical narrative, the story focuses on the fate of the *St Louis*, a cruise liner that set sail from Hamburg on 13 May 1939, with 937 passengers, most of whom were Jews in enforced exile from Nazi Germany. The refugees find no refuge in the allegedly free world and any possible welcome is inadequate. Potential liberation in Havana, for example, would have been limited to 250 fortunate passengers: 'Who would separate the clean from the unclean? Was it to be done by casting lots?' (Barnes 1990: 184) Barnes, again, alludes to the paradigmatic ark story but, in this narrative there is no dove bearing an olive branch and no refuge in a renewed world: Barnes notes, with understated pathos, that the passengers of the unwelcome vessel 'shared in the fate of European Jewry' (Barnes 1990: 188).

Does Barnes's emphasis on accident, random punishment, natural disaster, wilful ignorance of suffering and appalling acts of human cruelty suggest that *A History of the World in 10½ Chapters* is an atheist tract? The tone of this experimental narrative is certainly more theologically confrontational than that of *Staring at the Sun*. The deity makes occasional guest appearances throughout the collection of stories and few of them are conventionally pious. The clandestine woodworm is less than flattering in his oblique portrayal of Noah's God: the patriarch, we are told, was 'a very God-fearing man; and given the nature of God, that was probably the safest line to take' (Barnes 1990: 11). He even suggests that Noah's drunkenness (an episode narrated in Genesis 9. 21–27) was caused by his heavenly father (Barnes 1990: 30). 'What Barnes has done', argues Gregory Salyer, 'is to bring to speech the voices of history that have been silenced by the one voice that passes itself off as the voice of God' (Salyer 1991: 224). A later chapter revisits another biblical myth, the story of Jonah and the whale: God is referred to as both 'moral bully' and 'paranoid schizophrenic'; he is an implacably authoritarian figure who 'holds all the cards and wins all the tricks' (Barnes 1990: 176–77). In 'Shipwreck', Barnes speculates that the relative lack of well-known paintings of Noah's ark might be because 'artists agreed that the Flood doesn't show God in the best possible light' (Barnes 1990: 128). Religious believers of later stories and generations – in the nineteenth and twentieth centuries, respectively, Amanda Fergusson and Spike Tiggler, both pilgrims to Mount Ararat – are represented as sincere but obsessive zealots whose faith blinds them to historical reality. Similarly, in the tragic-comic story 'Upstream!' the legacy of Christian missionaries in South America is not one of grace and compassion.

All of these examples might imply that Barnes's novel presents a fair case against monotheism as violent, vengeful and obsolete. However, the narrative complicates easy assumptions about all readings of history – including facile denunciations of religious worldviews. Amanda Fergusson's austere judgment in 'The Mountain' of her companion, Miss Logan, as 'dismally unreceptive to the transcendental' is not true of *10½ Chapters*, despite its sometimes caustic scepticism (Barnes 1990: 156). And Barnes frequently blurs the line between disbelief and faith: in 'The Survivor', Kath reflects that, despite her lack of belief, she is 'tempted' to make a leap of faith: 'she was tempted to believe in someone watching what was going on . . . It wouldn't be such a good story if there was no-one around to tell it' (Barnes 1990: 103). 'Everything *is* connected', reflects Kath, 'even the parts we don't like, especially the parts we don't like' (Barnes 1990: 84). The intuition that all parts of life are associated resonates with a religious (but not necessarily Christian) worldview. Significantly, this idea is highlighted in a novel that thrives on contingency, chaos and, paradoxically, connection.

The possibility that Kath is suffering from paranoid delusions after the trauma of a violent relationship is important: it does not unequivocally diminish the credibility of her view so much as it emphasizes Barnes's focus on the lost, dispossessed and outcast. Similarly, the art-historical reflections on the relative absence of Noah's Ark from the Western tradition shifts to a reading of Michelangelo's interpretation of the story as part of the vast Sistine Chapel narrative. In this version, notes Barnes, the ark 'loses its compositional pre-eminence' (Barnes 1990: 138). The emphasis, instead, 'is on the lost, the abandoned, the discarded sinners, God's detritus' (Barnes 1990: 138). This is a metonym of Barnes's novel which champions the lost and discarded but, perhaps less obviously, it also resonates with the weight that the Jesus Christ of the gospels gives to the poor, dispossessed and unloved. In this sense, the narrative subtly recuperates an element of Christian theology while remaining suspicious of institutional creeds and expressions of faith.

The richest exploration of the mysterious nature of faith in the novel – and probably in all of Barnes's work to date – is the elliptical, audacious 'half chapter'. 'Parenthesis' begins with its restive narrator watching his lover sleep, guessing at her dreams and nightmares. He reflects on religion, art and love – a kind of pastiche of St Paul's trinity of faith, hope and love in 1 Corinthians 13 – and offers a robust defence of love. This phenomenon, he argues, is utterly anomalous, 'an excrescence, a monstrosity' to the apparently dark 'agenda' of 'history of the world'. Significantly, Barnes's defence of love prompts him to find a Christian analogy: 'Tertullian said of Christian belief that it was true because it was impossible. Perhaps love is essential because it's unnecessary' (Barnes 1990: 236). This echoes Jean's analogy for the mysterious nature of marriage in *Staring at the Sun*: 'Like whoever it was said they believed in God because it was absurd. I really understood that' (Barnes 1987: 117). Love, for Barnes, is not simply a Romantic, erotic force but a necessary mode of resistance to the oppressive forces of history: it can 'teach us to stand up to history, to ignore its chin-out strut. I don't accept your terms, love says . . . and by the way what a silly uniform you're wearing' (Barnes 1990: 240). Love takes on a quasi-religious force in this half chapter:

> Religion has become either wimpishly workaday, or terminally crazy, or merely businesslike – confusing spirituality with charitable donations. Art, picking up confidence from the decline of religion, announces its transcendence of the world . . . but this announcement isn't accessible to all, or where accessible isn't always inspiring or welcome. So religion and art must yield to love. It gives us our humanity, and also our mysticism. There is more to us than us. (Barnes 1990: 244)

Barnes's defence of love is lyrical, persuasive and moving but it is no more rational than an apologia for Christian faith: he acknowledges that 'love' too, will 'fail us' but that, 'we must still go on believing in it' (Barnes 1990: 246). Peter Childs notes that although love, for Barnes, 'represents the closest we may come to truth', he also 'distances himself from all certainties and raises an eyebrow at those who use reason and logic to bolster power or to alienate' (Childs 2009: 128).

The incongruous persistence of belief-against-the-evidence is another thematic connection between the stories in Barnes's nonconformist world history. And its final chapter, 'The Dream', focuses on the contradictory nature of human desires, needs and hopes. Whereas 'Parenthesis' begins with insomnia, the concluding chapter starts with its narrator reporting on a dream of waking (Barnes 1990: 283). The 'oldest dream of all' proves to be a vision of 'new' heaven, an afterlife full of shopping, culinary excess, sporting triumph and sex with celebrities. Perhaps most significantly, it is an iteration of eternity free from judgement – heaven appears to be utterly inclusive with even the most heinous individuals admitted to its precincts (the narrator has a brief, wordless encounter with Hitler). God also appears to be absent from this guilt-free Paradise. One reading of the narrative might suggest that the very concept of heaven is rooted in immature wish fulfilment.

However, the story itself suggests that contemporary consumerist aspirations are the real subject of Barnes's parody. The narrator recalls that his brother-in-law once said, after a holiday in Florida, that his ideal image of the afterlife is not 'Heaven' but 'shopping in America' (Barnes 1990: 286). A rather business-like angel wistfully tells the narrator that 'dreams of Heaven used to be a lot more ambitious' and that 'Heaven is democratic these days' (Barnes 1990: 300–01). Ironically, the craving for pleasure wanes and the narrator sheepishly confesses that what he really desires is to be judged, a wish granted by another heavenly bureaucrat with a rather disappointingly bland assessment: 'He said I was OK' (Barnes 1990: 294). 'The Dream' re-writes St John's vision in Revelation from the perspective of disenchanted, late twentieth-century consumer culture. The failure to envisage a dynamic, transcendent vision of the afterlife is not surprising: as a sublime phenomenon it necessarily lies beyond language. Yet Barnes's critique of a culture driven by atomized, individualist achievement and satisfaction – there is little evidence of love or intimacy in this dream – is one of secular damnation.

'The Eyes of Faith': *Arthur & George*

The profound apocalyptic disappointment registered in Barnes's representation of 'new' heaven has not diminished his interest in visions of the afterlife. *Arthur & George* embodies the novelist's continuing fascination with the shifting nature of creeds regarding the world-to-come in a modern, post-Darwinian world. The novel explores the complex interior life – and spiritual journey – of Sir Arthur Conan Doyle, most famous as the creator of Sherlock Holmes. In *Memories and Adventures* (1924) (an important intertext for Barnes's novel), the Edinburgh-born author describes his youthful unconversion (or 'spiritual unfolding') from the Christianity in which he had been raised by his Roman Catholic parents and Jesuit teachers:

> There are no worse enemies of true religion than those who clamour against all revision or modification of that strange mass of superbly good and questionable matter which we lump together into a single volume as if there were the same value to all of it. (Conan Doyle 2007: 25)

However, Conan Doyle is careful to state that his 'agnosticism . . . never degenerated into atheism' because 'he had a very keen perception of the wonderful poise of the universe and the tremendous power of conception and sustenance which it implies' (Conan Doyle 2007: 25). Indeed, the autobiography narrates the path that led this rationalist-materialist to become Britain's most famous exponent of Spiritualism and this theological journey is one of the novel's dual points of focus. Barnes's Arthur is a principled, privately anxious individual whose 'moral life belongs . . . in the fourteenth century' but whose 'spiritual life' is future oriented: 'The twenty-first century, the twenty-second? It all depends how quickly slumbering humanity wakes up and learns to use its eyes' (Barnes 2006: 284).

The other narrative in *Arthur & George* is Conan Doyle's extraordinary, but now largely forgotten, intervention in an appalling miscarriage of justice. The novelist's celebrated alter ego, the great consulting detective of 221b Upper Baker Street, in one of the early *Adventures of Sherlock Holmes* (1892), tells Dr Watson that 'life is infinitely stranger than anything which the mind of man could invent. We would not dare to conceive the things which are really mere commonplaces of existence' (Conan Doyle 1981: 33). *Arthur & George* narrates one such bizarre 'real life' crime and its consequences. In 1903, George Edalji, a respectable solicitor and the son of a Church of England minister, was found guilty of maiming livestock and labelled as the lead conspirator of a gang who waged a hate campaign against local farmers in the so-called 'Great Wyrley Outrages'. The case was radically flawed, engendered by racial hatred and the evidence against Edalji never convincing; in fact, the sadistic crimes continued even when the accused was in prison awaiting trial but the case concluded with an innocent man being condemned to seven years penal servitude. Barnes' exploration of a vanished England represents a much more searching engagement with the slippery, dangerous nature of national identity than was evident in his dystopian fable, *England, England* (1998).

Arthur & George flirts with pastiche and Barnes playfully appropriates the adventures of Doyle's detective: the interplay between the writer and his long-standing amanuensis, Alfred Wood, is explicitly modelled on the bantering dialogue of Holmes and Watson, for example. Barnes represents Doyle as a restless soul given to the same kind of melancholy as his literary alter ego: like his fictional sleuth, the writer needed constant intellectual stimulation and the novel implies that for all his sense of moral outrage, the case of George Edalji represented a desirable public challenge for Doyle in a moment of personal crisis. The novel also thrives on generating the same kind of readerly desire for tension and resolution perpetuated by detective novels.

In fusing historical event – the novel is interleaved with real letters, newspaper articles and government reports – with fictional evocation of character and consciousness, Barnes is engaging in a risky strategy. James Wood has claimed that fiction 'moves *in the shadow of doubt*, knows itself to be a true lie, knows that at any moment it might fail to make its case'; it is a form that demands that we capitulate, however, briefly, to an untruth (Wood 1999: xiv). Such a view would suggest that the novel, as a genre, cannot represent reality without deception. Indeed, as we witnessed in *10½ Chapters*, Barnes has regularly displayed a signature scepticism. Yet a key subtext of *Arthur & George* is its scepticism about facile scepticism and Barnes confronts prevailing ideas regarding belief and truth telling. The police who pursue George are doing so because they are convinced he is guilty; their confidence is based on shocking but then widespread ideas regarding race and national identity that would now be laughable (if we could only believe such superstitions had died a century ago). Doyle, after his first meeting with George, states unequivocally that he 'knows' his new friend is innocent. Both positions require acts of faith and only one can be correct. Barnes, like the legal system, presents evidence but ultimately demands that his reader make a leap of faith.

Tensions between logic and belief, evidence and instinct, law and justice shape the narrative. In Holmes, Doyle created an impossibly logical figure whose brilliant pursuit of the 'science of deduction' seems to personify modernity's confident rationalism but the author himself was drawn to the unknown or immaterial. The novel explores Doyle's escalating interest in 'psychical research' – his belief that contact with the dead was possible and provable – and demonstrates a sensitivity to this spiritual quest that might surprise readers of Barnes's more typically materialist fiction.

Doyle, in the novel as in life, is prepared to suffer the charge of 'derangement' for his public defence of 'the world of spirit' (Barnes 2006: 276). In Barnes's account, the writer saw no contradiction between science and his favoured form of spirituality:

> Science is leading the way, and will bring the scoffers low as it always does. For who would have believed in radio waves? Who would have believed in

X-Rays? . . . The invisible and the impalpable, which lie just beneath the surface of the real, just beneath the skin of things, are increasingly being made visible and palpable. The world and its purblind inhabitants are at last learning to see. (Barnes 2006: 277)

For more sceptical readers, however, the religious position that this judicious, knighted and commercially successful author adopted and maintained until his death in 1930 might be viewed as a direct contradiction to the strict logic of the detective genre that he, in large part, created. Yet detective stories – including *Arthur & George* – have a theological dimension: they embody what Frank Kermode has named 'end-determined fictions', narratives that are defined by their conclusions and that look towards a meaningful resolution (Kermode 1967: 6). At the novel's end, George Edalji attends a Spiritualist memorial meeting for Sir Arthur and, despite his incipient religious doubt, reflects that standing among thousands of people 'on a warm summer's afternoon . . . it was less easy to believe that this intense and complex thing called life was merely some chance happening on an obscure planet, a brief moment of light between two eternities of darkness' (Barnes 2006: 477). Arthur Conan Doyle was not satisfied that death represented the end of human identity: though both secularists and orthodox believers might baulk at his 'spiritist' creeds, Julian Barnes uses the story of a twin search for faith and justice to ask vital questions about the possibilities of belief in our own age. Ultimately, the novel brings together the secular, rational world of law with the phenomenon of faith in an echo of the epistle to the Hebrews: 'Now faith is being sure of what we hope for and certain of what we do not see' (Hebrews 11. 1). As George reflects on the encouragement of a believing Spiritualist to look for the spirit of the departed writer with 'the eyes of faith', it prompts him to remember Sir Arthur's own act of faith in his innocence (Barnes 2006: 499). In its delicate re-writing of two lives, *Arthur & George* is a novel open to promises bigger than those offered in either the frail language of human law or in the comforting rationalism of detective fiction.

'Missing God': *Nothing To Be Frightened Of*

Nothing to Be Frightened Of, Barnes's first published full-length work of non-fiction, echoes the traditions of spiritual autobiography that we might trace back to St Augustine's *Confessions* (c. 400) Barnes's lack of faith is not untypical of contemporary novelists but the focus of this memoir – the sobering fact of mortality and the questions it poses about God – creates a more unusual affinity with seventeenth-century Puritans and the Evangelical conversion narrative tradition of John Wesley and his successors. Despite Barnes's bold declaration of faithlessness as an undergraduate, *Nothing To Be Frightened Of* suggests that his attitude towards matters of faith has become far less sanguine with maturity

(Barnes 2009: 17). The narrative begins with a confession of religious nostalgia ('I don't believe in God, but I miss him' [Barnes 2009: 1]) that is immediately ironized by a citation from the author's brother, a confidently rationalist philosopher who pronounces such melancholy longing '[s]oppy' (Barnes 2009: 1).

Death, in various guises, is both villain and co-protagonist of *Nothing to Be Frightened Of*, the figure who has shadowed Barnes since his incipient bout of thanatophobia in late adolescence. A singular statistic haunts the writer: 'the death rate for the human race is not a jot lower than one hundred per cent', he acknowledges with clarity if not unique insight (Barnes 2009: 107). The title itself is taken from a diary entry written more than 20 years ago: 'People say of death, There's nothing to be frightened of'. They say it quickly, casually. Now let's say it again, slowly, with re-emphasis. 'There's NOTHING to be frightened of' (Barnes 2009: 99). We might expect a novelist to be afraid of nothing: fear of the blank page, of absence and the void signifies a creative bereavement. Yet Barnes's grief is connected with loss of life in all its rude, rough complexity rather than a love of the perfect symmetries of art. Although the young sceptic was, he reflects, happy to be free from anxieties about God as 'the Old Nobodaddy', it appears he has never entirely reconciled himself to the idea of finitude: 'No God, no Heaven, no afterlife' (Barnes 2009: 19).

If Barnes, or at least Barnes's *Nothing To Be Frightened Of*, has no faith in the truth claims of Christianity, he has still less sympathy for the subjective wishful thinking of detraditionalized, private iterations of belief that proliferate in a secular era: 'The notion of redefining the deity into something that works for you is grotesque' (Barnes 2009: 45). He, like Gregory in *Staring at the Sun* and the anonymous dweller of 'new' heaven, defies the consolations of 'milksop creeds' (an echo of his description of 'wimpishly workaday' religion in 'Parenthesis'). Unbelievers, he claims, are unlikely to be convinced by liberal, platitudinous spirituality: 'What's the point of faith unless you and it are serious – *seriously* serious – unless your religion fills, directs, stains and sustains your life?' Yet zealous devotion is similarly problematic because '"serious" in most religions invariably means punitive' (Barnes 2009: 81).

This non-fiction work echoes some of the anxieties expressed by characters in both *Staring at the Sun* and *10½ Chapters*. Barnes reflects, for example, on the interpretation of art as a consolation for 'those reduced creatures who now no longer dream of heaven' (Barnes 2009: 75). He also reiterates the critique of consumer-capitalist versions of Paradise embodied in 'The Dream': 'We encourage one another', he argues, 'towards the secular modern heaven of self-fulfilment' (Barnes 2009: 59). However, Barnes's narrative takes an altogether more sympathetic line regarding the attractions of belief, and its nuanced variations, than, for example, the militant 'New Atheist', Richard Dawkins, to whose arguments he alludes (Barnes 2009: 88–89). He also pays homage for example to Jules Renard – another literary thanatophobe – who argued that theology's greatest defence lies in its incommensurability with reason: '"Perhaps the fact that God is incomprehensible is the strongest argument for His existence"' (Barnes 2009: 52). Barnes, no enthusiast for church doctrine, even approvingly cites 'the old Jesuit definition of man as "*un être sans raisonnable raison d'être*. A being without a reasonable reason for being'" (Barnes 2009: 65).

For Barnes, spiritual doubt derives 'not from God's incapacity, but ours' (Barnes 2009: 89). The limits of human imagination, sympathy and decency may not, he acknowledges, be any bar to 'rescue through grace': 'Why should the inadequacy of man preclude the possibility of a spiritual afterlife?' (Barnes 2009: 90). He also enjoys the incongruous image of a post-mortal life for devout sceptics: 'The fury of the resurrected atheist: that would be something worth seeing' (Barnes 2009: 64). *Nothing To Be Frightened Of* also pursues the connections that Barnes makes in *10½ Chapters* between aesthetic and religious experience. Both texts offer a cautious, qualified celebration of art – including literature – not just as a kind of surrogate religion but as an endeavour that is intertwined with the quest for significance: 'art and religion will always shadow one another through the abstract nouns they both invoke: truth, seriousness, imagination, sympathy, morality, transcendence' (Barnes 2009: 76–77). For some sceptics, the God-shaped hole created by disbelief generated an unusual sensitivity to religion-inspired art: Stendhal, for example, is said to have 'fainted at great art' in a Florentine church' (Barnes 2009: 75). However, Barnes is unconvinced that a purely secular sensibility can truly appreciate theologically charged works of art. 'Missing God', he claims, 'is focused . . . by missing the underlying sense of purpose and belief when confronted with religious art' (Barnes 2009: 53).

Barnes argues that Christianity itself persisted for 2000 years neither as a result of social expectations or ecclesiastical rule but 'because it was a beautiful lie, because the characters, the plot, the various *coups de théâtre*, the overarching struggle between Good and Evil, made up a great novel' (Barnes 2009: 53). The loss of religion, Barnes concludes, is a cause of grief '[b]ecause it was a supreme fiction, and it is normal to feel bereft on closing a great novel' (Barnes 2009: 57). This phrase alludes to Wallace Stevens's poem 'Notes Towards a Supreme Fiction' (1947) and stresses the concept of religion as a human construct that responds to the ineffable. This foreshadows a more substantial engagement, in the memoir's final pages, with narrative as a quasi-religious form: 'Fiction wants to tell all stories, in all their contrariness, contradiction and irresolvability; at the same time it wants to tell the one true story, the one that smelts and refines and resolves all the other stories' (Barnes 2009: 241). People who embrace one of the world's monotheistic, scripture-based faiths are likely to adhere to 'one true story' but for doubting novelists such as Barnes, caught in a space of dynamic uncertainty, the real task is to explore 'the texture of the ground between the competing narratives' (Barnes 2009: 240). Rather than representing a secular society or English empiricism, Julian Barnes's work is frequently energized by a sensation of wonder, mystery that he perceives at work even in what he names in *Arthur & George* 'the daily, grimy, unmagical sublunary world' (2006: 501).

CHAPTER FIVE

Crossing the Channel: Europe and the Three Uses of France in Julian Barnes's *Talking It Over*

MERRITT MOSELEY

> **Chapter Summary:** Julian Barnes, the most Francophile of contemporary British writers, has engaged with France in a variety of complex ways. This chapter explores Barnes's interest in French cultural and literary traditions and situates his *oeuvre* in a wider European context, demonstrating the tensions that historically exist between England and France. It argues for the presence of three distinct representations of France in *Talking It Over* (1991): France as signifier of cultural sophistication; as a place of resort; and as a place associated with Eros. There is attention to the polyglossal technique of the novel, its reworking of classical French narratives, and a particular attention to Barnes's intertextual engagement with François Truffaut (1932–84), *Jules et Jim* (1962).

Julian Barnes: a Mid-Channel Author?

Any reader of Julian Barnes's work is aware that he is the most Francophile of contemporary British writers, and the idea of 'crossing the channel' has a particular resonance for Barnes, as evidenced by the title of his book of stories about France, *Cross Channel* (1996); or Chapter Seven, the central chapter of *Flaubert's Parrot*, also called 'Cross Channel'; or the story 'Tunnel' in *Cross Channel*; or the many evocative accounts of his own channel crossings scattered through his published works.

In *Flaubert's Parrot* (1984), Geoffrey Braithwaite likes to cross over to France for the quality of the light, which is different on the French side of the channel, and for

> those things you forget about until you see them again. The way they butcher meat. The seriousness of their pharmacies. The behaviour of their children in restaurants. The road signs (France is the only country I know where drivers

are warned about beetroot on the road: BETTERAVES, I once saw in a red warning triangle, with a picture of a car slipping out of control). *Beaux-arts* town halls. Wine-tasting in smelly chalk-caves by the side of the road. I could go on, but that's enough, or I'll soon be babbling about lime trees and pétanque and eating bread dipped in rough red wine. (Barnes 1984: 83–84)

In *Letters from London* (1995) Barnes is wistful about the coming Channel Tunnel. It

> will, I think, finally lose us something much more important [than the time that will be gained by the abbreviation of the trip]: a sense of crossing the Channel. Since the day, thirty-five years ago, when the family Triumph Mayflower was hoisted from the Newhaven dockside into the depths of the Dieppe ferry, I have done this trip scores of times, but I still remember the sense of quiet awe instilled by that first occasion. After the laborious business of loading came the wide-eyed scamper around the deck, the anxious examination of lifeboat cradles whose key joints seemed encrusted with fifty-four layers of paint, the bass saxophone growls as the boat pulled out, the cross-shock as you eased beyond the protection of the breakwater, the opening whoosh of spray in the face, the discovery of those extra handles in the lavatories to stop you falling over or in, the silhouette of honking gulls against the receding Sussex coast. (Barnes 1995: 324)

and on through the several stages of the voyage until

> the creak of damp ropes pulling tight, and the sudden anticipation of your first French smell – which turned out to be a mixture of coffee and floor disinfectant. (Barnes 1995: 324)

And the elderly man who, at the end of *Cross Channel*, is identified as its author, confirms these sad forebodings of the loss of a sense of transition, as he takes the tunnel but reminisces about the ferry. What has gone is the specialness of going to France. It has become too easy, thus too automatic, thus too meaningless.

Barnes's nostalgia for the old channel crossing is more than just the old fartery he acknowledges; it is an insistence that France remains different. Understandably, if the point of another country is to displace one's idealism and romanticism, to check one's nationalism or insularity, then there must be perceptible frontiers and a perceptible *difference*. Barnes insists on the importance of retaining 'occasional incomprehension and surprise' (Macintyre 2007). In this brave new Europe, one might miss the sense of national borders, with guards and passport checks and money to change, along with some inconvenience and disequilibrium, of traveling on the continent in the old days. Only where there are frontiers can thoughtful people cross them, intellectually and culturally. One's success in this role may be, at least superficially, deracinating. Barnes told an interviewer

> when I'm here in this country I sometimes find I'm half-accused of being too continental, too intellectual, too French. But when I'm over there, when I've ventured this line to them and said 'You know, in England they think I'm sort of European,' they say, 'Oh, no, no, no, no, you're very English, that's why we like you.' (Swanson 1996)

In this, Barnes resembles the late Alistair Cooke, who appeared on American television shows where he represented all that was most English but was reportedly considered by English people to be thoroughly Americanized. For people like Cooke, we have the term mid-Atlantic. Is there a term 'mid-Channel' for someone like Julian Barnes? There should be.

Le Plus Francophile des Auteurs Brittaniques Contemporaines

A discussion of the French connection in Barnes's work might profit from framing this relationship as part of a larger topic, the English and Europe, as it appears to an outsider. An interested American observer is likely to be bemused by British Eurosceptics, by the controversy over whether the UK should 'join' Europe, and by the question of English football teams getting 'into Europe'. In the United States, this country is seen as part of Europe. We understand that there are differences between England and other European countries but the idea of England as being anything other than European is strange to us. The question of whether Canada or the United States should become more wholeheartedly North American never arises. So there is some question, conceptually, about Julian Barnes and the European tradition, which suggests an opposition, and suggests that Barnes is more European or differently European than other British authors. Barnes confirms this when he tells French audiences, 'in England they think I'm sort of European' (Swanson 1996).

Barnes is inevitably associated with France. While he said in an interview some years ago, 'I think I'm the one middle-class English writer who loves France but doesn't have a house there' (Swanson 1996), he is nevertheless thoroughly at home there. His books are well received in France; he is a Commander de l'Ordre des Arts et des Lettres and has won the Prix Médicis. In a review of the French version of *Cross Channel*, *Outre-Manche* (2000), Gérard Meudal calls him *'sans conteste le plus Francophile des auteurs brittaniques contemporaines'* (Meudal 2000).

He has frequently called France his other country. In an interview, he explained that 'you need another country on which to project, perhaps, your romanticism and idealism', (Swanson 1996) a view also assigned to the Julian Barnes character, the elderly Englishman in *Cross Channel* who believes 'it was unhealthy to be idealistic about your own country, since the least clarity of vision led swiftly to disenchantment. Other countries therefore existed to supply the idealism' (Barnes 1996: 207). And in *Something to Declare* (2002), Barnes makes a related, though to my mind, more subtle point when he says that 'Knowing a second country means choosing what you want from it, finding antitheses to your normal, English, urban life' (Barnes 2002: xv).

Another reason to focus on Barnes and France as a way of approaching Barnes and the European tradition is because France is a synecdoche for Europe. The distinction between what is English and what is European – that antithesis Barnes wrote about – is at its most acute a matter of being different from France. Barnes has provided his own lucid accounting for this fact: to the French, he offers this explanation of British contempt:

> It's not really you . . . it's just that you are more than yourselves, you have become the symbol of all that is foreign; everything, not just Frenchness, begins at Calais. Whereas you may look across your different frontiers and be offered a choice of four great civilizations, we in our offshore islands are surrounded by you on one side and fish on the other three. No wonder we feel about you more strongly, more obsessively – whether as Francophile or Francophobe – than you feel about us. (Barnes 2002: xvi–xvii)

The British are obsessed by the French', he says somewhere else, 'whereas the French are only intrigued by the British. When we love them, they accept it as their due; when we hate them, they are puzzled and irritated but regard it rightly as our problem not theirs' (Barnes 1995: 320).

He also notes that 'Francophobia remains our first form of Europhobia' (Barnes 2002: xvi), presumably because for most English people France is their first taste of Europe. Historically, it was in France that they first encountered non-English words, non-English food, right-hand driving and, as Barnes amusingly recalls fearing during his own first visit as a teenager, 'garlic-chewing low-lifes who drank red wine for breakfast and cut their bread – and youngsters' throats – with pocket knives' (Barnes 2002: xii). People who dislike France are likely, for that reason, to distrust 'Europe', to fear closer integration, to clamor against real or imagined outrageous European Community (EC) directives, to exaggerate their objections to harmless differences, even to mount an indefensible defense of the great British sausage. The EC, most emphatically before it began to be enlarged and diluted, *was* France and its associates: inspired by the main architect of European Unity, Jean Monnet (1888–1979), dominated by Charles de Gaulle (1890–1970), who blocked the British when they overcame their reluctance to join the European Economic Community, reputed site of a lake of French wine and a mountain of French cheese, and headquartered in three French-speaking cities. The same reasoning leads in the other direction; as objection to France can foster anti-EC feelings, so one can move from opposition to the EC straight to anti-French emotionalism.

For many of the same reasons, Francophilia is the first form of English Europhilia. You can come at this from either end, as you can cross the Channel from the south or the north. People who enjoy the experience of France are enthusiasts, even if not indiscriminately, for Europe. That is France as synechdoche.

'Francophile' and 'Francophobe' have their uses, and can be hard to avoid as handy indicators of mental conditions which, though perhaps complex, do actually exist; but they suggest an overly simple and brutal dichotomy between two countries and between two mentalities. A more fruitful subject for inquiry is the *uses* to which France can be put by the English and particularly by the English writer.

One of those uses is as a gauge for the shortcomings of Barnes's own country. France is a set of symbolic markers that mean 'not England'. Barnes has commented on this aspect of his own Francophilia, at least in his early days:

> Doubtless there was an element of cultural snobbery in my initial preference for things Gallic: their Romantics seemed more romantic than ours, their Decadents more decadent, their Moderns more modern. Rimbaud versus Swinburne was simply no contest; Voltaire seemed just smarter than Dr. Johnson. Some of these early judgements were correct: it wasn't hard – or wrong – to prefer French cinema of the Sixties to ours. (Barnes 2002: xii–xiii)

A sharper and funnier account, because the self-awareness has a different flavor, is that of the young Christopher Lloyd in *Metroland* (1980) who, with his *copain* Toni, thinks of all things French in a purely oppositional way, as the measure of how stupid and bourgeois suburban England is in the early 1960s. The two seek out opportunities to score an *épat* or an *écras*; they do not just walk around town, they work at being *flâneurs* (despite the obstacles of having to do their *flânerie* along a street instead of a boulevard and having emerged from the tube station rather than the arms of a mistress). They enjoy calling someone *syphilisée* and having it misconstrued as *civilisée* (Barnes 1980: 16). For Chris and Toni, France is *art pour l'art*, liberated sex, French songs on long-wave radio, damp cobblestones and (imagined) spectral gaslight, a Bohemian hatred of the bourgeoisie, and most important, an intellectual life unavailable in Britain:

> We cared for its language because its sounds were plosive and precise; and we cared for its literature largely for its combativeness. French writers were always fighting one another – defending and purifying the language,

ousting slang words, writing prescriptive dictionaries, getting arrested, being prosecuted for obscenity, being aggressively Parnassian, scrabbling for seats in the *Académie*, intriguing for literary prizes, getting exiled. The idea of the sophisticated tough attracted us greatly. Motherlant and Camus were both goalkeepers; a *Paris-Match* photo of Henri de going up for a high ball, which I had sellotaped inside my locker, was as venerated as Geoff Glass's signed portrait of June Ritchie in *A Kind of Loving*. (Barnes 1980: 16)

Francophilia is both positive and negative (as is Francophobia). Every Francophile is a Francophile *about* something, not everything, and possibly more important a Francophile *against* something. Toni and Chris are clearly Francophiles against Metroland, as Matthew Taunton explores in Chapter One. They are also Francophiles against their own real selves, particularly Christopher, who is as shy, orderly, virginal and uncombative as his French heroes are the reverse.

One other position that needs little explanation is the jingoist or chauvinist English attitude toward France, or Francophobia, not much found among literary women and men, though Kingsley Amis and Philip Larkin were, if not Francophobes, at least Francophilophobes. One of the best accounts of the vulgar form of this attitude is to be found in Barnes's *Letters from London* (1995), where he anatomizes the 'toxic nationalistic mix of military caution, political snootiness and intellectual skepticism' (Barnes 1995: 317) that blocked the plan for the channel tunnel in the nineteenth century and the 'peddling of coarse national myth and beery racial demonizing' unleashed around the time of its completion in the 1990s (Barnes 1995: 321). An Englishman's difference from a Frenchman, on this tabloid account, helps him understand where his pride should lie. France is still defined as 'non-England', though the relative values of the dyad have been transposed. As one is a Francophile *against* somebody or something, one is a Francophobe *for* something, in this case a crude island-nation patriotism. To sneer at the French for rudeness or incomprehensible post-structuralist theory is to congratulate oneself. Thackeray liked to peddle a similar line a hundred and fifty years ago when he told his readers that they were much taller than Frenchmen, because they ate beef (Thackeray 1841).

Dickens, for whom France provided a handy venue for his extramarital hedonism, caught the tone of self-satisfied Francophobia in Chapter Eleven of *Our Mutual Friend* (1864–65), where a visiting Frenchman has to deal not only with a 'gentleman with the lumpy forehead' who speaks up to say only 'ESKER' but with the more self-confident Mr. Podsnap who corrects his English and then lists for him the unique qualities of an Englishman; after which Mr. Podsnap's 'face flushed as he thought of the remote possibility of its being at all qualified by any prejudiced citizen of any other country; and with his favourite right-arm flourish, he put the rest of Europe and the whole of Asia, Africa, and

America nowhere' (Dickens 1952: 132–33). Barnes's books are free, of course, from crude Francophobia – or crude Francophilia for that matter. For a fuller consideration of the ways in which France functions for Barnes, a closer look at one text will be useful, on the grounds that the use of France there has a synecdochic relationship to his work as a whole.

Three Uses of France: Talking It Over

Talking It Over (1991), published in France as *Love, etc.* (1992), 'uses' France in three distinct ways. One is as a marker of real or pretended sophistication. Another is as a place of resort. A third is vaguer and has to do with the triangular sexual relationship at the heart of the novel. They are a *way to talk*, a *place to go*, and a *kind of loving*, and they all build on an antithetical or oppositional cross-channel relationship.

One must begin by acknowledging that the polyglossal technique of *Talking It Over*, with its three major speakers and several minor ones all giving their divergent versions of events, makes judgment difficult. Thus, when Oliver recounts the wedding luncheon after Stuart's and Gillian's wedding, he reports, 'We had a perfectly frisky non-vintage champagne chosen by Stuart (brand? search me – *mis en bouteille* par *Les Vins de l'Oubli*)' (Barnes 1991: 12). How are we to balance his condescension with the later account of *his* wedding to Gillian provided by Mme Wyatt?

> The wedding was a disaster. It is impossible to exaggerate how much everything went wrong. I could not avoid noticing that the champagne did not come from Champagne. We began with some black food that would have been more appropriate for a funeral. (Barnes 1991: 219)

Mme Wyatt, Gillian, and Stuart all provide characterizations of Oliver that are at odds with each other and with his own self-presentation. Likewise, readers have different reactions. Michael Levenson, though he recognizes some ironic distancing, declares that 'Barnes lavishes his cleverness on Oliver' (Levenson 1991: 44). I have a different reaction. I yield to no one in admiring Barnes's cleverness, but, while we know he speaks French, why does his cleverness in his own voice never take the form of passages like this one: 'Oh God, poor old Ollie, up to his mucous membrane in a tub of *merde*, how crepuscular, how inspissated, how uncheerful' (Barnes 1991: 195) or 'who should step in but some *vieille flamme* of Herr Vinkel's, and this Fräulein had in tow none other than what turned out to be our own dear Gillian' (Barnes 1991: 28).

Oliver's use of French is part of a system of *épats*. He swanks to impress Stuart, his stolider friend, and to an extent (though not quite to the extent he imagines) he succeeds. Stuart, who prides himself on his honesty and wishes to do justice to Oliver, comments:

> Oliver impresses people. He talks well, he's traveled to distant lands, he speaks foreign languages, he's conversant with the arts – more than conversant – and he dresses in clothes which don't fit the contours of his body and are therefore declared to be fashionable by people in the know. All of which isn't like me. (Barnes 1991: 19)

But even Stuart is not always really *bouleversé*. When Oliver tells him rather incoherently that the man who (allegedly) introduced Stuart to Gillian 'dealt [him] a *tranche de bonheur*,' Stuart knows his role: '"A wotsit?" I asked, playing Dumb Stu. He smiled his smile, playing Sophisticated Ollie.' (Barnes 1991: 20)

Is it sophisticated to call Gillian's fashion error *'un désastre'* (33) or refer to his little 'seedling of *bonheur*' (44) or 'return *billets* from Gatwick' (80) or call Gillian's mother an 'old *vache*' (67) or remember his father working the *'mots croisés'* (139) in the paper or refer to Gillian's honeymoon as the *'lune de miel'* (79)? Surely, not *very* sophisticated. Camp, perhaps. He is capable of modest multilingual jokes – 'when *les frites* are down a marriage always consists of one moderate and one militant' (248) – but it is hard to concur with reviewers who seem to think that in Oliver Julian Barnes is giving free rein to his own European sophistication. Barnes does not write this way when writing as Julian Barnes – he is neither so determined to show off his French nor so effortful in his own cleverness – he does not need to.

Instead, Oliver is a rather lightweight Francophile, but, as we should expect, he is a Francophile *against* someone. In this case that someone is Stuart. We are meant – meant by Oliver, that is – to gauge the depths of Stuart's insularity and lack of experience by the contrast with Oliver's cultural references and French vocabulary. His overreliance on favorite words, particularly 'crepuscular' (which he resolves to stop using but cannot resist for long) is also an act of one-upsmanship, aggression against Stuart, as when he asks, 'How did he burst out of his crepuscular *oubliette* of unnoticeability on this occasion? I put this poser to him, though in a more tactful way, you understand' (Barnes 1991: 28).

When, after they marry, Oliver and Gillian go to live in southern France, his descriptions of life are romantic and exotic in the vein of Peter Mayle and *Toujours Provence*.

> So I motor carefully, nodding to the locals like minor British royalty. Past the dusty rhombus which is half village square and half café forecourt, where a couple of senior citizens sip their morning beverage from fat cups bearing the slogan of Choky. Past the racks of Totalgaz outside the *alimentation* and the faded ads painted on the side wall for BRILLIANTINE PARFUMÉE and SUZE. The names, the names! Then past the disused *lavoir* next to the little

bridge – *où sont les blanchisseuses d'antan?* – and swing onto the main road by the Cave Coopérative . . . This is the life, I tend to reflect as I romp through the vineyards. A little Cinsault, a peppering of Mourvèdre, a jolt of Malbec and a stiffy of Tempranillo: mix them up and make them nice, pop goes the weasel. (Barnes 1991: 238–40)

Gillian's later account of the village, like her evaluation of Oliver's romantic Peugeot, is more ordinary.

This is France in its second use, not as a tool for impressing others but as a place of resort. Gillian's first trip to France in *Talking It Over* is with Stuart, one month after their marriage but after Oliver has decided that he loves Gillian and plans to win her over. Stuart's description, which diverges from Gillian's mostly in their differing reports of how much rain fell, is simple:

We had a wonderful weekend break. Headed off down the motorway from Calais. Turned left when we felt like it, found ourselves somewhere near Compiègne. Stopped at a village as it was getting dark. A half-timbered family hotel with rooms off a creaky wooden balcony running round two sides of a courtyard. Of course we went to a little market and naturally we bought a couple of plaited strings of garlic which will go mouldy before we've finished them. So we'd better give some away. The weather was a bit damp, but who cares? (Barnes 1991: 107)

The point is not that Stuart's way of visiting, or appreciating, France is better than Oliver's. But it is less pretentious; though he speaks French (badly, it's true) he delivers his account in English, calling the motorway a motorway instead of an autoroute, leaving the circumflex off 'hotel'.

When, in another of the parallels that the plot provides, Oliver and Gillian move to France to escape the attentions of Stuart (in ironic counterpoint to the first weekend break undertaken by *Stuart* and Gillian, which is partly meant to get them away from Oliver), they go there to buy a house and live, despite Oliver's reluctance. They return to England only after Stuart follows them to France to spy on them; and this, too, is a reversal of the previous situation, when Oliver followed Stuart and Gillian to France to spy on them (or as he claims to believe, to get them home safely). There is a first time as tragedy, second time as farce quality to this repetition, since Stuart and Gillian are unaware of being stalked by Oliver or of Oliver's obsession with Gillian; while Oliver and Gillian cannot help knowing of Stuart's interest in their movements. In the first escape to France, the married couple is innocent in a way impossible for the second.

Finally, France and Frenchness provide a model of a distinctly non-English model of *l'amour*. François Truffaut once defined a 'nice, classical story' as 'A girl, two boys, in a neighborhood in Paris' (Brody 2008: 121). That seems to me a very French idea of a classical story; it is also, without the neighborhood in Paris, the kind of triangle at the heart of several of Julian Barnes's novels, including *Metroland*, where the wife's adultery is retrospectively acknowledged, and relegated with the words, 'it's really all all right' (Barnes 1980: 163), to *Before She Met Me*, in which the wife's quasi-adultery drives the husband to comic and eventually savage lengths. And of course there is *Flaubert's Parrot*, in which both the story of Geoffrey Braithwaite and the intertext of *Madame Bovary* (1857) turn on unfaithful wives. *Love, etc.* (2000), the sequel to *Talking It Over*, also turns on a triangular relationship between husband, wife, and friend, though friend and husband have been reversed.

Talking It Over is the kind of French 'nice, classical story' in which the husband's best friend falls in love with the wife and, after a period of agonizing equipoise, prevails, supplanting the husband. It regularly reminds readers of the film *Jules et Jim* (1962). 'Several reviewers' – as Vanessa Guignery points out, 'and many French ones – analysed the love triangle through a comparison with the famous film by French director François Truffaut (1932–84), *Jules et Jim* (1962)' (Guignery 2006: 82). More important, as she goes on to insist (Guignery 2006: 83) – and Barnes has also insisted (Guignery and Roberts 2009: 45) – are the differences between his novel and Truffaut's film. We should note two things about the relationship between film and novel. One is that the similarity is recognized by the characters in *Talking It Over*, but their references are strangely innocent about the adulterous relationship. Stuart mentions it first, in an odd way that suggests he may not know how the film ends: 'Three weeks later Oliver came back from somewhere exotic, and there were the three of us. All that summer. The three of us. It was like that French film where they all go bicycling together' (Barnes 1991: 24). Oliver's response is mostly to denigrate Stuart's taste in films, though he does identify Oskar Werner (Jules, the husband) with Stuart by claiming that they are both steatopygous; his recollection is 'they all go bicycling together and run across bridges and *lark about*, yes?' (Barnes 1991: 26). Oliver recalls it one more time (Barnes 1991: 221) as a referent for the two of them, himself and Stuart, working together against a common enemy, old girlfriend Val. The two men, that is, seem to remember *Jules et Jim* more as a film about homosocial larks than about adultery.

The second point is that, no matter how similarly steatopygous Stuart and Oskar Werner may be, there is nothing in *Talking It Over* like Jules's patient encouragement of his friend's affair with his wife Catherine, no scene parallel to the one where Jules writes to Jim begging him to hasten his visit, since Catherine is missing him, no guiltless indulgence by the apical woman, in this case Gillian. Instead Stuart's response is a mixture of impotent fury, making trouble for Oliver with his landlady, and head butting, followed by divorce. In other words, there is a French situation here, a nice, classical story, but the responses are Anglo-Saxon (Oliver wants Gillian entirely to himself as much as Stuart does – no Jim-style sharing for him, either).

One interviewer suggested that Barnes's fictional interest in sexual jealousy derives from French influence. He responded:

> I don't think my preoccupation with jealousy is French or French influenced. I frequently write about love, and therefore about jealousy. It's part of the deal; it's what comes with love, for most people, in most societies. Of course, it's also dramatic, and therefore novelistically attractive, because it's frequently irrational, unfair, boundless, obsessing and horrible for all parties. It's the moment when something deeply primitive breaks the surface of our supposedly grown-up lives – the crocodile's snout in the lily pond. Irresistible. (Guppy 2000–01: 79)

In *Talking It Over*, certainly, the jealousy exceeds what a French reader might expect; the contrast between that novel and a classical French story like *Jules et Jim* derives from the fact that it depicts the English cuckold as much more jealous, more unforgiving.

There is one important French voice in *Talking It Over* (aside from Mme Rives, late in the book, who says 'Sont fous, les Anglais' [Barnes 1991: 274]); that is Mme Wyatt, Gillian's mother, who is French. What are we to make of her? She stands, at least for several of the characters, for a liberated approach to sex. Moreover, she, like her daughter, has had an affair shortly after marriage. ' "Oh, how French", I hear you say. Oo-la-la' (Barnes 1991: 168). But to Mme Wyatt, this is not French: just human. She explains that the beginning of marriage is the most dangerous time for adultery because 'the heart has been made tender. *L'appetit vient en mangeant*. Being in love makes you liable to fall in love' (Barnes 1991: 168).

Mme Wyatt is a sort of French chorus to this English *ménage a trois*, dispensing French wisdom, some of it her own vintage and some of it from Chamfort's epigrams. From Chamfort she translates 'Love pleases more than marriage, in the same way as novels are more amusing than history' (145) and 'marriage comes after love as smoke comes after fire' (146) Mme Wyatt also shares the epigram (in *Love, etc.*) that Barnes has quoted elsewhere: 'Who was it who said that the chains of marriage are so heavy that sometimes it needs three people to carry them?' (Barnes 2000: 90). But that is a very French way of seeing, or kind of loving; it applies to *Jules et Jim*, perhaps, but not to *Talking It Over*, where a more English, or mid-Channel observation might be that the chains of marriage are so heavy that sometimes one husband has to be taken off for a substitute.

As Barnes insists, the French elements in his novels are not there to accord with fashion; they're not part of some system of binaries, or inserted in the support of Francophilia or Francophobia. The matter of France is not treated as the exotic, nor is it assimilated to familiarity (and his fondness for borders calls for the preservation of otherness); it is neither an occasion for 'funny foreigners' nor an offshore platform for irredentist attacks on the home country. Whether France and Frenchness figure in his novels as a cultural marker to arouse and appease longing or to put less cosmopolitan Englishmen in their places; as a model of adultery, more or less urbane; or as a place to go, a venue for finding 'antitheses to your normal, English urban life', the difference helps to define what it is not, specifically what is English, and in a way that seems both English and thoroughly European.

CHAPTER SIX

The Story of Julian Barnes's *The Porcupine*: an Epistolary ½ Chapter

DIMITRINA KONDEVA

> **Chapter Summary:** This chapter traces the formation of Julian Barnes's *The Porcupine* (1992) through an exchange of letters between the author and his Bulgarian publisher and translator during the writing process. Dimitrina Kondeva gives us a unique and intimate insight into Barnes's research methods as well as the creative processes that lie at the heart of his novelistic practice.

Julian Barnes's latest book, the collection of short stories *Pulse* (2011), was sent to his foreign publishers as a final draft with handwritten corrections by the author. His literary agents must have been so fascinated with his new collection that they immediately sent it to his foreign publishers without waiting for the corrected proofs to come out. As Barnes's Bulgarian publisher, I looked at the familiar font of his IBM typewriter and the familiar handwriting in biro and was thrilled – the scanned pages, though on a screen, reminded me of the time of our intensive exchanges of letters and faxes and the arrival of the second draft of *The Porcupine* (1992). Reading that draft 18 years ago was an enjoyable and intimate experience. While scrolling down the pages of *Pulse*, I was both nostalgically excited and slightly disappointed: are these stories old unpublished pieces from the typewriter era? I scrolled up to the contents page. Two or three titles had recently appeared in magazines; even before reading the rest I realized it was a new collection written in the author's old, reliable, more effort-taking way. When it comes to writing fiction, Julian still avoids the computer, which, in his opinion, 'tends to make things look finished sooner than they are'. I guess he resents the lack of emotion in the contact with something called 'a word *processor*'. This is just an assumption but it is my firm belief that whatever he starts writing, he does it with emotion.

Most of Barnes's literary critics and fans could probably name their absolute favourite among his works but my top pick often changes – it is always his latest book to be soon published or just published. Perhaps this shiftiness of feelings is due to my current involvement in the 'extension' or rather 'expansion' of the life of his books abroad. While translating *The Lemon Table* (2004), I could not think of more charming stories than 'The Revival' and 'The Fruit Cage' though during my long obsession with the 'Stowaway' and the whole *The History of the World in 10½ Chapters* (1989), unfaithfulness had seemed impossible. Then *Nothing To Be Frightened Of* (2008) appeared and reminded me of my passion for *Flaubert's Parrot* (1984) – it was like a charismatic, slightly melancholic cousin of a first love. And now the more I am getting to know the vital *Pulse*, the more I am attracted to it.

However, there is one novel by Barnes which has always been very special to me in many senses – *The Porcupine*. 'A life-changing book' sounds like a quote from a self-help manual or an inspirational guide but this novel did change my life even before its publication in Great Britain. It became the first title of a hastily set up independent company and sold 10,000 copies in a week, and given that Bulgaria's population is roughly one-tenth the population of Great Britain, it was a huge success.

Below is a personal story, an epistolary ½ chapter, about the creation of *The Porcupine* and its reception in the country depicted. The letters written by Julian were never meant for publication but should be of great interest to scholars examining his choice of themes, preliminary research, structuring of the plot, and so on. I had the rare chance and privilege to watch fiction being created by an acclaimed author. In one of his interviews, Julian says that he never discusses his books with anyone until they are finished. This is true even in the case of *The Porcupine* – I knew the subject and some of the characters at an early stage of their development but not the plot itself until I received the manuscript four months later.

The story begins with a letter about an embryo of a nameless novel. Or rather, it began a year earlier when Julian and his wife, the literary agent Pat Kavanagh (1940–2008), came to Bulgaria for the promotion of the Bulgarian translation of *Flaubert's Parrot*. They had travelled to other East European countries in the peaceful Cold War days. It was a gloomy November, a year after the fall of the Berlin Wall. Todor Zhivkov, the longest-ruling leader in Eastern Europe, had been dethroned. The Cold War was over and so was the peace of apathy. There were great shortages of food and petrol but an abundance of hope and fear. Capitalism had come but Communism hadn't gone away. The Communist party was in disgrace, yet, by changing its name, it was still in power. There were demonstrations, student rallies, hunger strikes, power cuts, queues for bread. And a long queue of readers who came to meet Julian Barnes. They were carrying candles in case the electricity went off. He must have been touched by their literary enthusiasm, moved by the conflicting emotions of the people 'living in interesting times'. People had heard that living in interesting times was a Chinese curse but they also believed that it was History's blessing. Barnes the writer was jotting down notes, Barnes the man was sitting on the floor of a crowded apartment long after midnight, discussing art and politics with young university professors, poets and editors. They were smart and intelligent; they demonstrated a sense of humour and self-irony. He was impressed and saddened. That night he was chain-smoking for the first time in his life. The visit lasted nine days.

Upon returning to London, Barnes wrote 'Candles for the Living' (1990), an emotional essay about the empty shops, the ration coupons and the political chaos, but mainly about the great expectations and apprehensions of the people living in the void between two systems. He kept in touch with his new acquaintances. He was interested in the political developments and in their private lives. It wasn't research for a novel. He didn't have such a 'script in mind' for almost a year.

The letter of 28 November 1991 was a surprise. It contained a request and a list of questions. Some were amusing and easy to answer, some needed research; most of them were factual, a few were interpretative. Anyone Julian knew in Bulgaria would have probably agreed to answer them but I was the first one he approached and could not miss that opportunity. I did not know how big all this was, in fact.

When asked to write something on *The Porcupine* and its coming into being, I realized it would be impossible to do so without first getting Julian's permission to quote some of his letters to me. He is renowned for his fondness of digging into great writers' correspondence and mixing bits of it with witty comments and invented stories. He applies this technique to reveal unknown facts about these writers in addition to more subtle creative goals. My goal does not involve any invention or alteration. It is to select some of the author's own comments on the questions and answers from a famous passage in *Flaubert's Parrot*: 'How do we seize the past? How do we seize the foreign past? We read, we learn, we ask, we remember, we are humble; and then a casual detail shifts everything' (Barnes 1985: 90).

If I have cut parts of the following letters, it is because they are too long or not related to *The Porcupine* and the process of seizing the foreign past . . . and present.

28 November 1991

. . .
I'm writing with a request, Dimitrina. I've just started writing something which may be a short novel or a long short story, I'm not sure. It just started in the middle of one night. It's about the trial of a deposed Communist leader in Eastern Europe, seen largely from the accused's point of view . . . at least, I think so. Now it's not set in Bulgaria, but obviously the trial of Zhivkov is

very useful to me, as none of the other Communist leaders has come up for trial. What I'd like, if it's at all possible, is any English-language accounts, comments, background material on his trial which as I understand it has started or is about to start. I'm attaching a list of the sort of things I'm interested in. Also, any English-language accounts of the life in your country since Pat and I visited. We have a vivid recollection of course, and since it's not B/ia in the book (it's nowhere named) I can invent things, but I'm interested in the texture of life in the period from the fall of Zhivkov until now. That may sound a bit vague, but if so it's because – as is often the case with research – I'm not sure what I'm after until I find it. Perhaps as I go on with the writing I'll be able to be more precise.

I hope you don't mind doing this. I saw Margaret Drabble and Michael Holroyd the other evening – they are leaving for Bulgaria in a couple of days to do a British Council tour and stay with the ambassador. . . .

How is the History of the World coming along? You know you can ask me any questions you like about it. Though as . . . you understand and remember my book better than I do, this may not be necessary.

I hope all is well with you. . . . I hope the fragmentation of the publishing company didn't mean fragmentation of friendships. Have the bees recovered?

With love,
Julian

Questions

Zhivkov. What is he actually being tried for?

Do the charges accurately represent what crimes he might have committed, or are they charges on which it will be easier to find him guilty?

Is he charged under the old (Communist) law, or under laws made since he was deposed?

What attitude has he taken towards the trial? Contempt? Involvement? Self-justification?

Is it on television? How much of it? Do people watch it, or do they prefer to ignore it? What happens during power cuts? (I have a scene in the book where students rush from one part of the city to the next so as not to miss live coverage of the Leader's trial – is this feasible?)

Do you think the trial is good/useful/necessary? A national purge? Or a way of distracting attention? Are others to be tried too?

Who is the prosecutor, defence counsel, judge in the case? I mean a) can you describe the rough structure of the court; b) can you indicate what these people were before they came to try the former leader of their country. Were they part of the Communist system of justice? What happened to the legal system after Zhivkov fell – was it shaken up or left in place?

Were there demonstrations about the trial? If so, by whom?

What are the main arguments a) for having the trial
                             b) *against having it*

Were these arguments heard in the parliament?
That's all to begin with!

By the time I received the above letter, Julian had obviously structured the book and had outlined the protagonists, the minor characters and some central scenes as well. 'Novels come out of life, not out of theories', he has said in an interview. (Freiburg 1999: 47) *The Porcupine*, still unnamed at that time, was going to be his first novel about current political matters. A book about history in the making needed more real-life facts than those dealing with distant history. The past gives the excuse of blurred memory and a writer has more liberty to invent. Barnes had already produced a trial in chapter 3 of *The History of the World in 10 1/2 Chapters*, 'The Wars of Religion', a brilliant farce of a trial. In the case of *The Porcupine* he had to construct a trial simultaneously with the real one (which was gradually also turning into a farce). Of course knowledge of the specific legal procedures and structure of the court was important to a writer with law education. However, like in all his works, reality and fantasy went hand in hand.

16 December 1991

Dear Dimitrina: More questions, I'm afraid. . . . . .
How do people swear in Bulgaria? I mean, the three main types of swearing in English are a) sexual; b) blasphemous; c) to do with shit. Is it the same?
I need the sort of names that apartments blocks are called. I remember that Rada lived in a block called 'Youth', and therefore the individual blocks in the complex were called Youth 1, Youth 2, Youth 3, and so on. What would other complexes be called: after aspirations/qualities; after Communist leaders, famous heroes?
Are there any public accounts of Zhivkov's meeting with Gorbachov in the course of which he offered to incorporate Bulgaria into the Soviet Union? Am I right in the first place that he did make the offer to Gorbachov? My notes say he suggested it first to Brezhnev, but also suggested it a second time.
At last there is a story in the British press about the Zhivkov 'trial', saying that it will probably not take place because he is ill, though as there is now evidence of his approval of secret police action against dissidents living abroad, he may well be tried in absentia *for the Markov murder. So the tense of some of the questions I sent you last time has changed: What would he have been charged with, Who would have tried him, How would the court have been constituted? And so on. I'm afraid I still need the answers!*
BUT: two things, Dimitrina: 1) I don't want you to waste time on this; only answer if you can do so easily, or just by asking someone else. 2) I don't want you to do it at all if it is painful for you. Rereading my notes from my visit to Bulgaria, I found a reference to a time when I was asking you questions about your country and it was as if I was sticking needles into you. So don't if it is painful.

I need a list of common Bulgarian Christian names and surnames. Say, 10 of each. Would you recognize a peasant from his/her name? If so, give me a couple or so.

How much was/is the weekly ration of rationed goods? No doubt it changes but how much cheese/flour/cooking oil etc?

One proposal, I remember, was for a 'moral trial'. Can you give me any details of what this might have consisted of? What charges, evidence, sentence? Or would it have been in absentia? *Who would have been the judges – professors of ethics?*

* * *

22 January 1992

Dear Dimitrina:
Many thanks for your long and extremely helpful letter. I have already put one sentence whole and untouched from it in my story – you will have to guess which when you read it.... Your list of names, answers and comments are most useful and at times eerily in tune with what I am doing. For instance, I had put the Red Army statue in Plovdiv into my text – transposing it to the capital city in my unnamed Balkan country and changing the posture of the soldier, and having people discuss whether or not it should be torn down – when up you come with your unprompted observations on Alyosha. I didn't know he was called that. He is in my story too now.

. . .

I very much like the proverb of covering the culprit in honey.

Also: was there a name for the special shops where the nomenklatura could buy otherwise unobtainable goods? And were there different degrees of access to such shops according to rank? How did it work?

It may have been a mistake to give me your fax number!

With love,
Julian

Whatever facts and comments I sent, Julian skillfully transformed them so they acquired metaphoric meaning. The following paragraphs from *The Porcupine* evolved from the removal of communist symbols (red stars, hammers-and-sickles) from government buildings, which Julian witnessed, and my brief account of a debate on taking down the huge granite Russian soldier mentioned in the above letter. (It still stands on the top of a hill in a major Bulgarian city.) He quickly transferred the statue of Alyosha to a marshalling yard in the capital of his fictional country and made a brilliant scene which deserves quotation at length:

Meanwhile, slowly, discreetly, the monuments were coming down all over the city. There had been partial removals before, of course. One year, bronze Stalins had been purged at a whisper from Moscow. They had been taken from their plinths in the night and delivered to a patch of waste ground near the central marshalling yard, where they were lined up against a high wall as if awaiting the firing squad. . . .

Now Stalin had company. Brezhnev, who favoured bronze and granite postures in life, and now happily continued his existence as a statue. Lenin, with worker's cap and inspiringly raised arm, the fingers clasping holy writ. Next to him the nation's First Leader, who in a permanent gesture of political subservience loyally remained a meter or so shorter than the giants of Soviet Russia. And now came Stoyo Petkanov . . .

Recently, there was talk of Alyosha joining them. Alyosha, who had stood on that low northern hill for almost four decades, his bayonet glittering fraternally. He had been a gift from the Soviet people; now there was a movement to return him to his donors. Let him go back to Kiev or Kalinin or wherever: he must be getting homesick after all this time, and his great bronze mother must be missing him badly.

But symbolic gestures can prove expensive. It had been cheap enough to sneak the embalmed First Leader out of his Mausoleum on a forgotten night when only one street-lamp in six was lit. But repatriating Alyosha? That would cost thousands of American dollars, money better spent on buying oil or mending the leaky nuclear reactor in the eastern province. So some argued instead for a gentler, local banishment. Pack him off to the marshalling yard and let him join his metallic masters. He would tower over them there, for he was the largest statue in the country; and that might be a small inexpensive revenge, the thought of those vain leaders discountenanced by his huge arrival. Others believed that Alyosha should stand on his hill. . . . Why not let him remain where he was? You did not have to agree with every monument. You did not destroy the Pyramids in retrospective guilt at the suffering of the Egyptian slaves. (Barnes 1992: 42–44)

In April 1992 came a letter enclosed in a parcel.

Dear Dimitrina:

Here is The Porcupine. *(When I studied Russian I remember a phrase – or at least the English translation we used to use for the phrase – which went: 'We must handle him/her with mitts of porcupine'. I remember it because it's very bad English: you'd say 'porcupine gloves'; but this was how some antique translator from the Russian had rendered Pushkin or Turgenev or whoever. I wonder if there is a similar phrase in Bulgarian.) This is a second draft, and I shall need to produce the final draft by the end of May. This will be mainly fine-tuning, as most of what I want to say is said here; but I am quite capable of altering even fairly big things up to the last minute (as I have done in the past).*

You will see that the country is not Bulgaria, though much of it resembles Bulgaria, that Petkanov is not Zhivkov, though he often speaks his lines (there is an additive of Ceausescu, of course), and that the trial, though it parallels Zhivkov's trial, is not his. Nevertheless, I do not expect you to read the book thinking, 'Gosh, what a strange and distant country Julian has imagined.' And so I ask you to read it with some apprehension on my part. Firstly, because you will probably exclaim, 'Well, that's not true', and 'That never happened', and worse, 'That couldn't have happened' as you read. I would ask you to point out whatever strikes you as impossible, implausible, wrong or bad. My second, and larger reason for apprehension is that part of me wonders if you will not take offence at the book. Who am I, a nine-day visitor who's never lived under Communism (despite travelling under it fairly widely), to steal your story like this? It is not anything I felt while writing the book (all such extra-literary worries are wonderfully put aside at that time), but I feel it now. How dare he steal our story – and then mess it up, I hear you say. Or, It's too gloomy, it's simply not true to the feelings in the country. I remember a letter Pat got from Julia Stefanova after my 'Candles for the Living' article appeared, in which, while being able to admire the piece objectively, she said that for her the reality was too raw, and that she didn't like what she had lived through being turned into 'fictional reality' (though I was trying to be factual). But how much more might such a person object to the 'fictional reality' of a piece of fiction like this? So you will tell me also, Dimitrina, if you are offended by The Porcupine.

If you are still planning to send me material from your meeting with the defence lawyers, please do so. It may still prove useful even if most of the book is already in place.

. . .

Oh, one more thing. Tell me if the names are OK. I think I am going to have to adjust one of the names of either Petkanov or Sarotov. I think a Western reader might want the names to be as different from one another as the characters are different from one another, and so one of them should have a name that doesn't end in -ov. Do all Bulgarian names end in -ov? If so, I might give him a more Russian-sounding name. Like Sorokhin or Solukhin, or something like that. Any ideas?

. . .

Spring has almost arrived; daffodils are out in the garden, as are lots of other flowers which only Pat knows the names of. . . . The other thing that's happening is a General Election, a week today; the process of the campaign has been extremely tedious, but the result is going to be fascinating. We could even have a stalemate, which would at least be more interesting than any other result.

I hope you smile from time to time at things you have wittingly or unwittingly contributed to The Porcupine.

With love,
Julian

* * *

11 May 1992

. . .

I am glad you accepted the dedication of The Porcupine.

. . .

* * *

1 June 1992

Dear Dimitrina:
Here is the final draft of The Porcupine. *I'm afraid there are quite a lot of changes; new names, some new sections at the end, bits added and subtracted all over the place, extra references to bees and honey, and so on. You will probably curse me as you find you have to collate every page (but then I did tell you the previous draft wasn't a final one).*
We've agreed to change Alyosha to Serozha (Seryozha?). I give you carte blanche to do similar things if they would grate on Bulgarian ears. And if you come across anything new I've put in where you immediately respond with 'No!' then perhaps you could fax me about it. I'll be copy-editing the book here in about 4 weeks, I should imagine.
I've got to the (necessary) stage where I can only see things wrong with the book, and mistakes on every page. But the one page on which there is no mistake is the dedication page.
Wouldn't it be wonderful publicity if Zhivkov sued for libel?

Affectionately,
Julian

Barnes loves to polish every phrase until it shines: 'Change "candle-flicker" to "match-flare"; change "enormous wreaths" to "wreaths as big as tractor tyres"; change (this is very important) "He would put them to trial" to "He had a different script in mind".' He searches for inconsistencies in the text and in the chronology of the events described and imagined even in the final proofs: 'Delete the year but leave the month & day; Change "fifteen years" to "nine years" – otherwise the chronology doesn't work.' Julian sent me such notes because I was already translating *The Porcupine* for the state-run publishing house I was working for. However, it had not yet bought the rights and all of a sudden I had a crazy idea to quit and start on my own. Almost all state-owned companies were crumbling down and keeping my job was as risky as losing it. I had a couple of colleagues who were also at professional crossroads. We hoped the new private printing houses would agree to produce *The Porcupine* without any advance and be paid after we sell it. But would the author agree to be published by *an idea* of a publishing house? Would he agree to have a paperback premiere before the hardcovers of 'Jonathan Cape' and 'Knopf'?

30 June 1992

Dear Dimitrina:
Congratulations. Now you are a businesswoman and an entrepreneuse as well as a publisher and translator. . . .

Pat has a bestseller for you, Fatherland *by Robert Harris, which is to be a huge seller everywhere.* . . .

I've given [Nicky Kennedy, Julian Barnes's foreign rights agent] your friend's fax number as if it were your office number. I think everyone should believe you have an ENORMOUS office in Sofia. Now you are a publisher – I mean an independent publisher – you will have to learn to exaggerate and conceal. This is the nature of the job.

With love,
Julian

In August, the translation was ready for printing. We had to publish the book soon because its launch had to coincide with the pronouncement of Zhivkov's verdict. I asked Julian to write a short preface for our edition which was going to precede the British one. Bulgarians could not be misled about the 'source' country and some might have difficulties with reading the book as fiction. It was not only a matter of historical and topographical similarities – those resemblances could more easily be accepted as metaphors and allegories. But the names could be a bigger obstacle to the Bulgarian readers' detachment though I myself had persuaded Julian to make them more locally applicable. Given the global use of English personal and geographical names, an imagined country with such names would not be perceived as Great Britain-based. But with its strictly local non-exportable names *The Porcupine* would seem definitely Great Britain-based to any Bulgarian. On the other hand, a Balkan-Russian-Polish-Czech mix of characters would have been more confusing for all the East Europeans. This lexicographic incongruity would have been almost unnoticeable for a Western reader, it might even have sounded delightfully exotic. However, I knew that Julian's initial idea to have a mix of pan-Communist names in order to make the country a nowhere-place would be an unnecessary distraction for the Slavic countries readership. He did not write a preface so we used a part of the following letter as introduction.

7 August 1992

Dear Dimitrina:

. . .

I don't know what I might say to the Bulgarian reader, except 'Don't forget that this is a novel'; but such a remark would insult the readers who are most likely to enjoy the book. If Aglika has taken offence . . . *, then no doubt lots of other people will take offence as well. I don't mind this: I expect people in the West will take offence as well; in fact, I've just had a long report from the libel lawyer at Jonathan Cape in which he concludes 'the main areas of risk are Gorbachev, Nancy Reagan, Frank Sinatra and the Queen' – he doesn't even mention Zhivkov suing me! So while I'm initially tempted to say something* *like 'You will probably recognize bits of your recent history but all this really takes place in the country of my and your mind', this would a) not pacify literalist readers, who will complain about reality being betrayed; and b) be completely obvious and therefore irritating to intelligent people who know what a novel is and how it differs from a newspaper report. I wouldn't want to sound either defensive or patronising. I'm not giving any newspaper interviews in English before the book appears because I want it to be there and say to the readers, 'Here I am, make of me what you will'.*

. . .

The Porcupine was written in pre-Google times and Julian asked insiders about specific details and recent facts but, above all, he was interested in people's attitudes and opinions. I don't think he would use the let's-Google-it research method even now because he is interested in individuals' 'inner voices' and their own truths rather than the ultimate Truth. *The Porcupine* is a complex novel about the guilt of the accused and the accusers, the ideological fanaticism and the dangers of being trapped in dogma. It deals with the personal interpretation of recent events. However, it appeared in Bulgaria at a time when things seemed either black or white as it often happens during bloody or velvet, red or orange revolutions. The participants might notice the nuances of the situation years later. Would they like a book about the elusiveness of truth and its various shades and tints? Wouldn't they want the one and only Truth?

Such apprehensions were not groundless. There were people who complained about 'minor implausibilities' in the narrative and some who did not want their 'country being explained by foreigners'. However, thousands were curious to read the first novel about the post-totalitarian time by a famous writer. Most of them admired it as far as I could judge by the reviews and my friends' praises. It was rumoured that Zhivkov had sent for a copy to read in prison and had enjoyed the book. Years later, a young girl wrote on Amazon.com: 'If you want to know anything about Bulgaria, this is where you should start from'.

Even now *The Porcupine* stands out as the most insightful novel about those turbulent years. The lack of historical distance and detachment is no longer an excuse for East European writers. Yet they continue with their sob stories about nostalgic emigrants longing for their beloved homeland but never coming back. Expats' soul-searching is an easy subject. The other popular genre here (in Russia as well) is the crime novel about local mafia thugs. I haven't heard of any good work of fiction about our recent history created by an insider. Let us hope that sooner or later some talented writer would rise to the challenge which Julian Barnes took up once.

CHAPTER SEVEN

Julian Barnes's *England, England* and Englishness

RICHARD BRADFORD

> **Chapter Summary:** Julian Barnes's *England, England* (1998) invokes a non-existent tradition of fiction that represents the emotional mythology of Englishness while Barnes is known for his Francophile affiliations. The novel presents us with a fictional Theme Park that distils national images and myths, run by an entrepreneur who treats England and Englishness as products for tourists. Englishness is represented as an empty illusion, but the chapter argues against approaches to *England, England* as a work of satire. Instead, Barnes's novel draws us with great delicacy toward the possibility that there is an authentic emotion among those who share a sense of belonging and a memory of the lost county.

The English novel, particularly since the mid-twentieth century, is by parts a misnomer, a chameleon and a delusion. There are thousands of novels written in English, including those which emphasize the various local, postcolonial and national variations upon a linguistic legacy, and some treat Englishness as a marginal, relatively insignificant element of other issues, such as the enigmatic, unaffiliated notion of region or class and historical mutation. Besides novels such as Andrew Cowan's *Pig* (1994) and James Hawes's *Speak for England* (2005), you will search in vain for works of contemporary fiction whose primary topic or organising principle is England or Englishness. Conversely, there are a considerable number of works, again written in English, whose authors and readers would happily accept as 'Welsh', 'Irish' or 'Scottish' fiction, principally because the sense of national identity that underpins their subject and setting is, if not easily definable, then at least robust and dynamic. Leaving aside the option of specifying the English novel as something that it is not, the only discernible sense of England as a driving force within recent fiction is not a sense of nation itself but rather of a region which, more by geographical circumstance than conscious awareness, happens to be English. In the late 1950s and early 1960s, Alan Sillitoe, David Storey, John Braine, Stan Barstow and Keith Waterhouse shifted the fictional focus away from London and the home counties toward the predominantly working class communities of the North and the Midlands. More recently, Graham Swift (in *Waterland*, 1983) has turned his attention to East Anglia, Julia Darling (*The Taxi Driver's Daughter*, 2003) to Newcastle-upon-Tyne, John Murray (*Jazz etc.*, 2003) to Cumbria and Niall Griffiths (*Wreakage*, 2005) to Liverpool. Nonetheless, London and its environs have dominated the fictional landscape over the past half century, for the simple reason that their vastness and density make them a far more suitable vehicle for fiction than their regional alternatives; the fact that London happens to be the capital of England, and indeed the entire UK, is entirely superfluous.

It is, therefore, doubly curious that Julian Barnes should have elected to write a novel exclusively about England and the historical, cultural political, indeed the emotional mythology of being English; firstly because he was invoking a non-existent tradition and secondly because Barnes himself had gained a considerable reputation as a writer with Continental, especially Francophile, affiliations. Both of his parents taught French, the household was almost bilingual and Barnes read Modern Languages (primarily French) at Oxford. He regularly disdains the suggestion of autobiographical elements in his fiction but Geoffrey Braithwaite of *Flaubert's Parrot* (1984), must have reflected something of Barnes's life: the middle-class professional Englishman content with his own state while equally preoccupied with the fascinating otherness of life and letters across the channel. Barnes's wider *oeuvre* is, while not ostentatiously experimental, certainly more closely aligned with the Continental taste for formal self-consciousness – novels alert to their status as such – than to the English conservative traditions that Modernists have found difficult to dismantle. Despite this, *England, England* (1998) addresses itself almost exclusively to its subject. Everything and every individual in the novel is a falsification, often a caricature, of questionable memories and nostalgic contrivances. Barnes's achievement is thus considerable. What his peers have said by implication and omission, he has relentlessly foregrounded: Englishness is an empty illusion.

The supposedly definitive features of English life and culture have been distilled into a Theme Park on the Isle of Wight, run by the entrepreneur Sir Jack Pitman. The standard retinue of architectural monuments – Big Ben, Buckingham Palace, and so on – plus figures from myth including King Arthur and Robin Hood and legendary presences such as Dr Johnson, played by actors, all perform their ordained, predictable and emasculated functions. It is this final ordination, that the essential aspects of Englishness must be reduced to inoffensive performance, which animates the book because the role players gradually begin to exchange representation for dangerous actuality. Robin Hood's merry men branch out into real poaching and theft and Dr Johnson sheds his tourist-friendly persona to become an angry depressive, no longer willing to indulge the intellectual vapidity of his paying guests. Anyone attempting to locate purposive or unambiguous allegory in all of this will, however, find themselves continually sidestepped.

There is a typically peculiar passage in which the King and Queen Denise – not actors but the real ones now obliged to supplement their diminished grandeur by performing in the Theme Park – are flying in their private plane from the mainland to the Isle of Wight. It is clear that they regard their duties with sanguine contempt: 'There'd been a script meeting at the Palace that morning and he'd practised his lines with Denise as they were waiting form take off. She'd nearly peed herself. She was a real best mate, Denise. But what was the point in paying good money if the audience didn't get it?' (Barnes 1998: 160). Barnes's peppering of this third-person account with touches of loutish demotic is an accurate reflection of the Royal Family's manner – somewhere between a parody of how they imagine that their subjects speak and an honest embittered acceptance of their belittled status.

Custom decrees that the flight is accompanied by two symbols of England's heroic past, a Spitfire and a Hurricane, the fighter aircraft which effectively defeated the Luftwaffe in the Battle of Britain. As outriders to the royal aircraft, they are clearly intended to remind us of such institutions as the Household Cavalry whose role as protectors of the monarch has been no more than ceremonial for two centuries and whose antique armoury and colourful attire last saw combat in the Napoleonic Wars. Barnes brings atrophied nostalgia to life by having the royal flight pestered by a small aircraft trailing a banner that reads 'SANDY DEXTER AND THE DAILY PAPER GREET HIS MAJ' (Barnes 1998: 161); these are representations of an invented media entrepreneur and his tabloid, by degrees fawning dedicatees of the Royal Family and in constant pursuit of any scandal that might attend it.

There is something endearingly elegiac in his presentation. Even those characters who should stand out as pitiable absurdities are, often quite brilliantly, endowed with an air of tragedy, figures cast adrift in a hinterland between private wish fulfilment and media-generated invention. The Theme Park is less a choreographed model of England than an assembly of working cultural motifs whose relationship to each other is assumed to be predictable. As the passage goes on to disclose, however, impulsiveness can intervene. The King is irritated and indicates his displeasure to Wing Commander 'Johnnie' Johnson in the *Spitfire* who, seized by the emotions of his Battle of Britain 'rehearsal', shoots down the offending aircraft:

> There was a long pause. Finally the King having through thought the matter over, came on the intercom. 'Congratulations, Wing Commander. I'd say, bandits discouraged' . . .
> 'Piece of cake, Sir', replied 'Johnnie' Johnson, remembering his line from the Battle's end.
> 'But I'd say that, on the whole, Mum's the word', added the King.
> 'Mum's the word, Sir'. (Barnes 1998: 162–63)

The King and 'Johnnie' are perplexed because the roles they have been programmed to play carry a residue of genuine emotion and commitment and for a moment the tabloid press becomes for them as threatening to civilized values as the Nazism of half a century earlier. Barnes is playing an ingenious game with the reader who will have witnessed the manner in which the popular press can manipulate perceptions of individuals, sometimes procuring for them a cult of celebrity and just as frequently destroying their public image – while seemingly remaining immune from any responsibility in this. Many readers will at some point have wondered how victims of tabloid scrutiny would, if they could, take revenge and 'Johnnie', equipped with machine guns, enacts a fair number of hypotheses.

Although *England, England* seems initially to be a parodic account of hollow nostalgia, a caricature of the illusions and falsities that constitute most people's notions of Englishness, it matures into a more fluid, surprising reflection upon the nature of collective identity. Examples of individuals such as 'Johnnie' and the King overriding the corporate plan while in some way abiding by its more emotive clichés segue eventually into the penultimate chapter where Martha Cochrane, employee of Pitman and puzzled witness to the narrative, finds herself in the Church of St Aldwyn conversing with what seems to be either a projection of herself or God:

> Into her mind came an image, one shared by earlier occupants of these pews. Not Guilliamus Trentinus, of course, or Anne Potter, but perhaps known to Ensign Robert Timothy Pettigrew, and Christina Margaret Benson, and James Thorogood and William Petty. A woman swept and hanging, a woman half out of this world, terrified and awestruck, yet in the end safely delivered. A sense of falling, falling, falling, which we have every day of our lives, and then an awareness that the fall was being made gentler, was being arrested, by an unseen current whose existence no-one suspected. A short, eternal moment that was absurd, improbable, unbelievable, true. Eggs cracked from the slight concussion of landing, but nothing more. The richness of all subsequent life after that moment. (Barnes 1998: 238)

Barnes, via Martha, stops the farcical procession of emptiness, confusion and despair and indicates that moments of certainty, all the more powerful for their brevity, are possible. Her pseudo-mystical experience is a passive, reflective version of the struggles that beset the likes of 'Johnnie' Johnson and his namesake the doctor, and can be read as attempts to act according to who they are within a world comprised almost exclusively of questionable myths. The closing chapter, 'Arcadia', involves a village fete. It is some time in the future, Martha is in her contented dotage and although most of the characters are still playing roles they now seem more comfortable in doing so, as if they have found a tolerable median between story and fact. Jaz Harris, for example, is the village farrier bedecked in a countryman's outfit 'which had hints of both Morris dancer and bondage devotee' (Barnes 1998: 242). Jaz was once an American lawyer but he has not so much reinvented himself as chosen a way of life far better suited to his temperament.

Barnes's novel involves a double bluff. He seems at first to select easy targets for caricature and satirical execution: predominantly England as an assembly of brand names and performances all capable of drawing cash from the credulous tourist. But by the conclusion, his characters have found among this chiaroscuro of impressions an England that is at once imperfect but compelling. In a period dominated by post-colonial guilt or sceptical indifference to nationality, this novel, peculiarly, offers a kindly, quirkily patriotic view of Englishness.

It is curious and exceptional in other respects. Englishness as a definable condition or state of mind is in truth a chimera. Geographically, legally, and politically 'England' is a definable entity, of sorts, but if we were to seek an answer to the question of what living in it or belonging to it, intellectually, culturally even emotionally, actually involves we would invest and waste our time in an exercise of shadow-chasing. This contention is tendentious and while this is not the occasion for an explanation of its social and political premises, it is borne out by representation of Englishness in the contemporary novel.

In the vast majority of novels set principally in England and comprised mainly of English characters issues of nationality or shared collective identity are of negligible significance. Graham Swift often seems an exception to this, but the impression is misleading. *Waterland* (1983) is without doubt pervaded by a sense of place. East Anglia in general informs the stylistic temper of the piece and the mood and behavioural inclinations of its characters. The Fens are brought startlingly, often disturbingly, to life but to extrapolate from their somewhat dour enigmatic features something that is characteristically English would be absurd. *Last Orders* (1996) is a funeral odyssey in which we listen to the interior monologues of the late Jack Dodd's oldest friends, randomly assembled histories of four Englishmen's lives. Each of them is a capsule of the social history of South East London of the previous half century, but like *Waterland* there are no ideological underpinnings. This particular region of England is presented in vivid miniatures yet the only subtext is that these are inseparable from the multiplicity of impressions and susceptibilities of the storytellers. The routine sociocultural clichés of cockneyism are flagged up only to be dismantled in a novel where subjectivity is far more powerful than any shared notion of region or nation. To treat is as in any way a representation of the state even of a particular aspect of Englishness would not only be an act of interpretive fraudulence but would do a gross injustice to Swift's status as a literary artist.

Adam Thorpe's widely acclaimed *Ulverton* (1992) is generally seen as an attempt to locate and represent the intangible qualities of Englishness but in this endeavour its method is self-limiting. For one thing, the focus is exclusively upon a rural community which has remained largely immune from the effects of urbanisation and the industrial revolution. It is, moreover, a historical novel comprised of 12 interlinked stories which offer accounts of life in the eponymous village from just after the Civil War to the present day.

The only other novels in which Englishness can be detected as something tangible, a state of mind upon which some sense of secure identity might be based, are those which treat it as existing on a scale between the loathsome and the abominable, such as in *Trainspotting* (1993) by Irvine Welsh. This novel is usually presented as having abstained from recognizable engagements with morality, ethics and national identity but beneath its anarchic sheen, there is an impressive stratum of calculation. It is not England and Englishness per se that is the target of this polemic but 'English aristocrats' (Welsh 1993: 190), a threadbare target but one guaranteed to draw an alliance of loathing from young politically self-conscious readers, English or otherwise. It disabuses us of the myth that the Irish are 'the trash ay Europe'. No, 'That's shite. It's the Scots. The Irish hud the bottle tae win thir country back, or at least maist ay it' (Welsh 1993: 190). This appears to be a drink-sodden rant, but gradually such apparently unfocused, discontinuous laments begin to acquire not only a precarious shape, but a cautious rationale. Welsh is inviting the reader, particularly the educated middle-class reader, to do some literary slumming and he uses the characters' linguistic registers as a cult signal, a means by which the reader might take part, vicariously, in a world where unspeakable and shamefully exciting things go on.

Barnes's presentation of the village fete seems by turns endearing and wholesomely absurd. But one should not mistake this, on his part, as a disclosure of sympathy for the country of his birth and upbringing. An exercise of disdainful pathos would be a more accurate assessment of his attitude. Barnes's vision of the village fair is, by turns endearing and absurd and 'Johnie' Johnson and Martha might be somewhat unreliable props to shore against the ruins of Englishness but they and the other inhabitants of *England, England* invite comparison with *Henry V* when compared with the visions of what it means to be English that we encounter in other novels of the past 20 years, ranging from the shameful, through the contemptible to the non-existent. Barnes's village fete should not be mistaken as a disclosure of sympathy for the country of his birth and upbringing. An exercise of disdainful pathos would be a more accurate assessment of his attitude.

Something about England

I have pointed out a number of the instances of farcical dystopianism that make up the texture of the novel and in this respect I run the risk of giving a false impression. To provide a full account of the breadth and complexity of this run on caricature, one would need to say something about virtually every paragraph in the book. While this testifies to Barnes's dexterity as a literary craftsman, it raises fundamental questions about his intentions. If, after reading *England, England* some hypothetical English patriot could sustain any sense of coherence in what the notion of Englishness involves, they would be possessed of almost superhuman resolution or be hopelessly self-deluded. It is a brilliant demolition job, made all the more effective by the accompanying tone of pity and compassion, albeit somewhat patronizing in both cases. But still, we have to ask, what exactly is its target?

Among the intelligentsia, circa 1998, few if any entertained ideals, or more accurately fantasies, about England, its nature, myths and history, remotely similar to those satirized; the sceptical mood of other novels which address this concept testify to that. There were many others resident in the England of 1998 whose literary interests and intellectual aspirations were very different from the kind of reader who might routinely purchase a new novel by Julian Barnes. Did he have this sort of person in mind when he decided to place within convenient walking distance reproductions of the grave of Princess Di, Big Ben, Buckingham Palace, Harrods and the Tower of London? It is quite possible that some gullible tourists from outside the UK might have their perception of England confirmed by such a retinue of recommended sites: consult the advertisements on a visitor-orientated tube map and this gallery of delights will indeed announce themselves as an index to the history and culture: if not of the country, then at least its capital. Surely, though, a novelist as sophisticated as Barnes would not stoop so low as to make fun of tourists or, even worse, base his satirical attack on the premise that these visitors are ill-educated buffoons. Worse still would be the implication that many of his fellow countrymen – though hardly, one imagines, his readers – exist in a state of part ignorance, part nostalgic falsehood epitomized by Martha and her like. History, we are informed, is taught in Martha's school by 'charts of History' (Barnes 1998: 12), a simplified rote of heroic events which pupils memorize but are not allowed to question. Her teacher, in a manner that is by degrees reverential and unintentionally farcical, tells the children 'tales of chivalry and glory, plague and famine, tyranny and democracy' (Barnes 1998: 12). This image of a curriculum based upon the glorification of the endemic national characteristics that built the Empire and protected the realm from Napoleon, the Kaiser and Hitler (Barnes 1998: 47) bears no resemblance whatever to the way in which history had been taught during the three decades up to 1998. From the 1960s onwards, the left-leaning relativistic model of English and British history that already prevailed in universities had displaced the chronological, fact-based curriculum.

There was, during the late 1990s, a steady dose of reports in such mid-range right-wing tabloids such as *The Daily Express* and *The Daily*

Mail on how pupils in state schools had for decades been indoctrinated by an anti-patriotic Leftist presentation of history and calls both from journalists and renegade populist politicians for children to be instructed in the heroic greatness of their shared national legacy. Generally speaking, such proposals involved models just as selective and absurd as those to which Martha and her peers are subjected. No one within the prevailing political consensus, Left and Right, took them seriously, and if Barnes did indeed have these projects in mind as he composed the novel then he was tilting at very derelict windmills. It is just remotely possible that he was recollecting the 1950s. He was born in 1946 and would have been at primary and secondary school during a period when few, if any, questioned the heroism of England and Britain in World War II and even perceived the demise of the Empire and regret. I should, however, revise my description of Barnes's school experience. He went to prep and public schools: these were very conservative in their practices but far more enlightened than the dreadful institutions experienced by Martha. So unless he was recalling the educational backgrounds of his less-privileged peers, which would involve on his part a degree of condescension and guess work, then this too is an example less of satire than unfocused hyperbole.

The novel presents a chiaroscuro of national images and myths that in 1998 was relevant only to a small number of individuals who, like Pitman and his cohorts and advisors, treated England and Englishness as a product with a customer base drawn almost exclusively from those who had no personal experience of it as a place or a historical narrative. In the year of its publication, or more pertinently during the two previous years during which it evolved, very few people in England cared about or even took casual cognizance of what England meant or was. I cannot claim to speak on behalf of a collective state of mind, but I would aver that most people who happened to have been born and brought upon in England would, if consulted in 1998 on what the notion of Englishness involved, confess to contentment in belonging to something agreeably indefinable. I suspect that Barnes too sensed this and, subtly, signalled it in a creation of Mark, a figure who appears out of synchronisation with the rest of the cast. He treats with impatient contempt the various attempts to shoehorn Englishness into nostalgic myths or to lament the loss of what it might once have meant. Constantly, he rejects the definitions mooted by other members of Pitman's advisory committee to which he belongs. He is the sceptic, contending at one point that Englishness is essentially 'about keeping reality and illusion separate' (Barnes 1998: 111). Notably he never offers an alternative to the proliferation of illusions discussed by the committee; the 'reality' he implies is too diverse and amorphous for definition. This is his vision of what Englishness involves – his mantra is often repeated 'I am English' (Barnes 1998: 111) – and one I would contend that he shares with his author. Barnes had written the national coming-of-age novel. In his view, England at the end of the 1990 had despatched to her past, had come to regard with generous amusement, the self-constructed images and mythologies of its heritage; hence the somewhat farcical rather than ominous mood of the satire. Being English meant in 1996–98 being comfortably unaffiliated: aware of the events and constructions of the past but not viscerally attached to any of them. As Barnes said in an interview shortly after the novel's publication, 'Getting Barnes history wrong is part of becoming a nation' (Denning: 1998).

At the time of its publication, the novel was optimistic, and not inaccurate. Sadly it was not prescient. As Barnes brought it to its conclusion, the New Labour Government was putting in place legislation which encouraged mutual antipathy and tribalism among the nations of the Union. Devolution was not intrinsically flawed in principal. In practice, however, it has left the one nation of the UK, or at least, many of its citizens, unhappy at what they perceive as the benefits, often financial, of non-Englishness. There is no room here for a serious discussion of the non-literary ramifications of 'being English', post-1998, but one has only to note the proliferation of St George–cross flags in gardens and on roofs – a phenomenon that did not exist before Devolution – to be reminded that a considerable number of the 'English' are presently engaged in an embittered search for what Barnes had celebrated as a comedic gallery of redundant illusions.

There is a remarkable, very moving passage in the first chapter of the novel in which Martha recollects her favourite childhood game, a lambent emotional link with her absent father who deserted the family before she reached her teens. It is a jigsaw, called 'The Counties of England' (Barnes 1998: 5). She was never quite able to finish the puzzle because

> a piece would always be missing. Leicestershire, Derbyshire, Nottinghamshire, Warwickshire, Staffordshire – it was usually one of them – whereupon a sense of desolation, failure, and disappointment at the imperfection of the world would come upon her, until Daddy, who always seemed to be hanging around at this moment, would find the missing piece in the unlikeliest place. What *was* Staffordshire doing in his trouser pocket? How could it have got there? And she would smile her Nos and-head shakes at him, because Staffordshire had been found, and her jigsaw, her England, and her heart had been made whole again. (Barnes 1998: 5–6)

From a hand much less subtle than Barnes's, such a passage might beg for explanation, the unpicking of registers of private loss from the broader fabric of a fragmented, forgotten nation. But such a reading would do a gross injustice to a piece of prose that might have been borrowed periphrastically from a poem. One is reminded particularly of what is, arguably, the most English of all poems written by an English poet, Edward Thomas's 'Adlestrop' (1917). As the train draws up at a deserted country station the speaker, Thomas, is bewitched by a sense of simply being part of the landscape,

> willows, willow-herb, and grass,
> And meadowsweet, and haycocks dry,
> No whit less still and lonely fair
> Than the high cloudlets in the sky.
>
> And for that minute a blackbird sang
> Close by, and round him, mistier,
> Farther and farther, all the birds
> Of Oxfordshire and Gloucestershire. (Thomas 1917: 8–16)

Throughout the poem, Thomas balances a temptation to forget that anything exists apart from the beautiful anonymity that seems about to swallow the train and its passengers against an equal compulsion to record, remember the experience: he attempts the latter by fixing upon names. 'What I saw/was Adlestrop – only the name', and implicitly lifts himself above this place and its signpost, to imagine where it actually is in the landscape of his native country, near the border between, 'Oxfordshire and Gloucestershire'. The notion of telescoping a transient sense of belonging into something concrete – variously county borders, place names, a map jigsaw puzzle – preoccupies Martha and Thomas. Barnes disclosed in an interview that 'In my younger days I spent a lot of time criss-crossing England in search of second hand books (Cathedral towns were always very good sources for some reason – perhaps the clergy read widely.)' (Anonymous: 2005). As an individual, Barnes's probably the most determinedly enigmatic of all contemporary authors, willing to talk about his interests in literature and comments on all manner of issues in the public eye but on his personal life and history, rigorously costive. It would then be presumptuous to treat Martha's sense of loss as a reflection of something that her creator feels about England. Yet, leaving such auto-fictional possibilities aside, it is still the case that Martha in moments such as this causes a sensation of something other than empty nostalgia, a feeling that despite the ravages of Pitman there might still be something about England – something too private to be extrapolated to a shared national mood, let alone a patriotic consensus – that can evoke for the reader unalloyed emotion. When, aged 25, Martha meets her father again and finds that he recalls nothing of her jigsaw games, she experiences a sensation of resentment and betrayal greater than anywhere else in her dismal narrative. 'She would always blame him for that . . . she would always blame him for that' (Barnes 1998: 25). The 'that' is the irreconcilable break with a past that lives only in her memory, a record now denied by the man with whom she once shared it. Towards the end of the novel, Martha, via the narrator, reflects again upon the power of memory and the tragic consequences of its fragmentation:

> The operation of memory was becoming more random; she had noticed that . . . this was your brain hinting at what you didn't want to know: that you had become the person you were not by explicable cause and effect, by acts of will imposed on circumstance, but by mere vagary. (Barnes 1998: 250)

Routinely, and lazily, *England, England* is treated as a work of satire, its targets abidingly self-selecting and open for ridicule. While it is certainly the case that Pitman's obsessive re-merchandising of what most readers would already treat as ludicrous symbols of a questionable legacy is the motor for the book that Barnes with great delicacy also draws us, often against our better judgement, toward the possibility that there might just be something, albeit wonderfully intangible, that touches a genuine emotion among those who share something of Martha's attachment to her jigsaw puzzle, perhaps a sense of belonging so beautifully evoked by Thomas and by Martha herself in her memory of the lost county.

CHAPTER EIGHT

Matters of Life and Death: The Short Stories of Julian Barnes

PETER CHILDS

> **Chapter Summary:** In *The Lemon Table* (2004) Julian Barnes talks through his stories about living at a pensionable age and the sense of dread before an unknowable future. This chapter looks at the short-story collection's overall sardonic take on 'rage and age', as well as several stories that embrace more sanguine attitudes and assert equanimity if not defiance before the dying of the light. *The Lemon Table* collection is read alongside the 'memoir' *Nothing To Be Frightened Of* (2008), which focuses on Barnes's reflections on living with intimations of death and with the thoughts of those who write about the afterlife, immortality and oblivion. In the second half of the essay, comments are offered on Barnes's bittersweet recent stories, which contribute towards his 2011 collection *Pulse*.

'It's almost like storytelling, the way he invents it. . . . He invents it, but I know it's true, because I now remember it'. (Barnes 2005: 167)

'Why did some people forget what they needed to remember, and remember what was best forgotten?' (Barnes 2010: n.p.)

Regularly chided for publishing books in one genre that a critic thinks belong in another, Julian Barnes is among a handful of novelists who have been *accused* of writing short stories. Most well known in this regard is his novel *A History of the World in 10½ Chapters* (1989), a book of disparate but connected narratives whose title advertises not (short) stories but *chapters*. The assertion of there being a rogue 'half-chapter' among them immediately punctures any attempt seriously to debate the book's categorization beyond Barnes's own view that the novel can contain whatever the author puts in it. Many, but by no means all, of Barnes's 'self-categorized' short stories are collected together in two themed volumes, *Cross Channel* (1995) and *The Lemon Table* (2004), with a third to be published, like the present study, in 2011: *Pulse*. The first book is an episodic inquiry into aspects of the British and Irish experience in France but it is the second collection, assembling stories on death and ageing first published between 1996 and 2003, that will occupy more of the discussion in this chapter before a consideration of Barnes's latest stories, which contribute to the third collection.

In Barnes's eschatology, there are two deaths. The first is the death of youth, the second the death of old age (Barnes 2008: 42). When he was himself approaching the first he wrote his sophomore collection of stories, *The Lemon Table*, which concerns the disconsolations of mortality. At publication, Barnes, born in 1946, was still not yet pensionable, as he notes elsewhere: 'at the age of 58, I published a collection of short stories dealing with the less serene aspects of old age' (Barnes 2008: 97).

That comment was published in 2008 in the 'memoir', as the book jacket calls it, that serves as a non-fiction companion piece to *The Lemon Table*. A book about books, anecdotes, and thoughts about final things, as well as Barnes's own experiences of mortality, this meditation on the second death is pointedly entitled *Nothing To Be Frightened Of*, echoing Arthur Conan Doyle's first memory at the very start of *Arthur & George* (2005) of being shown his grandmother's corpse, perhaps 'to impress upon the child that death was nothing to be feared' (Barnes 2005a: 3). That frightening 'Nothing', which Barnes says is the most exact, true and meaningful word according to Renard (Barnes 2008: 100 and 164), was first discussed as 'Big D' (Barnes 2008: 196) in Barnes's all-too convincingly autobiographical debut *Metroland* (1980). In that first novel it is not so much dying as death that Barnes's protagonist Christopher Lloyd fears: 'I wouldn't mind Dying at all, I thought, as long as I didn't end up Dead at the end of it' (Barnes 1981: 54). Unsurprisingly for those familiar with Barnes's later work, it also transpires that the principal solace for mortality in *Metroland* is the oxymoronic weak promise of temporary immortality offered by art.

While Chris Lloyd's nighttime fears are largely solitary, silent experiences in *Metroland*, *The Lemon Table* is so called because Barnes demanded of himself that each story *talk about* the shortcomings of old age in the expectation of an unhappy ending. We find in the final story, 'The Silence', taking its cue from the lemon's supposed representation of death in Chinese symbolism, that the original Lemon Table was a convivial discussion group that Sibelius attended in a Helsinki restaurant in the 1920s, where it was 'obligatory – to talk about death' (Barnes 2005: 206; Barnes 2008: 23–24).

Barnes's collection is thus nominally obliged to discuss death, and in at least some of the stories there are artists contemplating mortality, about which their art seems to provide little consolation. For example, Barnes's octogenarian Sibelius thinks: 'so much work, talent and courage, and then everything is over . . . To be misunderstood, and then to be forgotten, such is the artist's fate' (Barnes 2005: 209). The story ends with the composer calling for a lemon, having earlier declared that he wishes the slow movement of his Fourth Symphony to be played at his funeral while he himself is 'to be buried with a lemon clasped in the hand which wrote those notes' (Barnes 2005: 211). After an assortment of musings, music, and ageing chattering characters, *The Lemon Table* thus concludes with 'The Silence', inaudibly echoing Hamlet's last words and E. M. Forster's view that even in life 'a perfectly adjusted organism would be silent' (Forster 2000: 145).

In terms of his second story collection's thematics, one leitmotif is sounded by Barnes's reference to Sibelius's Fourth symphony. The work was referred to by one critic it seems as a 'bark bread symphony', a phrase alluding 'to the days when the poor used to adulterate flour with finely ground bark' (Barnes 2005: 211). Which is to say that Sibelius's symphony 'expressed a sullen and unpleasant view of life in general' (Barnes 2005: 211) for the critic. This resonates because 'Bark' is the title of one of the earlier stories in the collection: the narrative of an epicure who gambles on outliving his peers, but finds only sorrow, bitterness, and a loss of *bon vivant*. Here again, bark represents at best a sense of resignation and at worst a sour negativity as a gastronome chooses dietary austerity while others drink 'life-shortening concoctions' (Barnes 2005: 129). At the tale's conclusion, he finally gnaws miserably on a piece of bark while listening to his adult son's 'prattle' and 'idiocies' (Barnes 2005: 136). The man, who has previously enjoyed reflecting 'contentedly on the folly of those around him' (Barnes 2005: 123), dies with his linen nightcap in his hand, the equivalent of Sibelius's lemon.

'Bark' is set in nineteenth-century France and focuses on an elderly widow, Delacour, who falls for a young maid at the new bathhouse called Jeanne. He employs her for sex, in which, he has read, it is healthy to indulge moderately. The bathhouse has been 'built as a matter of hygiene and general beneficence' by 40 subscribers, one of whom urges Delacour to 'renounce' his sexual arrangement; but Delacour is too much in love: 'Nothing in those experiences of my youth advised me of the possibility that carnal delight might lead to feelings of love. I imagined – no, I was sure – that it was always the other way round' (Barnes 2005: 131). That Jeanne is the illegitimate daughter of the other subscriber is also not something Delacour discovers until the man dies, by which time Jeanne is pregnant. Delacour, who has spent his later life studying the law, concludes that the world is making 'less sense than it should' (Barnes 2005: 135). Reason has not brought happiness: his gambling, which others thought a vice, 'seemed the application of a logical scrutiny to human behaviour', his gourmandism, which others saw as indulgence, 'seemed a rational approach to human pleasure' (Barnes 2005: 136). Delacour has found that his rational approach to life is insufficient: 'we make such certainties as we can' (Barnes 2005: 132) but nature and appetite make other choices. At the end of applying the rational exercise of free will to life, Delacour has no appetite left and he is discovered dead, having seemingly lost the will to live. Observing the inadequacy of his rationalism, he has concluded that while he may have chosen how to approach his love of gambling, food and Jeanne, these were not desires that he chose to have. The corresponding section of *Nothing To Be Frightened Of* conjectures that while 'we might think we are free in acting as we want, we cannot determine what it is that we want', and Barnes quotes Einstein's contention that 'a Being endowed with higher insight and more perfect intelligence ... would smile about man's illusion that he was acting according to his own free will' (Barnes 2008: 117). Here as elsewhere the later memoir illuminates the earlier stories, not explaining them but revealing their concerns in fresh light.

Of direct relevance to Delacour's insight, later in the same section of *Nothing To Be Frightened Of,* Barnes also observes, 'There is What We Know (or think we know) To Be The Case, There is What We Believe To Be The Case (on the assurance of others whom we trust), and then there is How We Behave' (Barnes 2008: 177). This comment attaches a significance to another of the stories of self-deception and reflection on life's illusions in *The Lemon Table*: 'The Things You Know'. In this story, two widowed women, regular dining companions, persist in a convenient but uneasy relationship whose polite familiarity is based on duplicity and condescension as each knows disreputable secrets about the other's dead husband but declines to disabuse a friend's shining memories out of a misplaced sense of superiority. As in 'Bark', the story develops a strong flavour of bitterness as the women have not chosen their friendship and each takes an acidic pleasure in unhappy knowledge of the other.

Like 'Bark', 'The Revival' is a story of renunciation and last love which also asks 'whether the heart drags in sex, or sex drags in the heart' (Barnes 2005: 94). Barnes has already noted elsewhere of his protagonist Turgenev that 'after the age of forty, the basis of life is renunciation' (Barnes 2002: 211; cf. Barnes 2008: 89–90). In 'The Revival' he positions the Russian author as 'a connoisseur of the if-only', and therefore a writer who favoured the 'past-conditional' (Barnes 2005: 95). By contrast, the present tense for Turgenev lets in 'too much reality', the thing that T. S. Eliot's poem 'Burnt Norton' (1936) said human kind could not bear very much of. Barnes here anatomizes the fiction writer's preference for the conditional tense in opposition to the taste of the modern world of reality TV and 24-hour news reporting for constant non-fictional, factual actuality. In this story he also draws a contrast between what he sees as the mystery, desire and imaginings of love beside the conquests and consummation of sex.

In *Nothing To Be Frightened Of,* Barnes reconsiders his own choice of the conditional tense in the light of his philosopher brother's suspicion and rejection of it. His brother sees the conditional as simply hypothetical, making anyone's indulgence of it irrational. However, like

Turgenev, Barnes himself feels that the hypothetical – imagining what might or might have been the case – is a useful guide to action. Because indulging the conditional encourages us to act as we think others might wish (instead of merely doing what we want), there is also an ethical dimension that impinges on the social contract's faith in reciprocity. So, when the undertaker asks Barnes if religious symbols should be removed from the walls of the crematorium in which his mother lies, he answers that 'I thought that this is what she would have wanted' (Barnes 2008: 5). His brother perceives this as a 'hypothetical want of the dead', doubly objectionable to the rationalist because it is both conjectural and passé: out of date because attributed to someone who no longer has preferences, let alone preferences that are simply speculative. According to Barnes, his philosopher brother thinks we can only do what we want and 'to indulge the maternal hypothetical was as irrational as if he were to pay attention to his own past desires' (Barnes 2008: 6).

With regard to what often emerges as conjectural criticism, Barnes warns critics that they make a common error in believing the 'imagined world is really much closer to the writer's life than he or she cares to admit' (Barnes 2008: 244), but what is always apparent from his writings is that the imagined world draws raw material for refining from memories, forgotten or remembered, as when parents' wishes to be scattered in the wind in 'The Fruit Cage' (Barnes 2008: 178) are realized by the scattering of Barnes's own parents' ashes after a three-leg journey that he, his niece, and his brother chose to undertake between them (see Barnes 2002: xvii and Barnes 2008: 210). In that story, too, a blackbird has its neck wrung in the cage, presaging a key reminiscence of chicken strangling at the start of the later memoir (Barnes 2008: 4). Arguably, the novelist in Barnes's world seems to work like the twice-told legend of the gunshots that are 'extra' in 'The Story of Mats Israelson', and which tourists pay for in order 'to awaken the echoes' in the passages of the Falun mines (Barnes 2005: 31 and 47). Many characters in *The Lemon Table*, from Sibelius in his Silence to Turgenev in his Revival, try to reawaken the echoes, usually unsuccessfully, just as Barnes reawakens stories from other writers and from his own life, in order to mine the truths hidden between different versions or pastiches of the past. Or, as expressed in a quotation Barnes attributes to Stravinsky: '"I wonder if memory is true, and I know that it cannot be, but that one lives by memory nonetheless and not by truth"' (Barnes 2008: 228).

Sex, ageing and death, laced with miscommunication, deception and humiliation, overhang almost all the stories in *The Lemon Table*. In 'Hygiene', the narrator is an aged and sexlessly married war veteran deluded over his annual liaisons with 'Babs' (in fact a prostitute, now dead) on the occasion of his regimental dinner in London. In 'Appetite', a 75-year-old retired dentist expresses his sexual tastes in the most graphic terms to his ruminative nurse-turned-second-wife who indulges his previous love of food by reading him recipes that are met, on his bad days, by profanities – and while he is the one suffering from Alzheimer's, she is the one who can no longer recall their life together or even 'what we were like in bed together' (Barnes 2008: 172).

With many of Barnes's central characters expressing or exhibiting connoisseur tendencies, the temptations and unreliable pleasures of food is another recurrent element. A story such as 'The Fruit Cage' therefore brings many of the book's concerns together through its metaphoric title – a fruit cage protects what is inside from poaching animals but also incarcerates – and its cautionary tale of an 80-year-old man who leaves the narrator's mother to live with a local widow, for 'physical' reasons, but stays in touch with his wife. The tug-of-war *ménage a trois* ends with the man hospitalized – by accident or assault in his wife's kitchen – with the warring women, to each of whom he thinks he is married, seeing him on alternate days in his *cage aux fruits*. He has severe memory loss and is paralysed down one side, with the left half of his face 'twisted like the bark of a tree' (Barnes 2008: 198), invoking once more one of Barnes's images of the potential bitterness of old age.

Despite the collection's overall sardonic take on 'rage and age', the book's working title, several stories in *The Lemon Table* also embrace more sanguine attitudes and assert equanimity if not defiance before the dying of the light (Barnes 2008: 181). 'Knowing French' is composed of a series of letters written over three years to 'Barnes' by Sylvia Winstanley, an octogenarian lady from an 'Old Folkery' called Pilcher House. Sylvia encounters the author when proceeding alphabetically through the fiction aisles of her public library, or 'Lie brewery'. As a current reader of *Flaubert's Parrot* (1984) and a bilingual lover of Flaubert's *Un Coeur Simple* (1877), she has decided to contact 'Dr Barnes' (as though he is Dr Geoffrey Braithwaite) to discuss the synchronicity of putting down Barnes's novel and then observing 'a large grey parrot in its cage' (Barnes 2005: 140). Taking up the discussion in *Flaubert's Parrot* (Barnes 1985: 66), Sylvia remarks on the coincidence of *perroquets* but not on the similarity between the grey parrot's position and her own (Barnes pointedly has 'cage(d)' appear three times in four lines (Barnes 2008: 140). Sylvia's wry sense of humour and continued lively interest in people epitomize her view that 'Knowing French' applies 'to all aspects of life (Barnes 2005: 152), because '*Grammer*' is ultimately less important than being able to inquire, understand and communicate. In the interstices of Sylvia's letters we also find responses to communications from Barnes that chime with statements in *Nothing To Be Frightened Of* or in the novels, as with the comment from *Metroland* quoted above: 'You write that you are not afraid of dying as long as you don't end up dead as a result' (Barnes 2005: 153). Sylvia's problem is, however, not only to be surrounded by the dying and those who may ask 'Am I dead yet?' (Barnes 2008: 153), but also to be without anyone to join her at the proverbial Lemon Table, because 'There's nobody here to talk to about death' (Barnes 2005: 153). 'Barnes' therefore fits this bill but is also someone who, unlike her fellow 'incarcerees' (Barnes 2005: 141), is neither deaf nor mad.

Another story of frustration, bordering on fury, is 'Vigilance'. This is the piece most full of rage and ends with its vituperative narrator trying to attend amid the noise of other concertgoers to Sibelius's violin concerto (Barnes 2005: 120). Focused on a gay curmudgeon whose sexual frustration vents itself in spleen, 'Vigilance' concerns a demonstratively disgruntled 62 year old who wages a war against all the rustlers, coughers, and talkers who interfere with his listening pleasure. His quieter, milder counterpart is found in the first story of *The Lemon Table*, about an 'ageing geezer . . . afraid of sex' (Barnes 2005: 21). 'A Short History of Hairdressing' opens the collection and charts the movement of a man called Gregory from youth to senior citizenship through his experiences at the 'Barnet Shop' (Barnes 2005: 18), chronicling the changes in his hirsuteness, which ends with 'long mattressy eyebrow hairs' and 'thinning hair he'd soon have to comb more carefully' (Barnes 2005: 16, 21). The story also archives changes in his life, which amount to little that he considers important because he is simply 'one who stayed at home, went to work, and had his hair cut. His life, he admitted, had been one long cowardly adventure' (Barnes 2005: 20). In the third part of Gregory's story, with two grown-up children, he has been married longer than his hairdresser has been alive and his one act of rebellion, or 'timid victory', is to decline after 40 years the rear view of his 'short back and sides', achieving at least a '[r]evolt against the tyranny of the bloody mirror' (Barnes 2005: 22, 3).

Challenging the signs of ageing and the promise of death may be small rebellions, but that visceral and primal revolt against the conditions of the universe is the fundamental driving force of Barnes's second story collection – and also of his later memoir. Barnes records how his very being is repulsed by the inevitability of total, eternal annihilation: it is a certainty and a conditional in which all wants will become merely the future wishes of the dead, sooner or later to be forgotten. *The Lemon Table* does not despair at this, however, because observing the capacity to exercise intelligence and humour forces a realization that individuals may both live as if they were not going to die and periodically sit at the lemon table to reflect on the advantages of mortality. This is like Sylvia Winstanley, who puts forward as good a case for death and dying as Barnes is able to muster anywhere in *Nothing To Be Frightened Of*:

> Main reasons for dying: it's what others expect when you reach my age; impending decrepitude and senility; waste of money – using up inheritance – keeping together brain-dead incontinent bag of old bones; decreased interest in The News, famines, wars, etc.; fear of falling under total power of Sgt. Major; desire to Find Out about Afterwards (or not?). (Barnes 2008: 151)

That 'Barnes' in his second-story collection and his memoir cannot elsewhere provide a better answer is not a shortcoming, merely a necessity. This is chiefly because, as he notes, death happens to us for no other reason than because the universe happens to us. Sylvia Winstanley also adumbrates her main reasons for not dying, but can think of nothing more than rebelling against the expectations of some people (another kind of revolt against the 'mirror') while avoiding anguish to others. She concludes that, distressing though it may be for all involved, there are more reasons for dying than not, and so death ought to be nothing to be frightened of. Sibelius adds, with the occasionally mordant wit that marks the spirit of *The Lemon Table*: 'Cheer up! Death is round the corner' (Barnes 2008: 211).

Barnes has also written several short stories this century that resonate with a sense of different pulses: the rhythmical throbbing of the heart, a short burst of sound, or a musical beat. With an interspersed series of *tableaux vivants* focused on evenings 'At Phil & Joanna's', these stories are brought together in the 2011 collection *Pulse*, whose title is in part an intimation of life and the measured pace of continued living after Barnes's stories around the lemon table.

'Trespass', first published in *The New Yorker* in 2003, epitomizes the determined but dogged spirit of an indomitable life as a 31-year-old walker called Geoff, recently split up from Cath, starts a new relationship with a casual acquaintance, Lynn. Geoff's happiness, and his perception of his previous life with Cath, revolves around the organization of hiking trips. We soon learn in the story that Geoff decided not to join the Ramblers when he became single, but it is the socialist origins of that collective movement that first intimates the significance of the story's title: 'He told her about the trespass on Kinder Scout in the nineteen-thirties: how walkers and hikers had come out from Manchester in their hundreds to the Duke of Devonshire's grouse moors to protest against lack of access to the countryside' (Barnes 2003: n.p.). Another instance of trespassing becomes clear as Geoff repeatedly tries to organize and clothe Lynn, taking a presumptuous and controlling role in their hikes. Her resistance to his invasion of her 'space' earns his nickname for her as 'Miss Duke of Devonshire' (Barnes 2003: n.p.). Their incompatibilities become more evident as Geoff discovers that Lynn is, for example, both a smoker and someone attracted by paragliding. Their relationship ceases after the independent and free-spirited Lynn screams into the sky at a cliff edge on one of their walks – because she feels like it. Geoff is uncomfortable with this inexplicable spontaneity and the narrative ends with him making out an application to join the Ramblers. A story about the lines between private and public, and the individual's right to protect or make incursions into personal space, 'Trespass' sets up a number of themes and leitmotifs that resonate with other stories that are collected in *Pulse*.

The first story in Barnes's third collection, and another tale of second starts, 'East Wind' focuses on 37-year-old divorced estate agent, Vernon, blessed with two children, a rented flat, and 'a quiet job' (Barnes 2008b: 67). Like Geoff, he also embarks on a new relationship. However, while Lynn remained essentially a mystery to Geoff, Vernon discovers considerably more information about the woman he dates. At first, Vernon believes Andrea is Polish, one of many migrants who have moved to southeast England from Eastern Europe since the expansion of the European Union member states. As their relationship develops, Vernon's curiosity about Andrea's seeming meekness leads him to pry into her personal possessions by copying a key to the rented house in which she lives and making an entrance in her absence. Again the narrative line pursues a scenario in which one person invades someone else's space while trying to forge a new relationship after earlier disappointment. However, whereas 'Trespass' concludes somewhat comically by highlighting a new couple's incompatibility, here the story ends far more disturbingly when Andrea one day flees the coastal town and her job as a waitress. Having discovered Andrea is East German by origin, Vernon tracks down information about her through an internet search and discovers a sinister truth:

> There had been a state recruiting scheme. Girls were picked out when they were as young as eleven. . . . She had some school lessons, but was mostly trained to swim and swim. It was a great honor to be a member of the Dynamo: that was why she'd had to leave home. Blood was taken from her earlobe to test how fit she was. There were pink pills and blue pills. Vitamins, she was told. Later, there were injections – just more vitamins. Except that they were anabolic steroids and testosterone. It was forbidden to refuse. The training motto was "You eat the pills or you die." The coaches made sure she swallowed them. . . . Vernon had to look up terms like "virilization" and "clitoris hypertrophy," then wished he hadn't. He didn't need to look up heart disease, liver disease, ovarian cysts, deformed children, blind children. (Barnes 2008b: 72)

Vernon learns this had all taken place in the 1980s, before the fall of the Berlin Wall: 'They doped the girls because it worked. East German swimmers won gold medals everywhere, the women especially' (Barnes 2008b: 72). Thus, Vernon thinks he has learned Andrea's secret but he is also made aware of both the complexity and the difference of personal lives enmeshed with political history. The story's title itself most likely refers with irony to Mao Tse-Tung's speech at the 'Moscow Meeting of Communist and Workers' Parties' in November 1957 that the 'East Wind prevails over the West Wind', when the success of the Soviet space program suggested to him that Eastern Europe was now technologically superior to the West (Duiker and Spielvogel 2010: 787).

A third contemporary story published in 2008 is '60/40', one of the series of four glimpses into life 'At 'Phil & Joanna's' that punctuate the stories in the first half of *Pulse*. It focuses on a wide-ranging dinner-table conversation between London liberals at the time of the U.S. presidential nominations. Aside from framing comments by a first-person narrator at the start and end, the story is made up of dialogue in the ebb and flow of assertion, speculation, and opinion. A group of ex-smokers, the diners criticize the hypocrisy of those who make money from the tobacco industry: 'Governments telling people it's bad for them while living off the tax. Cigarette companies knowing it's bad for people and selling their stuff to the third world because of getting sued here' (Barnes 2008a: 24). Later when someone says that smokers cost the health service least, the topic returns: ' "Stigmatising smokers, taxing the fuck out of them, making them stand on street corners in the rain, instead of thanking them for being the nation's cheap dates". "It's the hypocrisy of it all" ' (Barnes 2008a: 25). The story shares an observation with 'Trespass' at one point when someone comments that low-tar cigarettes are 'more dangerous' (Barnes 2008b: 24), echoing Geoff's assertion to Lynn that 'low-tar cigarettes are, in fact, just as bad for you' because they make you inhale more deeply to get the nicotine' (Barnes 2003: n.p.). Importantly, 'Trespass' is also echoed when someone says that passive smoking is 'more a metaphor, really. Like, don't invade my space' (Barnes 2008a: 25). Also a metaphor, the title '60/40' arises when one diner decides their level of resistance to the Iraq war was 60/40, and someone else later announces that this is also their view on Obama's chances of being elected. The title stands as a marker of anti-fundamentalism; an index of liberal values and opposition to totalitarianism, the Iraq invasion, emphasizing free speech, pro-equality, anti-state interference, and an ethos of 'don't invade my space' (Barnes 2008a: 25).

Published a year earlier than the three discussed above, 'Marriage Lines' is a second story of a walker. It concerns a newly widowed man who returns to the Scottish island where he and his partner used to holiday in the Hebrides. He stays with their usual hosts, Calum and Flora, a couple whose wisdom seems to outstretch his own. When he departs the island, he realizes he will not return because the trip has not eased his grief, a truth Calum already grasped. The story ends with the lines: 'And in the months and years ahead, he expected grief to teach him many other things as well. This was just the first of them' (Barnes 2007: 323). The title comes from an explanation given by Calum's wife:

> Flora had taken out of a drawer an old sweater which had belonged to her grandfather. She laid it on the kitchen table, ironing it with her palms. In the old days, she explained, the women of these islands used to tell stories with their knitting. The pattern of this jersey showed that her grandfather had come from Eriksay, while its details, its decorations, told of fishing and faith,

of the sea and the sand. And this series of zigzags across one shoulder . . . represented the ups and downs of marriage. (Barnes 2007: 320)

Another intimation of rhythms and pulses, the highs and lows of married life are here presented, like lines on a cardiograph, in the pattern of knitted zigzags, which also proclaim a place of origin and belonging. The pattern's truth is made most plain by the widower's inability to move on from his bereavement in contrast to the confidence of his earlier visits with new wife: 'they would be different from everyone who had ever got married before' (Barnes 2007: 320).

In 2009, Barnes first published two historical short stories subsequently included in the second half of *Pulse*. The stories are both somewhat in the manner of Hawthorne and both concerned with disability and synaesthesia. 'The Limner' tells of a deaf and speechless painter, Wadsworth, working on the portrait of a collector of customs, Tuttle. The painter observes far more than he communicates: 'Wadsworth did not see that speaking was in itself a promoter of virtue. His own advantages were only two: that he could represent on canvas those who spoke, and could silently perceive their meaning' (Barnes 2009a: n.p.). The story's title is a word applied to untrained and unnamed artists in the United States who took commissions from colonial America's merchants and traders wishing to imitate the portraits of the landed gentry to show their prosperity and success. However, Wadsworth decides that when he:

> provided his clients with their portraits, it was habitually the first time that they had seen themselves as someone else saw them. Sometimes, when the picture was presented, the limner would detect a sudden chill passing over the subject's skin, as if he were thinking, So this is how I truly am? (Barnes 2009a: n.p.)

Uninterested in being shown as he is, bombastic and bullying, Tuttle responds to his portrayal by asking Wadsworth for 'more dignity' in the painting. As a departing gesture, Wadsworth finally confers a questionable 'dignity' on Tuttle's portrait by making false touches, such as adding a beard. He then leaves on his mare, who he decides will serve as the subject of his last painting. Hoping there might be both painting and continued deafness in Heaven, his last act of the story is given in the final line: 'Wadsworth shouted into the silence of the forest' (Barnes 2009a: n.p.). Seemingly a reaction to the pomposity and conceitedness of Tuttle, this expression of feeling also echoes Lynn's scream in 'Trespass'.

Barnes's second historical story treats of musical, cosmological, and human accord. ' "Music seeks harmony . . . just as the human body sees harmony." . . . The music of the human body was heard when it too was in a state of harmony, the organs at peace, the blood flowing freely and the nerves aligned along their true and intended paths' (Barnes 2009c: 100).

'Harmony' is a narrative set in the late eighteenth century, but with a contemporary, reflective narrator who observes that practices like the suppression of details such as names and dates in stories

> would have been a routine literary mannerism at the time; but they also tactfully admit the partiality of our knowledge. Any philosopher claiming that his field of understanding was complete, and that a final, harmonious synthesis of truth was being offered to the reader, would have been denounced as a charlatan; and likewise those philosophers of the human heart who deal in storytelling would have been – and would be – wise not to make any such claim either. (2009c: 100)

The story line focuses on a physician known simply as M – and a blind noblewoman, Maria Theresia von P–, who becomes a patient under the doctor's cure by magnetism. Another slightly dark Romantic story in the mould of Hawthorne, Poe or Hoffmann, 'Harmony' hinges on quasi-scientific progress in metaphysics: 'in his doctoral thesis *De planetarum influxu*, he had proposed that the planets influenced human actions and the human body through the medium of some invisible gas or liquid' (2009c: 106). Like 'The Limner', where a man does not speak or hear, in 'Harmony' a woman can neither see nor smell. However, as the doctor's influence on the patient proves effective, Maria Theresia's ability to play the piano diminishes and her parents grow concerned for her ability to attract patronage and fame. They remove her from the doctor's tutelage, he returns to his practice and for 40 years they do not meet again: Maria Theresia sinking into the blindness that secured her living, but losing the close relationship with the doctor that had begun to cure her condition. The suggestion is that love, or human empathy, can lead to physiological benefit, and that this is a kind of harmony of human spirits that reaps physical benefit.

Two last stories demonstrating the breadth of Barnes's emotional range have appeared more recently. 'Sleeping with John Updike' (2010) is a contrasting companion piece to 'The Things you Know' from *The Lemon Table*. Again two long-standing female friends are more polite to each other than they sometimes wish to be: 'Jane was embarrassed when Alice referred to herself as an artist rather than a writer, and thought her books strove to appear more highbrow than they were; Alice found Jane's work rather formless, and at times bleatingly autobiographical' (Barnes 2010: n.p.). They are both moderately successful writers who have developed together as authors while following the parallel paths of their private lives. Returning on a train from a literary festival, they reassure each other on their successes and correct each other's memories when appropriate, while the narrator fills in the backstory of their long association as a 'good team' (Barnes 2010: n.p.) for their publisher's promotional events. Jane has 'got religion' (Barnes 2008: n.p.), of a liberal and permissive kind, while Alice exhibits a mildly pessimistic pragmatism:

> Life, she thought, was mostly about the gradual loss of pleasure. She and Jane had given up sex at about the same time. She was no longer interested in drink; Jane had stopped caring about food – or at least its quality. Alice gardened; Jane did crosswords, occasionally saving time by filling in answers which couldn't possibly be right. (Barnes 2010: n.p.)

Seeing themselves as ladies of a certain age, their lives are still in full flow but, as with most of these stories of looking back more than forwards, there is a degree of melancholy and stoicism tempering the continued enjoyment of the rhythm of life. The narrative conveys a sense that the pulse of their careers and lives is slowing – 'Their own sales were holding up, just about' (Barnes 2010: n.p.) – and the story concludes by suggesting that Jane and Alice need one another, like they need other dependencies or stimulants: alcohol, religion, and, previously, sex. One friend is serious and responsible, the other life affirming but with a depressive tendency.

> Alice found herself wondering if it were better to take life seriously or lightly. Or was that a false antithesis, merely a way of feeling superior? Jane, it seemed to her, was a person who took life lightly, until it went wrong, when she reached for serious solutions like God. Better to take life seriously, and reach for light solutions. Satire, for instance; or suicide. Why did people hold so fast to life, that thing they were given without being consulted? All lives were failures, in Alice's reading of the world, and Jane's platitude about turning failure into art was fluffy fantasy. Anyone who understood art knew that it never achieved what its maker dreamed for it. Art always fell short, and the artist, far from rescuing something from the disaster of life, was thereby condemned to be a double failure. (Barnes 2010: n.p.)

Like 'East Wind' and 'Trespass', 'Complicity' is a story of a divorced man starting out again on a new relationship, and it is also a story, again reminiscent of 'Trespass' and '60/40', that touches on the pleasure of smoking, from which the story in part takes its title: smoking has become a clandestine, conspirator's habit. Barnes is someone, by the way, who says he smokes one cigarette a day, taking the connoisseur's rather than addict's approach. The narrator explains later his use of the term that gives the story its title: 'I used the word "complicity" a bit ago. I like the word. To me, it indicates an unspoken understanding between two people, a kind of pre-sense, if you like' (Barnes 2009b: n.p.). It is a tale, also, that alludes to the title of Barnes's third story collection: 'Later, looking back, we will fetishize and celebrate the first date, the first kiss, the first holiday together, but what really counts is what happened before this public story: that moment, more of pulse than of thought, which goes, Yes, perhaps her, and Yes, perhaps him' (Barnes 2009b: n.p.). Not forgetting the nothingness that awaits, in these stories the pulse of life, music, and nature suggests that the principal subjects of Barnes's latest stories are affirmation and reaffirmation in the rhythm and renewal of existence. 'Complicity' itself develops on a positive note, and by its end there is more hope than anxiety about a possible future relationship. Here, the future hangs in the balance on a date – 'The film passed; her mobile didn't pulse' – but with optimism to the fore by the story's close: 'And then I touched her' (Barnes 2009b: n.p.).

Along with the eight stories discussed here, Barnes has included several previously unpublished stories in *Pulse*: 'Gardeners' World', 'Carcassonne', the title story, and three more snapshots of evenings at Phil and Joanna's. Together they represent a largely affirmative collection of positive connections despite the disappointments, misunderstandings, and failings that Barnes presents as pauses between the hopeful heartbeats.

CHAPTER NINE

'All Letters Quoted Are Authentic': The Past After Postmodern Fabulation in Julian Barnes's *Arthur & George*

CHRISTINE BERBERICH

> **Chapter Summary:** Steeped in historical research yet informed by fictional knowledge made possible only by the novelistic imagination, Julian Barnes's *Arthur & George* (2005) moves away from his earlier postmodern historical metafictions such as *Flaubert's Parrot* (1984) and *A History of the World in 10½ Chapters* (1989) to reinvent the traditional historical novel, as well as its author. Whereas Barnes's early playful and experimental engagement with historical metafiction contributed to shaping high postmodernism, at the beginning of the twenty-first century the author again proves a significant influence on the transformation of our conception of the relationship between the past and the present.

'How do we seize the past?' (Barnes 1985: 90) This is the key question that Julian Barnes asks in *Flaubert's Parrot* (1984), which takes as its subject the problematic nature of understanding history through narrative representation. In the novel, narrator Geoffrey Braithwaite goes in search of authenticity in the life of the French writer Gustave Flaubert (1821–1880). *Flaubert's Parrot*'s postmodern attitude to the past is primarily shaped by self-referential commentary, such as Braithwaite's remarks that 'the past is autobiographic fiction pretending to be a parliamentary report' and that 'we must look at the past through coloured glass' (Barnes 1985: 90; 94). The novel leaves us with the sense that history is not something that we can possess or know, but it is only a process, something that we can desire but never actually attain because historical artifacts and texts are fundamentally unreliable, making the past at best an unreliable fiction and at worst completely inaccessible. In *Flaubert's Parrot* any quest to 'find the author' leads to great uncertainty, and the novel leaves us with competing narratives, historical relativity and epistemological speculation, which thwart any attempt at retrieving the Author.

It is no wonder then that Barnes's early work was regarded as exemplary of postmodernism: it clearly emphasises the constructedness of any narrative – whether historical or novelistic, and argues that all of our relationships to the world are 'narrated' and, to some extent, textual. In her classic work on postmodern fiction, Linda Hutcheon groups *Flaubert's Parrot* with Salman Rushdie's *Midnight's Children* (1981), labelling these novels 'historiographic metafictions', which she defines as 'novels which are both intensely self-reflexive and yet paradoxically also lay claim to historical events and personages' (1988: 5). More recently, Frederick Holmes noted that Barnes's fiction 'displays a self-reflexive postmodernist scepticism' and 'restless fictional experimentation' (Holmes 2009: 12; 14).

Dominic Head introduces an interesting paradox into these routine accounts of Barnes as a postmodernist: 'The different perspectives on Flaubert that Barnes assembles indicate that biographical writing may be a distinctly unreliable form of historical record. Yet the book remains a celebration of Flaubert the writer as personality, not just a shadowy figure from whom notable texts are known to have emanated' (Head 2006: 16). Indeed, Head notes that besides addressing the problem of history, Barnes's interest lies in understanding 'the relationship between art and life' (Head 2006: 15). This relationship was not exclusively of interest to the postmodernists, but it is an obsession first and foremost of modernist writers ranging from such as James Joyce to Djuna Barnes; a tradition which starts with the Parisian excursions of Charles Baudelaire (1821–1867) in the second half of the nineteenth century. As Matthew Taunton demonstrates in Chapter One, Baudelaire plays a central role in Barnes's first novel, *Metroland* (1980), suggesting that Barnes's work is more complex than the postmodernist account suggests.

Barnes's engagement with the problem of understanding our relationship to history runs throughout his *oeuvre*, and, just like its author has continuously transformed himself, so has his thinking about the problem of the past. Barnes's novel *Arthur & George* (2005), for instance, goes in search of another author, Arthur Conan Doyle (1959–1930), yet the result is markedly different from *Flaubert's Parrot*.

The novel tells the real-life story of George Edalji, a Birmingham solicitor of mixed Parsee and Scottish parentage who, in 1903, was sentenced to seven years' hard labour for allegedly mutilating cattle and other livestock in the area surrounding his native village of Great Wyrley, Staffordshire. In 1906, Sir Arthur Conan Doyle, world-famous creator of Sherlock Holmes, became interested in the case and began his own investigations that led him to conclude – and to vociferously campaign for – Edalji's innocence which culminated, in 1907, in the publication of an 'eighteen-thousand word pamphlet called "The Story of Mr. George Edalji"' (Stashower 1999: 258). Edalji was, eventually, granted a partial pardon (after serving three of his sentence's seven years) and resumed his unprepossessing and quiet life as a solicitor until his death in 1953. Although little known today, his case contributed largely to the formation of the Court of Criminal Appeal in 1907 (Guignery 2006: 132).

Just as Conan Doyle before him, Barnes accidentally stumbled across the story of George Edalji. In Barnes's case it was while reading a book about the Dreyfus case in France. Barnes's curiosity to find out more about the mysterious livestock mutilations soon turned to frustration, as he explains in an interview:

> So I thought that I wanted to read about it and try to find something about it and, to my amazement, I went on the Internet and Googled it and went to Abebooks and all that, and no one had written about it, no one had touched it since the day nearly a hundred years previously when Conan Doyle wrote his article [in support of George Edalji]. So it was part out of frustration that there was nothing written about it that I thought I might write something. (Fraga 2006: 134)

In contrast to *Flaubert's Parrot* and *A History of the World in 10½ Chapters* (1989), *Arthur & George* is, at first glance, a gentle historical novel seemingly set apart from Barnes's earlier work by both the modified realism created by the third-person narrator and, more importantly, a different attitude to the past. The novel appears considerably more straightforwardly historical in the sense that it is less experimental and self-reflexive. Elsa Cavalié has remarked that '*Arthur & George* signals a temporal as well as a generic shift in Barnes's fiction, for it forgoes the patently postmodern conundrum for a more subdued approach of story-telling and what one might call a "retro-Victorian" style' (Cavalié 2009a: 89). This suggests yet another shift in Barnes's work and establishes *Arthur & George* as a novel that attempts to re-create its historical setting rather than continuing postmodern fabulation. Richard Bradford notes that *Arthur & George* belongs to a new kind of historical novel, written by

> more astute practitioners [who] are beginning to tire of the assumption that the nineteenth century comprised only the limitless trove of recoverable guilty secrets.... Barnes adheres scrupulously to the well-documented facts and never employs inventive license to suggest that the prejudices that underpinned the case were any less or more severe than disclosed in the documentary accounts. Instead he creates a modestly elegant novel out of a very real collision of actuality and literary mythology. Doyle steps into the fiction as a figure who closely resembles his own creation, and while this carries a trace of postmodern whimsy there is compelling resonance of a very real character driven by a respect for truth and justice. (Bradford 2007: 95–96)

Bradford's reference to Barnes's 'collision of actuality and literary mythology' is interesting because it suggests a successful merging of factual historical research and imaginative investment as well as Barnes's exploitation of exiting mythologies surrounding Conan Doyle.

Barnes's attitude to history in *Arthur & George* is certainly more 'serious' than in the earlier work, and there is a clearer respect for the boundary between fiction and factuality compared to, for instance, *England, England* (1998).

Arthur & George is a historical novel set, predominantly, in Edwardian England, with Sir Arthur Conan Doyle as one of its twin protagonists. And, initially, *Arthur & George* does indeed appear straightforward in its reconstruction of an Edwardian crime investigation. By doing this, Barnes's novel immediately seems to mirror what Conan Doyle himself helped to rise to fame: the detective novel.

The opening lines of the novel, which introduce us to Conan Doyle as a small boy whose curiosity leads him to walk in on his first corpse, is worth quoting because they open a window onto Barnes's renewed engagement with history: 'A child wants to see. It always begins like this, and it began like this then. A child wanted to see' (Barnes 2006: 3). Within once sentence, the shift from the present into the past tense makes us descend from the experiential present tense into a historical self-consciousness. The first person narrators of Barnes's early work are replaced by a third-person narration, and with it we have moved from foregrounded subjectivity to a restrictive third-person consciousness. Yet the opening passage contains more clues about Barnes's changed approach:

> A small boy and a corpse: such encounters would not have been so rare in the Edinburgh of his time. High mortality rates and cramped circumstances made for early learning. The household was Catholic, and the body that of Arthur's grandmother, one Katherine Pack. Perhaps the door had been deliberately left ajar. There might have been a desire to impress upon the child the horror of death; or, more optimistically, to show him that death was nothing to be feared. (Barnes 2006: 3)

Here we have a clear sense that we are not only confronted with a narrating historical consciousness but also with a historiographic consciousness. The narrator presents the facts within a clear historical framework, while the 'Perhaps' suggests clearly where knowledge spills over into speculation and extrapolation. In the authorial voice, however, we also get a hint from Barnes, whose memoir on death and religion, *Nothing To Be Frightened Of* was published in 2008.

In *Arthur & George*, Barnes similarly acknowledges his debt to existing sources and research in his attempt to re-create an authentic Edwardian 'feel' to the world of his two protagonists. Setting the tone and creating the atmosphere for the story was as important to him as narrating George Edalji's story in the first place. Barnes says that

> I wanted them to be real people so I had to get inside their heads to start off with. I suppose my way of getting into that period and evoking that period for readers today is to do it through the way the characters think and the way that they talk and through the language of the prose rather than amassing a great amount of historical detail. There are occasional references to clothes or furniture, but not really very many. That seems to me a very ponderous way to write a historical novel. You can do a lot more using just a few words that give you the period. (Fraga 2006: 135)

Arthur & George starts inside the consciousness of one of the protagonists: the third-person indirect discourse Barnes uses in the opening section starts in the mind of 'Arthur' as a little boy (Barnes 2006: 3); an interesting narrative strategy, as it alerts the reader to the 'reinvention' component of the story, its fictional element. It also links in with the biographical element of *Arthur & George* – narrating a life in chronological order – but reinforces the novel's double perspective. As readers, we will 'see' what Arthur and George respectively see. The conclusions from these snippets are up to us and this, effectively, changes the reader-writer contract. Barnes provides the narrative framework, but the readers can themselves assume the role of investigators – assessing this piece of evidence here, or weighing up that newly emerging detail there.

This way of conjuring up a historical period is what sets *Arthur & George* apart from more traditional historical novels that go into considerable period detail. One may think, here, of the work of Philippa Gregory, Edward Rutherfurd and even Hilary Mantel. Instead *Arthur & George* emphasizes the detective theme: Barnes has fashioned a novel in which the creator of the world's greatest fictional detective investigates a real-life case which is now, in turn, researched and embellished by Barnes and pieced together by each reader.

This reading of the novel is reinforced by the inclusion of some illustrations – but the marked *exclusion* of others. This brings to mind other contemporary novelists, and the German writer W.G. Sebald (1944–2001) in particular, who complicate rather than gloss over our complex relationship to history. Sebald's work includes numerous photographs scattered throughout the text in order to create a deliberately *false* sense of authenticity. The reader, inevitably, clutches at these photographs as supporting the truth of Sebald's narrative – only to be confronted with statements warning of the unreliability and 'manipulatibility' of photographs, and, by extension, historical narratives. By contrast, *Arthur & George* includes two images – one a reproduction of the frontispiece of George Edalji's 1901 publication *Railway Law for the "Man in the Train"*

(Barnes 2006: 93), the other of George's invitation to Sir Arthur Conan Doyle's wedding with Miss Jean Leckie (Barnes 2006: 444,) plus a drawing of the potential mutilation weapon (Barnes 2006: 406). When naming its author, the frontispiece of George's book brilliantly conveys his pride in his achievements and in his seemingly secure position as a pillar of society quite literally upholding law and order: 'George E. T. Edalji, Solicitor, Second Class Honours, Solicitors' Final Examination, November 1898; Birmingham Law Society's Bronze Medallist, 1898' (Barnes 2006: 93).

However, the novel does *not* contain any images from the actual crime scenes around Great Wyrley; nor does it include any illustrations of any of the alleged 'evidence' (a cast of a footprint, for example, supposedly matching George's shoe). By contrast, Kate Summerscale's *The Suspicions of Mr Whicher* (2005) also re-creates a real-life murder, of Francis Saville Kent, a three-year old boy inside his middle class home in Wiltshire. In contrast, this novel provides its readers with photographs of the Kent family and the investigating police officers, with sketches from the court trial as well as with detailed floor plans and photographs of the house at Road Hill where the gruesome events took place in 1860, shocking the nation and influencing writers such as Dickens, Collins and Arthur Conan Doyle himself. Summerscale thus helps her readers visualize the setting and characters involved. Barnes could have made use of visual aids to provide his readers with a glimpse of the past but chooses not to, not even offering as much as a photograph of his two protagonists (although he mentions, in the afterword, that a photograph of George Edalji can now be found in the vestry of Great Wyrley Church [Barnes 2006: 504]). Ana-Karina Schneider has argued that '*Arthur & George* thematises the tension between seeing and believing, that which is empirically demonstrable and the persuasive power of narratives' (Schneider 2009: 51). Barnes shows in his novel, and in his sparing use of descriptions or illustrations, that we do not necessarily need to see in order to believe.

Despite leaving so many gaps and blank spaces for the reader to fill, clearly much social and historical research has gone into *Arthur & George*. Barnes occasionally resorts to more tangible props to get the tone and feel of the period exactly right. This again emphasizes the fact that *Arthur & George* offers something new, an ingenious combination of realism and postmodern historiography. *Arthur & George* is the only Barnes novel to date to feature a substantial and very detailed Author's Note (Barnes 2006: 503–5), one which seems to reinforce the research element of the novel at the expense of the fictional and, inevitably, speculative component of it. Barnes states that, barring some exceptions, '*all letters quoted, whether signed or anonymous, are authentic; as are quotations from newspapers, government reports, proceedings in Parliament, and the writings of Sir Arthur Conan Doyle*' (Barnes 2006: 505). This list suggests that *Arthur & George* is not just another historical novel, but a genre-defying hybrid. In *Arthur & George,* fact and fiction converge and intermingle in a way that makes it difficult, or maybe even irrelevant, for the reader to discern the dividing line.

Alden has summarized this way of writing as trying 'to demonstrate what fiction *can* do with history that history *cannot*' (Alden 2009: 59), such as creating atmosphere rather than presenting facts, or breaking up a strict chronology or linear narrative pattern by interspersing varying perspectives. What the reader has to be aware of at all times is that Barnes does not create *the* version of the past in *Arthur & George,* but *two* versions: Arthur's and George's. Conan Doyle's life and work are well-documented and thoroughly researched by, for example, Daniel Stashower and Andrew Lycett, but little is known about the personal life of George Edalji, the novel's second protagonist, and this is where Barnes the historical researcher inevitably has to make way for Barnes the novelist, the creator of the *fictional* character George Edalji who only might also bear resemblance to the *real* George Edalji.

Despite Barnes's intensification of historical research and a more subdued style, many of the themes prevalent in *Arthur & George* bear close resemblance to themes he developed in earlier novels. At the forefront of these are themes of memory and identity, both personal and national, and the notion of 'Englishness'. Barnes explores these themes in order to express Edwardian anxieties that challenge, in particular, the mythical notion of a secure English identity as yet unscathed by two world wars, and his novel thus has important political dimensions. Whereas many twentieth-century novels depict the Edwardian era as some kind of Indian summer of English supremacy and unchallenged greatness, Barnes depicts, in particular, Edwardian Englishness as an unstable concept, one that is not necessarily, as common myth would have it, innate and inimitable, but, on the contrary, one that is laboriously studied and painstakingly applied – a façade, rather than a nation's pride.

This can be seen clearly in Barnes's construction of his protagonists. Both Conan Doyle and Edalji consider themselves English though neither *is* English by birth: Conan Doyle is of Scottish extraction; Edalji of mixed Scottish and Parsee stock. The fact that Conan Doyle and Edalji pride themselves on their Englishness does not hide the fact that both of them assume their Englishness through careful study. In the case of Arthur, this began with his schooling:

> Irish by ancestry, Scottish by birth, instructed in the faith of Rome by Dutch Jesuits, Arthur became English. English history inspired him; English freedoms made him proud; English cricket made him patriotic. . . . For Arthur the root of Englishness lay in the long-gone, long-remembered, long-invented world of chivalry. (Barnes 2005: 31)

For Arthur, Englishness is a conscious choice. However, the attentive reader cannot but wonder, even at this early stage, if Arthur's fervent Englishness is not bound to be disappointed. In particular the sentence 'English freedoms made him proud' seems to suggest that, by the end of the novel, Arthur might no longer feel so secure about alleged English freedoms. And decades after the case, Conan Doyle did indeed remark in his diaries that 'After many years . . . I can hardly think with patience on the handling of this case [of George Edalji]' (in Stashower 1999: 259) that clearly irrevocably weakened his belief in the English justice system.

The situation is different for George. His 'Englishness' is instilled into him by his Parsee Father Shapurji in what resembles a repetitive mantra:

'George, where do you live?'
'The Vicarage, Great Wyrley.'
'And where is that?'
'Staffordshire, Father.'
'And where is that?'
'The centre of England.'
'And what is England, George?'
'England is the beating heart of the Empire, Father.' (Barnes 2006: 23)

As a narrative device, this exchange is reminiscent of the similar indoctrination into Englishness that Martha Cochrane experiences in *England England* when, together with the other children in her class, she has to 'chant' important historical dates repeatedly:

55BC (clap clap) Roman Invasion
1066 (clap clap) Battle of Hastings
1215 (clap clap) Magna Carta
1512 (clap clap) Henry the Eight (clap clap)
Defender of Faith (clap clap) . . . .
1940 (clap clap) Battle of Britain
1973 (clap clap) Treaty of Rome. (Barnes 1998: 11)

Barnes's rendition of national identity acquisition is playful but nevertheless conveys the idea of indoctrination. The rhythmic clapping ensures that the children do not even have the time to think about what it is they are chanting. Similarly, in *Arthur & George*, Shapurji's catechism leaves George no opportunity for queries either. National identity is thus absorbed unquestioningly. While Barnes's work is historical, it still raises important questions about national identity that resonate with contemporary assumptions about belonging and naturalization. Barnes clearly points out nationality's artificiality, its often laborious acquisition, and its early imprint on impressionable children.

The above dialogue between George and his father also highlights the fictional component of Barnes's work. Whereas Conan Doyle's childhood and upbringing have been chronicled in detail, George's childhood is very much a blank, giving Barnes the creative licence to fill in gaps. A dialogue between George and Shapurji Edalji could have taken place like this but verisimilitude is not Barnes's aim; it is to shape the interests of his narrative.

Throughout the novel, Barnes offers his readers a multitude of similar examples of how fact, historical research, and fiction – artistic licence – merge. One case in point is the description of Sir Arthur's wedding to Jean Leckie, the woman he had secretly loved for many years while nursing his first wife, Touie, who suffered from consumption. The section starts with the aforementioned reproduction of the wedding invitation George receives. From there, it moves to a description of the wedding itself, the venue, the flowers that adorn the chapel ('the chancel is decorated with tall palms; groups of white flowers are arranged at their base' [Barnes 2006: 445]) and the clothes the bride and groom wear (one of the few instances where clothes other than those allegedly worn during a crime are described in any detail), thus painting a very detailed and realistic picture of the events of the day:

> Arthur wears a frock coat and white waistcoat, with a large white gardenia in his buttonhole. . . . The Mam . . . wears grey brocade. . . . Jean's dress, semi-Empire style with a Princess front, is made of ivory silk Spanish lace, its designs outlined with fine pearl embroidery. The underdress is of silver tissue; the train, edged with white crêpe de Chine, falls from a chiffon true-lovers' knot caught in with a white horseshoe of white heather; the veil is worn over a wreath of orange blossom. (Barnes 2006: 445–46)

It is in particular the lengthy description of Jean's dress which is striking. This is exactly the kind of (historical) information contemporaries of Sir Arthur would have been regaled with in their daily papers the day after the wedding. However, we have to realize that not all of this information might have been available at the time: would contemporary newspapers really have printed details about the fabric of Jean's underdress? To potentially blur the line between the two further, Barnes reproduces contemporary media reports as part of the final paragraph describing the wedding when George, deeply impressed by the splendour of the preceding day's wedding events, buys *The Times* and the *Daily Telegraph* for their descriptions and interpretations of the nuptials:

> One paper listed his name between those of Mr Frank Bullen and Mr Hornung, the other had him between Mr Bullen and Mr Hunter. He discovered that the white flowers he had been unable to identify were called *lilium Harrisii*. Also that Sir Arthur and Lady Conan Doyle had afterwards

left for Paris, en route to Dresden and Venice. 'The bride,' he read, 'travelled in a dress of ivory white cloth, trimmed with white Soutache braid, and having a bodice and sleeves of lace, with cloth over-sleeves. At the back the coat was caught into the waist with gold embroidered buttons. In front, folds of the cloth fell softly at either side of a lace chemisette. The dresses were by Maison Dupree, Lee, B. M.' He scarcely understood a word of this. It was . . . mysterious to him . . . (Barnes 2006: 450)

Barnes's own style in describing the wedding venue and the outfits perfectly mirrors this, showing once more how he interweaves factual information gained in archival research with fictional additions – here, in particular George's utter bewilderment at what he reads.

From the initial report-style account of the wedding, the narrative focus then repeatedly shifts on to George – and, more importantly, George's assumed feelings and emotions during the wedding reception, his anxieties at knowing 'no one there except Sir Arthur, whom he has met only twice, and the bride, who briefly shook his hand at the Grand Hotel, Charing Cross' (Barnes 2006: 446), his 'surprise and considerable relief' (Barnes 2006: 447) when people actually *do* come up to speak to him and his amazement at the amount of champagne consumed ('more champagne than George has ever seen poured in his life' [Barnes 2006: 447]). The shift is one from factual account to fictional interpretation of it, and this is strongly concluded in the rendition of Sir Arthur's *factual* wedding speech which includes the statement ' . . . and among us this afternoon I am delighted to welcome my young friend *George Edalji. There is no one I am prouder to see here than him* . . . ' (Barnes 2006: 447–48) and George's fictional reaction to it: 'he had no idea where to look, but realizes that it doesn't matter anyway' (Barnes 2006: 448).

Barnes is careful not to paint too one-sided a picture of George Edalji and the Great Wyrley slasher case. This is where the novel clearly differs from the coverage of the Edalji case in the media at the time, when newspaper coverage about Edalji was largely negative. The novelistic form, by contrast, is considerably more subtle, and Barnes thus restricts his detailed and *realistic* descriptions to events that have been chronicled in detail elsewhere and can be checked. The 'blanks', the 'gaps' that the reader can fill in, he leaves when there is no evidence, no one sufficiently proven truth. The structure of his novel – most commonly one chapter dedicated to Arthur, the next to George – juxtaposes two very different characters and presents both their impressions and emotions. As Holmes has pointed out, 'Barnes's undramatized third-person narrator does not correct their misperceptions and prejudices in order to provide readers with a broader understanding of reality' (Holmes 2009: 59). We are being presented with differing interpretations that fuse to become the same story – reading Sir Arthur's findings and his interpretation of events in one chapter, only to be confronted with George's reactions to them in the next. And whereas Sir Arthur usually feels smugly triumphant about his investigations, George often reacts with surprising reticence and even surliness to Sir Arthur's boundless enthusiasm: 'And it was all, George decided, the fault of Sherlock Holmes. Sir Arthur had been too influenced by his own creation' (Barnes 2006: 426). George's considerably more subdued reaction to Sir Arthur's investigations alerts the reader to the fact that not all might be as clear-cut and 'logical' as Sir Arthur assumes or as Sherlock Holmes finds in his fictional cases. In fact, as Vanessa Guignery has pointed out, 'the frontier between Sir Arthur as investigator and defender of an innocent victim, and Conan Doyle as writer, becomes blurred . . .' (2006: 130). Importantly, this strategy helps to remind the readers that they are, indeed, reading a *novel*, a work of fiction, in which even the characters, George Edalji in particular, are feeling like 'a character in a novel' (Barnes 2006: 416).

Simultaneously, Conan Doyle unearths a number of relevant facts the police have been ignoring during their investigations. However, he is also confronted with negative evidence about George, for example when Anson, the Chief Constable of Staffordshire, informs Conan Doyle about rumours regarding George's alleged gambling debts that George has run up (see Barnes 2006: 377) and he even produces a letter, supposedly authored by George himself, begging for money to pay off debts to moneylenders filing bankruptcy against him. While Conan Doyle nonchalantly dismisses this information and disregards the evidence of the letter, the information is there for the reader to and assess independently. Barnes seems to hint that there might have been more to the Edalji case than Conan Doyle was prepared to see. Stashower reports that

> Recent investigations suggest that the final chapter of the Edalji case has yet to be written. "He was of irreproachable character," Conan Doyle insisted. "Nothing in his life had ever been urged against him." Subsequent research indicates that Edalji may not have been entirely pure of heart. Rumours of gambling debts and misappropriation of client funds have surfaced, indicating that the story may yet take another twist. As a 1907 editorial in the *New York Times* noted: "[Conan Doyle] may have been misled by the literary artist's natural desire to round out his story perfectly. Truth may be stranger than fiction, but it usually lacks what is known in literature as 'construction'". (Stashower 1999: 259)

In this instance, it can be argued, there is considerable self-reflexivity at work in Barnes's novel. These examples highlight how easily narratives can be manipulated, and, consequently, how unreliable they can be. Barnes offers his readers various kinds of evidence to put together and assemble the jigsaw that was the Wyrley Lifestock Massacre piece by piece. However, he leaves out one vital piece – a conclusive ending that, once and for all, exonerates George of all blame. George is released from prison and acquitted of the crime of mutilating cattle and horses but the sentence accusing him of having authored malicious letters targeting his family and himself is upheld, and Sir Arthur's proposals for potential culprits for both offences are studiously ignored by the authorities. By putting Conan Doyle's findings in favour of Edalji alongside other evidence, Barnes paints a complex and multi-faceted picture of Edalji that corresponds with the ambiguous ending of the novel:

> [George] gazes through his succession of lenses, out into the air and beyond.
> What does he see?
> What did he see?
> What will he see? (Barnes 2006: 501).

The three different tenses that Barnes uses to end his novel on are symptomatic of the uncertainty regarding not only the Edalji case, but historical events in general. As readers, finding out about the case over a hundred years later, we can never know the entire truth; we can only assume, conject and hypothesize.

Ending the novel on a series of questions hints at what Alden terms 'the contradiction inherent in historical fiction, that of being simultaneously fictional *and* based in reality' (Alden 2009: 61) There are some questions that simply cannot be answered retrospectively. As Schneider points out, '*Arthur & George* could thus be read as a recuperative virtuoso performance of an old story that both meets and problematizes the expectations of twenty-first century audiences' (2009: 51). Twentieth-century readers, in particular those used to the self-reflexive historiographic metafictions of the 1980s and 1990s, would not necessarily expect closure and finality. What Barnes provides instead, is all the evidence he could find – in a way that allows his readers to make up their own minds.

By mixing fiction with factual accounts and original sources, by offering some illustrations but leaving out others, by offering evidence pro and contra the accused, Barnes has created an intricately crafted historical novel, a hybrid of a detective novel, a *Bildungsroman* for its two protagonists, and a biographical novel. Simultaneously, though, it questions all of these conventions: the 'detective' is ultimately defeated as he cannot come up with a convincing solution; and while some of the biographical information is steeped in historical research, many gaps have been filled by fictional hypotheses. And with this, Barnes asks his readers to critically assess all narrative and take nothing for granted.

AFTERWORD

Seeing and Knowing with the Eyes of Faith

ANDREW LYCETT

For months, before it was published, I imagined that *Arthur & George* (2005) was a biography of Sir Arthur Conan Doyle. I did not know the title at the time, but I was convinced that Julian Barnes was writing a life of the creator of Sherlock Holmes. These circumstances rather coloured my attitude to the novel, though I think I have now come to see more dispassionately.

It happened like this. In June 2004, I was invited to the South of France for the hundred birthday party of Lesley Blanch, the author best known for *The Wilder Shores of Love* (1954), her colourful history of women who found romance in the Arab world.

Unfortunately I was not able to go. But when I next spoke to her on the telephone, I told her I had just been commissioned to write a new biography of Conan Doyle. Lesley replied that this was interesting because another of her friends, Julian Barnes, who had attended her party, had been locked in conversation there with a woman who ran a Sherlock Holmes Museum in Switzerland, and the reason, so far as she understood, was that the author of *Flaubert's Parrot* (1984) had recently embarked on a life of Conan Doyle.

I thought this was unlikely. Barnes basically wrote novels and short stories. However, as attested in this collection of essays, he was fascinated by biography, and its relationship to fiction, and he often turned his hand to biographical essays on writers such as Flaubert and de Maupassant in the *Times Literary Supplement* and other journals.

Nevertheless, I could not be sure. For months, as I embarked on my research, I fretted that Barnes might be beavering away in competition, and this would be disastrous as he was so much more talented and celebrated than I.

I discussed this with Ion Trewin, my editor at my publisher Weidenfeld & Nicolson. Some time the following January he informed me that he had been talking to Pat Kavanagh, the tenacious, much loved agent who was Barnes's wife. (She, sadly, died in 2008). In the course of their conversation, she had told him that her husband had just finished his new novel over the Christmas holiday. I had no further information, but at least it was a novel, and I could begin to relax as I continued to go about my research.

Before long, details of this new novel began to emerge. It was about the Edalji affair. In July 2005 (in time to take its rightful place on the Man Booker Prize short list) this book was published to acclaim.

I must have been one of the first people to purchase a copy. I was immediately struck by how closely Barnes kept to Conan Doyle's life. Here were the general details of the Victorian author's childhood which I had been reading in various biographies, including stories of heroic ancestors and medieval chivalry which he imbibed at his mother's knee. Here too was more precise information about the young boy's reading, such as his love of the adventure stories of Captain Mayne Reid. Barnes surely made up the fact that young Arthur dipped into Mayne Reid's *The Rifle Rangers: or Adventures of an Officer in Southern Mexico* (1850), for I know of nothing which indicates this particular title was on his reading list. However, it is true that, in his autobiography *Memories and Adventures* (1924), Conan Doyle referred to Mayne Reid as his favourite author and he did mention a book called *Scalp Hunters* as his favourite book. Barnes repeats this, giving the book its full name, *The Scalp-Hunters: or Romantic Adventures in Southern Mexico* (1860). I imagine that, as an assiduous researcher, he might have checked the details of the original 1851 edition in the British Library catalogue.

As Conan Doyle's biographer, I was particularly interested in reading about one of the great unresolved conundrums in his life: his relationship with his second wife, Jean Leckie. The background is that, while still a struggling GP in Southsea in 1885, Conan Doyle married Louise Hawkins, the quiet and undemonstrative sister of one of his patients who died. In 1893, when he was at the height of his fame following the publication of the first two series of Sherlock Holmes stories, Louise was diagnosed as suffering from tuberculosis. He seemed to do everything he could and should to help prolong her life, even moving to a new house in Hindhead, Surrey, because it was considered healthy.

However, in 1898 he met young Jean Leckie, who was healthy, attractive and socially active, and he fell deeply in love with her. This relationship caused bitter divisions in his family, with his mother siding with Jean (largely because, in her eyes, her boy could do no wrong) and his sister Connie and her husband, the novelist E. W. Hornung, showing disapproval, particularly after they saw Sir Arthur promenading with his paramour at a cricket game at Lord's. However, Conan Doyle pleaded his innocence, saying his liaison with Jean was platonic, and this made all the difference between guilt and innocence (which, in another context, was the issue in the Edalji affair).

From a biographer's point of view, this had great potential. If I could find evidence that Conan Doyle was lying, it would puncture his reputation as an Edwardian man of honour. So I went about my business, looking, for example, at unpublished letters and public records.

There was little among the former (the result of assiduous weeding by the family). However, in the latter I found that, in March 1901, Conan Doyle spent the weekend with Jean at the Ashdown Forest Hotel in Sussex. Unfortunately for him the census was taken during that very period. Somewhat oddly, however, it showed that the couple was accompanied on this romantic interlude by Arthur's mother, Mary. So, although this suggests that the relationship must have been consummated, it still cannot be said for certain.

Barnes did not have this material. He keeps closely to the accepted version of events, presenting Conan Doyle as an honourable man, wrestling with a moral dilemma which pitched his love for a young woman against his responsibility to a dying wife. However, Barnes does allow occasional departures from the script, as when Conan Doyle first meets Jean and is so attracted that he has an embarrassing ejaculation in his trousers.

On another occasion, in *Arthur & George* but not in the records, Conan Doyle experiences a rare moment of uncertainty in his relationship with Jean. They have been discussing his growing interest in spiritualism and he is gratified that she agrees with him that a Guardian Spirit looks over their relationship. However, he feels something is lacking. As Barnes puts it, 'He needs an earthly witness to their love. He needs to offer proof. He takes to forwarding Jean's love letters to the Mam'. (Barnes insists on calling her 'the Mam', but there is no evidence that this was Conan Doyle's name for his mother, whom he addressed as 'Mam' (without the definite article), 'Mammie' or, earlier, 'Mama'.)

So Sir Arthur visits his mother in Ingleton, Yorkshire. Barnes takes some artistic licence, putting him on the 10.40 train from St Pancras, which I do not believe he could have known – in much the same way that, earlier, he has his hero and Jean gambolling happily around various West Riding tourist attractions, including the Twiss Valley and Pecca Falls, and climbing Ingleborough together.

On this occasion Conan Doyle is alone and in a sour mood, which he duly conveys to his mother. How can I know Jean loves me? he asks. 'If only I could prove it, if either of us could prove it'. His mother replies bluntly, 'Women often prove their love in a way that has been done many times'. It is clear that she means that they give physical expression to their emotions; they make love. But Arthur is still not satisfied. Turning Jean into his mistress would not prove her love, he argues; it might even show the opposite, by compromising his honour. And he adds, 'Proof normally depends on action. What is singular and damnable about our situation is that proof depends on non-action.'

This is just another line of approach to the book's main theme which, as Christine Berberich and Andrew Tate argue in their different ways in this volume of essays, is about the nature of knowledge. At the time Conan Doyle's interest in spiritualism is growing. He is dismayed to find that Jean takes a snobbish attitude, complaining that the people who indulge in it are rather 'common' (Barnes 2005: 192). But his sister Connie has a different complaint – that it is fraudulent. Sir Arthur agrees: 'True prophets are always outnumbered by false – as Jesus Christ himself was. There is fraud, and trickery, even active criminal behaviour' (Barnes 2005: 194).

But he goes on to affirm that he no longer trusted faith. 'I can only work with the clear light of knowledge' (Barnes 2005: 194.) And he adds, 'The whole point of psychical research is to eliminate and expose fraud and deceit. To leave only what can be scientifically confirmed. If you eliminate the impossible, what is left, however improbable, must be the truth' (Barnes 2005: 194).

That last statement is of course a famous (and, in my opinion, fatuous) observation of Sherlock Holmes, underlining the extent to which Barnes seeks to align his Conan Doyle with the fictional detective. What is significant is the way in which Conan Doyle truly thought, in *Arthur & George* as in real life, that, following his earlier experiments into extra sensory perception, he had arrived at a scientific religion – one where the results of observation lead to the accumulation of knowledge. Just like Sherlock Holmes, really.

Of course *Arthur & George* is a book about two men, the second of whom, George Edalji, is much less known. So Barnes has to work harder to re-create the inner life of this half-Parsee solicitor, whose trial on charges of animal mutilation is so central to the story. Conan Doyle's defence again centres on the nature of evidence, as he dismisses the reports of witnesses to show that Edalji was so myopic that he would not have been able to see to perform the crimes of which he was accused.

However *Arthur & George* is more than a mystery story. After Jean's death, Edalji is surprised to be invited to Sir Arthur's wedding to his new wife Jean in September 1907. In this context I can confirm something that Berberich notes: Barnes's description of this ceremony did indeed echo reports of the event in *The Times* and other newspapers, even down to details of the underdress. In this context, as she further suggests, Barnes, with his knowing, not quite postmodern style, continues to investigate the significance of attested (or observed) pieces of information: they might be true or they might not.

The licence which an author takes in filling in the resulting gaps establishes one of the crucial differences between fiction and non-fiction, or between a novel and a biography. Berberich even toys with the idea that Barnes is creating some sort of hybrid where 'fact and fiction converge and intermingle in a way that makes it difficult, or maybe even irrelevant, for the reader to discern the dividing line' (p. 123).

Interestingly, she also draws attention to Barnes's use of two illustratons as an example of his approach to giving authenticity to his novel (and also providing the sense of a clue which is crucial to the detective story). One of these intertextual insertions is a copy of the wedding invitation from the Conan Doyles to Edalji. She is probably unaware that this is not a replica of the actual invitation, which I have seen, but is (presumably) a computer-generated mock-up of this document – nearly the same, with an attempt to use the same cursive script, but in fact tellingly different. This manipulation of the image adds another teasing dimension to the ongoing investigation of what is real and what is not.

To return to Barnes's text: in a crucial chapter at the end of the book, we meet Edalji again as he prepares to enter the Albert Hall to attend a spiritualist memorial service for Sir Arthur who has recently died (on 7 July 1930). With his problems with sight, Edalji fiddles with his binoculars and examines the Albert Memorial. 'He swept slowly up the Memorial, above the levels at which art and science and industry held sway, above the seated figure of the pensive Consort, up to a higher realm. The burred knob was hard to control, and sometimes there was a mass of unfocused foliage filling the lens, but eventually he emerged at the plain vision of a chunky Christian cross' (Barnes 2005: 339).

In the Hall, the medium conducting the service reveals that Sir Arthur is present, and this information is widely acknowledged. So is he there, or not? Those who believe in spiritualism say they can see him. Edalji is confused and can only reflect, as Barnes puts it, again in quasi-Christian terms, 'Sir Arthur, a man of the highest integrity and intelligence, believed in events of the kind George has just been witnessing; it would be impertinent for George in this moment to deny his saviour' (Barnes 2005: 354).

Edalji finds he needs again to resort to his binoculars to try to observe what everyone else is claiming. A woman turns and tells him he will not see Sir Arthur that way. 'You will only see him with the eyes of faith' (Barnes 2005: 355). And Edalji realizes that there is indeed some truth in this: Sir Arthur had taken up his case because he believed in his innocence and in a sense 'knew' it. Belief or a measure of faith had been central to the process of proving he was not guilty – all rather different from the process of gathering and sifting evidence which seems so crucial to the work of a consulting detective such as Sherlock Holmes.

However as anyone who reads Holmes soon understands, the sleuth is much more than a calculating machine: his investigations may seem to hinge on the scientific analysis of observable criteria, but they are brought to their conclusion by more human qualities, including hunches and intuition.

And so it is with novels and biography, which both stand at different places in the spectrum between objective and imaginative truth. Back in 2005, I remember wondering if, given its palpable use of factual information, *Arthur & George* should have been entered for the Man Booker Prize for Fiction at all. If I had any doubts then, I do not any longer. In this book, as in everything he does, Barnes was playing with and quietly expanding on the conventions of storytelling.

REFERENCES

Works Cited by Contributors

Introduction: 'Julian Barnes and the Wisdom of Uncertainty, Sebastian Groes (Roehampton University) and Peter Childs (University of Gloucestershire)

Barnes, J. (1980), *Metroland*. London: Jonathan Cape.
—(1984), *Flaubert's Parrot*. London: Jonathan Cape.
—(1986), *Staring at the Sun*. London: Jonathan Cape.
—(1989), *A History of the World in 10½ Chapters*. London: Jonathan Cape.
—(1995), *Cross Channel*. London: Jonathan Cape.
—(1991), *Talking It Over*. London: Jonathan Cape.
—(1992), *The Porcupine*. London: Jonathan Cape.
—(1995), *Letters from London*. London: Picador.
—(1998), *England, England*. London: Jonathan Cape.
—(2002), 'Introduction', in A. Daudet, *In the Land of Pain*, London, Jonathan Cape, v–xv.
—(2004), *The Lemon Table*. London: Jonathan Cape.
—(2005), *Arthur and George*. London: Jonathan Cape.
—(2008), *Nothing To Be Frightened Of*. London: Jonathan Cape.
—(2011), *Pulse*. London: Jonathan Cape.
Bradford, R. (2007), *The Novel Now: contemporary British fiction*. Oxford: Blackwell.
Bradley, A., and A. Tate (2010), *The New Atheist Novel*. London: Continuum.
Childs, P. (2005), *Contemporary Novelists: British Fiction since 1970*. Basingstoke and New York: Palgrave Macmillan.
David, L. (2008), 'We made up the Bible as a good novel', *Liverpool Daily Post*, 11 June, 18–19.
Forster, E. M. (1934), *Abinger Pageant*. London: Abinger.
—(1940), *England's Pleasant Land*. London: Hogarth.
Guignery, V. (2006), *The Fiction of Julian Barnes: A Reader's Guide to Essential Criticism*. Basingstoke: Palgrave Macmillan.
Head, D. (2006), *The Cambridge Guide to Literature in English*. Cambridge: Cambridge University Press.
Holmes, F. (2009), *Julian Barnes*. Basingstoke: Palgrave Macmillan.
Kriegel, V. (1988), *The Truth about Dogs*. London: Bloomsbury.
Kundera, M. (1999), *The Art of the Novel*. London: Faber and Faber. First published in English in 1988. Originally published in French as *L'art du roman* in 1986 by Editions Gallimard.

Pateman, M. (2002), *Julian Barnes*. Tavistock: Northcote House.
Pearsall, S. (2008), 'Julian Barnes', *Private Eye magazine*, 1207, 4–17 April, 26.
Powys, J. C. (1932), *A Glastonbury Romance*. New York: Simon and Schuster.
Rhys, R. (1966), *Wide Sargasso Sea*. London: Andre Deutsch.
Stoppard, T. (1966), *Rosencrantz and Guildenstern are Dead*. New York: Grove Press.
Stout, M. (1992), 'Chameleon Novelist', *New York Times Review of Books*, 22 November, http://www.nytimes.com/books/01/02/25/specials/barnes-chameleon.html [Accessed 6 June 2009].
Woolf, V. (1941), *Between the Acts*. London: Hogarth.

Filmography
(1996), *Love, etc.* Dir. Marion Vernoux, adapted by Dodine Herry.
(1997), *Metroland.* Dir. Philip Saville, adapted by Adrian Hodges.

Adaptations
(2005), *Arthur & George.* First performed 19 March 2005 by Birmingham Repertory Theatre, adapted by David Edgar.

Chapter One: The *Flâneur* and the Freeholder: Paris and London in Julian Barnes's *Metroland*, Matthew Taunton

Barnes, J. (1990), *Metroland*. London: Picador. First published by Jonathan Cape in 1980.
—(1997), 'Out of Place', *Architectural Digest*, 54 (5), 36–38.
Baudelaire, C. (1995), 'The Painter of Modern Life' in *The Painter of Modern Life and Other Essays*, trans. J. Mayne (2nd Edn.). London: Phaidon, 1–41.
Benjamin, W. (2006), *The Writer of Modern Life: Essays on Charles Baudelaire*, Jennings, M. W. (ed.). Cambridge, MS and London: Harvard University Press.
Bowlby, R. (1988), *Feminist Destinations and Other Essays on Virginia Woolf*. Oxford: Basil Blackwell.
Carey, J. (1992), *The Intellectuals and the Masses: Pride and Prejudice among the Literary Intelligentsia, 1880–1939*. London: Faber & Faber.
Debord, G. (2006), 'Theory of the Dérive', in J. Morra and M. Smith (eds). *Visual Culture*, Vol. 3, *Spaces of Visual Culture*. London: Routledge, 77–81.
Evans, E. J. (2004), *Thatcher and Thatcherism* (2nd Edn.). London: Routledge.
Flint, K. (1986), 'Fictional Suburbia', in P. Humm, P. Stigant and P. Widdowson (eds). *Popular Fictions: Essays in Literature and History*. London: Methuen.
Frampton, K. (1992), *Modern Architecture: A Critical History* (3rd Edn.). London: Thames and Hudson.
Frankl, G. (1974), *The Failure of the Sexual Revolution*. London: Khan & Averill.
Grossmith, G. and W. (1995), *The Diary of a Nobody*. Oxford: Oxford University Press.
Guignery, V. (2006), *The Fiction of Julian Barnes: A Reader's Guide to Essential Criticism*. Basingstoke: Palgrave Macmillan.

Hobsbawm, E. (1994), *Age of Extremes: The Short Twentieth Century, 1914–1991*. London: Michael Joseph.
Parsons, D. L. (2000), *Streetwalking the Metropolis: Women, the City, and Modernity*. Oxford: Oxford University Press.
Ross, K. (2002), *May '68 and its Afterlives*. Chicago: University of Chicago Press.
Sartre, J. P. (1969), *Being and Nothingness*. Trans. H. E. Barnes. London: Routledge.
Taunton, M. (2009), *Fictions of the City: Class, Culture and Mass Housing in London and Paris*. Basingstoke: Palgrave Macmillan.

Filmography
(1997), *Metroland*, Dir. P. Saville.

Chapter Two: Inventing a Way to the Truth: Life and Fiction in Julian Barnes's *Flaubert's Parrot*, Ryan Roberts

Barnes, J. (1976), 'Sparring Partners', *The New Statesman*, 8 October, 492.
—(1980a), 'Flaubert's Refrigerated Heart', *The Sunday Times*, 30 March, 41.
—(1980b), 'Very Clean', *The New Statesman*, 11 April, 561.
—(1982a), 'Double Bind', *London Review of Books*, 4 (10), 3–16 June, 22, 24.
—(1982b), 'One of a Kind', *London Review of Books*, 4 (3), 18 February–3 March, 23–24.
—(1983a), 'Flaubert and Rouen', *Listener*, 110 (2822), 18 August, 14–15.
—(1983b), 'Flaubert's Parrot', *London Review of Books*, 5 (15), 18–31 August, 20–21.
—(1983–4a), 'Eyes of Blue'. Unpublished manuscript. Julian Barnes Papers 1971–2000. Harry Ransom Humanities Research Center, University of Texas at Austin. Box 5, Folder 2, Gathering 15. August 2003.
—(1983–4b), 'Flaubert's Parrot: Some Unanswered Questions [Raitt notes]'. Unpublished manuscript. Julian Barnes Papers 1971–2000. Harry Ransom Humanities Research Center, University of Texas at Austin. Box 5, Folder 1, Gathering 1. August 2003.
—(1983–4c), 'Flaubert's Parrot[: Some Unanswered Questions]'. Unpublished manuscript. Julian Barnes Papers 1971–2000. Harry Ransom Humanities Research Center, University of Texas at Austin. Box 5, Folder 2, Gathering 11. August 2003.
—(1983–4d), 'Flaubert's Parrot'. Unpublished manuscript. Julian Barnes Papers 1971–2000. Harry Ransom Humanities Research Center, University of Texas at Austin. Box 5, Folder 2, Gathering 13. August 2003.
—(1985), 'The Follies of Writer Worship', *New York Times Book Review*, 17 February, 1, 16–17.
—(1990), *Flaubert's Parrot*. New York: Vintage International. Originally published by Jonathan Cape in 1984.
—(2004), 'Knowing French', in *The Lemon Table*, New York: Alfred A. Knopf, 137–58.
—(2005), 'When Flaubert Took Wing', *Guardian*, 5 March, 30.

Guignery, V. (2002), 'Julian Barnes in Conversation', *Cercles*, 4, 255–69.
Guignery, V. and R. Roberts. (2009), 'Julian Barnes: The Final Interview', in Guignery, V. and R. Roberts (eds), *Conversations with Julian Barnes*. Jackson, MS: Univ. Press of Mississippi, 161–88.
Guppy, S. (2001), 'The Art of Fiction CLXV', *The Paris Review*, 157, 54–84.
Joseph-Vilain, M. (2001), 'The Writer's Voice(s) in *Flaubert's Parrot*', *Q/W/E/R/T/Y: Arts, Litteratures et Civilisations du Monde Anglophone*, 183–88.
Moseley, M. (1997), *Understanding Julian Barnes*. Columbia: University of South Carolina Press.
Pateman, M. (1998), 'Is There a Novel in This Text? Identities of Narrative in *Flaubert's Parrot*', in Morel, M. (ed.), *L'Exil et l'allégorie dans le roman anglophone contemporain*. Paris: Ed. Messene/Collection 'Dire le Récit', 35–47.
Sartre, Jean-Paul. (1981), *The Family Idiot: Gustave Flaubert 1821–1857*. Translated by Carol Cosman. Chicago: Chicago University Press.
Sartre, Jean-Paul (1971), *L'Idiot de la famille: Gustave Flaubert de 1821 à 1857*. Paris: Gallimard.
Walsh, J. (1984), 'Faction, Fiction and Flaubert'. *Books and Bookmen*, 20–21.
Wilson, K. (2006), "Why aren't the books enough?': Authorial Pursuit in Julian Barnes's *Flaubert's Parrot* and *A History of the World in 10½ Chapters*', *Critique* 47 (4), 362–74.

Chapter Three: 'A preference for things Gallic': Julian Barnes and the French Connection, Vanessa Guignery

Anon. (2009), 'He's Turned Towards Python', in V. Guignery and R. Roberts (eds), *Conversations with Julian Barnes*, Mississippi, University of Mississippi Press, 27–30. First published in 1998.
Barnes, J. (1982), 'Double Bind', *The London Review of Books*, 3–16 June.
—(1983), 'Flaubert and Rouen', *The Listener*, 110, 18 August, 14–15.
—(1985), *Flaubert's Parrot*. London, Picador. First published by Jonathan Cape, 1984.
—(1990), *Metroland*, London, Picador. First published by Jonathan Cape, 1980.
—(1992), *Talking It Over*, London, Picador. First published by Jonathan Cape, 1991.
—(1995), *Letters from London 1990–1995*, London, Picador.
—(1996), *Cross Channel*, London, Jonathan Cape.
—(1998), *England, England*, London, Jonathan Cape.
—(2000), 'Influences – Single-Handed', *New Yorker*, 25 December–1 January, 114–15.
—(2002a), *Something to Declare*, London, Picador.
—(2002b), 'Introduction', in Alphonse Daudet, *In the Land of Pain*, London, Jonathan Cape, v–xv.
—(2002c), Papers, Harry Ransom Humanities Research Center, Austin, Texas.
—(2003a), 'Hate and Hedonism. The Insolent Art of Michel Houellebecq', *New Yorker*, 7 July, http://www.newyorker.com/archive/2003/07/07/030707crbo_books [Accessed 7 Jule 2009].

—(2003b), 'Flashes of Wisdom in an Age of Chaos', *Guardian*, 4 October, 34.
—(2006a), 'The Rebuke', *Guardian*, 30 September.
—(2006b), Addition to his Papers, Harry Ransom Humanities Research Center, Austin, Texas.
—(2008), *Nothing To Be Frightened Of*, London, Jonathan Cape.
—(2009), 'On We Sail', *The London Review of Books*, 31.21, 5 November, 25–28.
Barth, J., 'The Literature of Replenishment. Postmodernist Fiction', *Atlantic*, 245.1, January 1980, 65–71.
Bloom, H. (1973), *The Anxiety of Influence*, London, Oxford University Press.
Bouillaguet, A. (1996), *L'Écriture imitative. Pastiche, parodie, collage*, Paris, Nathan Université.
Connor, S. (1996), *The English Novel in History: 1950–1995*, London, Routledge.
Eliot, T.S. (1920), *The Sacred Wood: Essays on Poetry and Criticism*, London, Methuen.
Freiburg, R. (2009), 'Novels Come out of Life, Not out of Theories': An Interview with Julian Barnes, in V. Guignery and R. Roberts (eds), *Conversations with Julian Barnes*, Mississippi, University of Mississippi Press, 31–52. First published in 1999.
French, M. (2008), 'Mike Interviews: Julian Barnes', *The View from Here*, 4 April, http://www.viewfromheremagazine.com/2008/04/mike-interviews-julian-barnes-part-1-of-html [Accessed 12 September 2009].
Guignery V. and Gallix, F., (eds). (2001), 'Julian Barnes at the Sorbonne. 14th November 2001', *Études britanniques contemporaines*, 21, December, 107–32.
Guignery, V. and Roberts, R., (eds). (2009), *Conversations with Julian Barnes*, Mississippi, University of Mississippi Press.
Gutleben, C. (2001), *Nostalgic Postmodernism: The Victorian Tradition and the Contemporary British Novel*, Amsterdam and New York, NY, Rodopi.
Hayman, R. (2009), 'Julian Barnes in Interview', in V. Guignery and R. Roberts (eds), *Conversations with Julian Barnes*, Mississippi, University of Mississippi Press, 3–6. First published in 1980.
Herbert, S. (2008), 'Julian Barnes: Not Dead Yet, just Dying', *The Sunday Times*, 16 March.
Holmes, F. M. (2008), *Julian Barnes*, Basingstoke, Palgrave Macmillan.
Hutcheon, L. (1988), *A Poetics of Postmodernism. History, Theory, Fiction*. New York and London, Routledge.
Jameson, F., 'Postmodernism, or the Cultural Logic of Late Capitalism', *New Left Review*, 146, July/August 1984, 53–92.
Kastor, E. (1987), 'Julian Barnes' Big Questions', *Washington Post Book World*, 18 May, 1+.
Moseley, M. (1997), *Understanding Julian Barnes*. Columbia, University of South Carolina Press.
Porter, H., 'The Heart of a Man of Letters', *The Independent on Sunday*, 2 April 1995, 6.

Rafferty, T., 'Watching the Detectives', *Nation*, 241:1, 6–13 July 1985, 21–22.
Salgas, J.-P., 'Julian Barnes n'en a pas fini avec Flaubert', *Quinzaine Littéraire*, 463, 16–31 May, 13.
Sterne, L. (1985), *The Life and Opinions of Tristram Shandy*. Harmondsworth, Penguin. First published in 1759–1767.
Stout, M. (1992), 'Chameleon Novelist', *New York Times*, 22 November 1992, section 6, 28+.
Swanson, C. (1996), 'Old Fartery and Literary Dish', *The Salon Interview*, 13 May, http://www.salon.com/books/int/1996/05/13/interview/index.html [Accessed 12 September 2009].
Wilde, P. (2009), 'Interviews: Julian Barnes', in V. Guignery and R. Roberts (eds), *Conversations with Julian Barnes*. Mississippi, University of Mississippi Press, 96–100. First published in 2002.

Chapter Four: 'An Ordinary Piece of Magic': Religion in the Work of Julian Barnes, Andrew Tate

Augustine. (2008), *Confessions*. Trans. Chadwick, H. Oxford: Oxford University Press.
Barnes, J. (1987), *Staring at the Sun*. London: Picador. Originally published by Jonathan Cape in 1986.
—(1989), *A History of the World in 10½ Chapters*. London: Picador.
—(2006), *Arthur & George*. London: Vintage.
—(2009), *Nothing To Be Frightened Of*. London: Vintage.
Bradley, A. and Tate, A. (2010), *The New Atheist Novel: Fiction, Philosophy and Polemic after 9/11*. London: Continuum.
Brown, C. (2001), *The Death of Christian Britain: Understanding Secularisation, 1800–2000*. London: Routledge.
Childs, P. (2009), 'Beneath a Bombers' Moon: Barnes and Belief'. *American, British and Canadian Studies*, 13, December. 120–29.
Conan Doyle, A. (1981), *The Adventures of Sherlock Holmes*. London: Penguin.
—(2007), *Memories and Adventures*. Ware: Wordsworth. Originally published by Hodder and Stoughton in 1924.
Eagleton, T. (2005), *The English Novel*. Oxford: Blackwell.
Head, D. (2002), *The Cambridge Introduction to Modern British Fiction, 1950–2000*. Cambridge: Cambridge University Press.
Joyce, J. (2000), *Dubliners*. London: Penguin. Originally published in 1914.
Pateman, M. (2002), *Julian Barnes*. Tavistock: Northcote House.
Salyer, G. *(1991)*, 'One Good Story Leads to Another: Julian Barnes's *A History of the World in 10½ Chapters*'. *Literature and Theology*. 5 (2), 220–33.
Woods, J. (1999), *The Broken Estate: Essays in Literature and Belief*. London: Jonathan Cape.
Wu, D. (1998), *Romanticism: an Anthology*. Oxford: Blackwell.
Yeats, W. B. (2000), *The Collected Poems of W. B. Yeats*. Ware: Wordsworth.

Chapter Five: Crossing the Channel: Europe and the Three Uses of France in Julian Barnes's *Talking It Over*, Merritt Moseley

Barnes, J. (1996), *Cross Channel*. London: Jonathan Cape.
—(1984), *Flaubert's Parrot*. London: Jonathan Cape.
—(1995), *Letters from London*. London: Jonathan Cape.
—(1992), *Love, etc.* Trans. R. Las Vergnas. Paris: Éditions Denoël. French translation of *Talking It Over*.
—(2002) *Metroland*. London: Picador. Originally published in 1980.
—(2000), *Outre-Manche*. Trans. J.-P. Aoustin Paris: Éditions Denoël. French translation of *Cross Channel*.
—(2002), *Something to Declare*. London: Picador.
—(1991), *Talking It Over*. London: Jonathan Cape.
Brody, R. (2008), *Everything is Cinema: The Working Life of Jean-Luc Godard*. New York: Metropolitan Books.
Dickens, C. (1952), *Our Mutual Friend*. Oxford: Oxford Illustrated Dickens. First published 1864–65.
Flaubert, G. (1857), *Madame Bovary*. Paris: Revue de Paris and Michel Levy Freres.
Guignery, V. (2006), *The Fiction of Julian Barnes*. Houndmills: Palgrave.
Guignery, V. and R. Roberts. (2009), 'Julian Barnes: The Final Interview', in Guignery, V. and R. Roberts (eds), *Conversations with Julian Barnes*. Jackson, MS: University Press of Mississippi.
Guppy, S. (2001), 'The Art of Fiction CLXV', *The Paris Review*, 157, 54–84.
Levenson, M. (1991), 'Flaubert's Parrot: *Talking It Over* by Julian Barnes', *New Republic*, 16 December. 42–45.
Meudal, Gérard. <<http://www.amazon.fr/Outre-Manche-Julian-Barnes/dp/2070410072 >> [Accessed 18 October 2008].
Swanson, C. (1996), 'Old Fartery and Literary Dish', *Salon*, http://www.salon.com/weekly/interview960513.html [Accessed 16 October 2009].
Thacheray, W. M. (1841), 'Memorials of Gormandising', *Fraser's Magazine*, June. It is collected in *The Works of William Makepeace Thackeray*, vol. 13, 1899.

Filmography
(1962), *Jules et Jim*. Released 17 May, Dir. F. Truffaut, for Les Films du Carrosse.

Chapter Six: The story of Julian Barnes's *The Porcupine*: an Epistolary ½ Chapter, Dimitrina Kondeva

Barnes, J. (1985), *Flaubert's Parrot*. London: Picador. First published in 1984 by Jonathan Cape.
—(1989), *A History of the World in 10½ Chapters*. London: Jonathan Cape.
—(1990), 'Candles for the Living – Julian Barnes in Bulgaria', in *London Review of Books*, 12 (22), 22 November, 6–7.
—(1992), *The Porcupine*. London: Jonathan Cape.

—(2004), *The Lemon Table*. London: Jonathan Cape.
—(2008), *Nothing To Be Frightened Of*. London: Jonathan Cape.
Freiburg, R. (1999), 'Novels come out of life, not out of theory', in Freiburg, R. and J. Schnitker (eds), *Do you Consider Yourself to be a Postmodern Author?* Hamburg and London: Munster, 39–66.

Chapter Seven: Julian Barnes's *England, England* and Englishness, Richard Bradford

Anonymous (2005), 'An Interview with Julian Barnes', Authors' Corner on Abebooks website, http://www.abebooks.co.uk/docs/authors-corner/julian-barnes.shtml [Accessed 10 July 2010].
Barnes, J. (1984), *Flaubert's Parrot*. London: Jonathan Cape.
—(1988), *England, England*. Cape, London: Jonathan Cape.
Darling, J. (2003), *The Taxi Driver's Daughter*. London: Viking.
Denning, P. (1998), 'Inventing England,' *The Irish Times* 8 September, http://www.ireland.com/scripts/search/highlight.plx?TextRes=Julian%20barnes&Path [Accessed 7 July 2010].
Griffiths, N. (2005), *Wreckage*. London: Jonathan Cape.
Murray, J. (2003), *Jazz etc*. London: Flambard.
Swift, G. (1996), *Last Orders*. London: Picador.
—(1983), *Waterland*. London: Heinemann.
Thomas, E. (1917), E. Longley (ed.). *The Annotated Collected Poems*, Bloodaxe Books, 2008; First published in 1917.
Thorpe, A. (1992), *Ulverton*. London: Secker and Warburg.
Welsh, I. (1993), *Trainspotting*. London: Secker and Warburg.

Chapter Eight: Matters of Life and Death: The Short Stories of Julian Barnes, Peter Childs

Barnes, J. (1981), *Metroland*. London: Robin Clark. Originally published by Jonathan Cape in 1980.
—(1985), *Flaubert's Parrot*. London: Picador. Originally published by Jonathan Cape in 1984.
—(1996), *Cross Channel*. London: Picador.
—(1998), *England, England*. London: Jonathan Cape.
—(2002), *Something to Declare*. London: Picador.
—(2003), 'Trespass', *New Yorker*, 24 November, http://www.newyorker.com/archive/2003/11/24/031124fi_fiction [Accessed 6 July7 2010].
—(2005), *The Lemon Table*. London: Picador. Originally published by Jonathan Cape in 2004.
—(2005a), *Arthur & George*. London: Jonathan Cape.
—(2008), *Nothing To Be Frightened Of*. London: Jonathan Cape.
—(2007), 'Marriage Lines,' *Granta* 100 (Winter 2007): 317–23.

—(2008a), '60/40', *Guardian*, 2 August, 22–25.
—(2008b), 'East Wind', *Sunday Times* (Magazine), 30 November, 65–72.
—(2009a), 'The Limner', *New Yorker*, 5 January, http://www.newyorker.com/fiction/features/2009/01/05/090105fi_fiction_barnes [Accessed 7 June 2010].
—(2009b), 'Complicity', *New Yorker*, 19 October, 72–77.
—(2009c), 'Harmony', *Granta* 109, Winter, 97–122.
—(2010), 'Sleeping with John Updike', *Guardian*, 23 January, http://www.guardian.co.uk/books/2010/jan/23/julian-barnes-new-short-story [Accessed 7 June 2010].
Duiker, W. J. and J. J. Spielvogel (2010), *World History: Volume 2, Since 1500*, Sixth Edition. Boston: Wadsworth.
Forster, E. M. (2000), *A Passage to India*. Harmondsworth: Penguin. First published in 1924.

Chapter Nine: The Past After Postmodern Fabulation. Fact and Fiction in Julian Barnes's *Arthur & George*, Christine Berberich

Alden, N. (2009), 'Words of War, War of Words: *Atonement* and the Question of Plagiarism', in S. Groes (ed.), *Ian McEwan: Contemporary Critical Perspectives*. London and New York: Continuum, 57–69.
Barnes, J. (1985), *Flaubert's Parrot*. London: Picador. First published in 1984 by Jonathan Cape.
Barnes, J. (1998), *England, England*. London: Jonathan Cape.
Barnes, J. (2006), *Arthur & George*. London: Vintage. First published in 2005 by Jonathan Cape.
Bradford, R. (2007), *The Novel Now*. Oxford: Blackwell.
Cavalié, E. (2009a), 'Constructions of Englishness in Julian Barnes's *Arthur & George*', *American, British and Canadian Studies*, 13, December, 88–100.
Cavalié, E. (2009b), "Unofficial Englishmen': Representations of the English Gentleman in Julian Barnes's Arthur & George', in F. Reviron-Piégay (ed.), *Englishness Revisited*. Newcastle: Cambridge Scholars Publishing, 352–64.
Childs, P. (2005), *Contemporary Novelists: British Fiction Since 1970*. Basingstoke: Palgrave Macmillan.
Fraga, X. (2009), 'Interview with Julian Barnes (2006)', in V. Guignery and R. Roberts (eds), *Conversations with Julian Barnes*. Jackson, MS: University of Mississippi Press, 134–47.
Guignery, V. (2006), *The Fiction of Julian Barnes. A Reader's Guide to Essential Criticism*. Basingstoke: Palgrave Macmillan.
Guignery, V. and R. Roberts, (eds). (2009), *Conversations with Julian Barnes*. Jackson, MS: Mississippi University Press.
Holmes, F. M. (2009), *Julian Barnes*. Basingstoke: Palgrave Macmillan.

Hutcheon, L. (1988), *A Poetics of Postmodernism. History, Theory, Fiction*. London: Routledge.
Jeffries, S. (2009), 'It's for Self-Protection (2005)', in V. Guignery and R. Roberts, (eds), *Conversations with Julian Barnes*. Jackson, MS: University of Mississippi Press, 129–33.
Kucala, B. (2009), 'The Erosion of Victorian Discourse in Julian Barnes's *Arthur & George*', *American, British and Canadian Studies*, 13, December, 61–73.
Lycett, A. (2009), *Conan Doyle. The Man Who Created Sherlock Holmes*. London: Phoenix. First published in 2007.
McEwan, Ian (2006), 'An Inspiration, Yes. Did I copy from another author? No'. *Guardian*. 27, November, 1–2.
Moseley, M. (1997), *Understanding Julian Barnes*. Columbia, SC: University of South Carolina Press.
Pateman, M. (2002), *Julian Barnes*. Tavistock: Northcote House.
Schneider, A. (2009), 'Competing Narratives in Julian Barnes's *Arthur & George*', *American, British and Canadian Studies*, 13, December, 50–60.
Sebald, W. G. (1996), *The Emigrants*. London: The Harvill Press. Translated by M. Hulse.
Stashower, D. (1999), *Teller of Tales. The Life of Arthur Conan Doyle*. New York: Henry Holt.
Summerscale, K. (2008), *The Suspicions of Mr Whicher; or The Murder at Road Hill House*. London: Bloomsbury Publishing.
Stout, M. (1992), 'Chameleon Novelist', *New York Times Magazine*. 22 November, 29; 68–72; 80.
Taylor, J. B. (1997), 'Structure of Feeling', in *Dictionary of Cultural and Critical Theory* Online Version, http://www.blackwellreference.com/public/tocnode?id=g9780631207535_chunk_g978063120753522_ss1–37 [Accessed 6 June 2010].
Walter, N. (2009), 'Our Mutual Friend,' *Guardian*, 2 July. http://www.guardian.co.uk/books/2005/jul/02/bookerprize2005.bookerprize [Accessed 6 April 2010].

Afterword, Andrew Lycett

Barnes, J. (2005), *Arthur & George*. London: Jonathan Cape.
—(1984), *Flaubert's Parrot*. London: Jonathan Cape.
Blanch, L. (1954), *The Wilder Shores of Love*. London: John Murray.
Conan Doyle, A. (1924), *Memories and Adventures*. London: Hodder and Stoughton.
Reid, M. (1850), *The Rifle Rangers: or Adventures of an Officer in Southern Mexico*. London: Routledge.
—(1860), *The Scalp-Hunters: or Romantic Adventures in Southern Mexico*. London: Routledge.

FURTHER READING

I Primary Works

Novels
(1980). *Metroland*. London: Jonathan Cape.
(1982). *Before She Met Me*. London: Jonathan Cape.
(1984). *Flaubert's Parrot*. London: Jonathan Cape.
(1986). *Staring at the Sun*. London: Jonathan Cape.
(1989). *A History of the World in 10½ Chapters*. London: Jonathan Cape.
(1991). *Talking It Over*. London: Jonathan Cape.
(1992). *The Porcupine*. London: Jonathan Cape.
(1998). *England, England*. London: Jonathan Cape.
(2000). *Love, etc*. London: Jonathan Cape.
(2005). *Arthur and George*. London: Jonathan Cape.

Memoir
(2008). *Nothing To Be Frightened Of*. London: Jonathan Cape.

Under the Pseudonym of Dan Kavanagh
(1980). *Duffy*. London: Jonathan Cape.
(1981). *Fiddle City*. London: Jonathan Cape.
(1985). *Putting the Boot In*. London: Jonathan Cape.
(1987). *Going to the Dogs*. London: Viking.
(1991). *The Duffy Omnibus*. Hammondsworth: Penguin. – The above novels are included in this book.

Collected Short Stories
(1995). *Cross Channel*. London: Jonathan Cape.
(2004). *The Lemon Table*. London: Jonathan Cape.
(2011). *Pulse*. London: Jonathan Cape.

Uncollected Short Stories/Writings
(1975). 'A Self-Possessed Woman'. *The Times Anthology of Ghost Stories*. London: Jonathan Cape, 132–49.
(1981). 'On the Terrace', in *Punch*. 28 October, 746–48.
(1982a). 'One of a Kind', in *London Review of Books*, 4: 3, 18 February–3 March, 23–24.
(1982b). 'The Writer who Liked Hollywood', in *New Statesman* (2 July), 18–20.
(1986). 'The 50p Santa: A Duffy Detective Story' (as Dan Kavanagh) in *Time Out*, 19 December 1985 – 1 January, 12–13.
(1991). 'U' in Spender, S. (ed), *Hockney's Alphabet*. London: Faber and Faber.
(1993). '1981', *21* (21 Picador Writers Celebrate 21 Years of Outstanding International Writing). London: Picador, 91–109.
(1994). 'Trap. Dominate. Fuck.', in B. Buford (ed.), *Granta 47 'Losers'*. Basingstoke: Macmillan.
(1994). 'Hamlet in the Wild West', in *Index on Censorship*, 23: 4–5, September, 100–3.

Non-fiction
(1995). *Letters from London*. London: Picador.
(2002). *Something to Declare*. London: Picador.
(2003). *The Pedant in the Kitchen*. London: Jonathan Cape.

Translations
(1988). Kriegel, V. *The Truth about Dogs*. London: Bloomsbury.
(2002). Daudet, A. *In the Land of Pain*. London: Jonathan Cape. Translation, introduction and notes. Originally published in French in 1930.

Selected Articles and Journalism
(1981). 'The Giving of Offence', in *Times Literary Supplement*. 23 October.
(1983). 'Remembrance of Things Past', in *Observer*, 24 July, 22.
(1984a). 'To Suit the Occasion', in *Times Literary Supplement*, 3 February, 113.
(1984b). 'Curious Case of Infidelity', in *Observer*, 7 October, 24.
(1985). 'The Follies of Writer Worship', in *New York Times Book Review*, 90, 17 February 1, 16, 17.
(1986). 'Once in Love with Emma', *New York Times Book Review* 91, 21 December, 10.
(1987). 'Life in the Slow Lane', *New York Times Book Review* 92, 4 October, 13–14.
(1988). 'Playing Chess with Arthur Koestler', in *Yale Review,* 77: 4, Summer, 478–91.
(1989). 'Prince of Poets: *Selected Letters of Stephane Mallarme*', in *New York Review*, 9 November, 10–14.
(1990). 'Candles for the Living – Julian Barnes in Bulgaria', in *London Review of Books*, 12: 22, 22 November, 6–7.
(1992). 'The Proudest and Most Arrogant Man in France: *Letters of Gustave Courbert*', *New York Review*, 22 October, 3–5.
(1992). 'How Much is That in Porcupines?', in *The Times*, 24 October, 4–6.
(1993). 'Unlikely Friendship', in *New York Review of Books* 40 (11), 10 June, 5–6, 8, 10, 12.
(1994a). 'The Modernizer', in *New Yorker* 70 (26), 22–29 August, 66–71.
(1994b), 'Romancing Flaubert', in *New York Review of Books* 41, 26 May, 12–16.
(1994c). 'Romancing Flaubert: *Rage and Fire: A Life of Louise Colet, Pioneer Feminist, Literary Star, Flaubert's Muse*', in *New York Review*, 26 May, 12–16.
(1995). 'Odilon Redon', in *Modern Painters*, January, 14–18.
(1996). 'Grand Illusions', in *New York Times Book Review*, 28 January, 9.
(1997a). 'O Unforgetting Elephant', in *New York Review of Books,* 44: 1, 9 January, 23–7.
(1997b). 'Dept. of Dreams: European Solutions to Travel', *New Yorker* 73 (10), 5 May, 90, 92–93, 96–97, 109.
(1997c). 'Paris in the Twentieth Century', *New York Review of Books*, 27 January, 4.
(1997d). ''O Unforgetting Elephant', in *New York Review of Books* 44 (1), 9 January, 23–27.
(1998a). 'No One Suffers as Much', in *Times Literary Supplement*. no. 4994, 18 December, 3–5.

(1998b). 'A Love Affair with Color', *New York Times Book Review*, 29 November, 6.

(1998c). 'The Wise Woman', *New York Review of Books*, 22 October, http://www.nybooks.com/articles/archives/1998/oct/22/the-wise-woman/ [Accessed 5 October 2008].

(1999a). 'One Famous Writer brought him a piece and was told it might serve as cat litter', *Guardian*, 17 April, http://www.guardian.co.uk/books/1999/apr/17/julianbarnes [Accessed 9 September 2007].

(1999b). 'A London View', *Granta*, Issue 65, *London: The Lives of the City*, 176.

(2000a). 'The Afterlife of Arthur Koestler', *New York Review of Books*, 47: 2, 10 February, 23–25.

(2000b). 'Influences: Single-Handed', *New Yorker*, 25 December, 114.

(2000c). 'The Hardest Test: Drugs and the Tour de France', *New Yorker*, 21 and 28 August, 94, 96–100, 102–103.

(2002a). 'French Farce', *Guardian (Review)*, 3 May, 2.

(2002b). 'Pronoun Overboard', *New Yorker* (8 April): 32–33.

(2002c). 'The Worst Reported War Since the Crimean', *Guardian*, 25 February, http://www.guardian.co.uk/media/2002/feb/25/broadcasting.falklands [Accessed 5 July 2008].

(2002d). 'Life Support', *Observer*, 24 February, http://www.observer.co.uk/life/story/0,6903,655997,00.html [Accessed 7 July 2009].

(2003a). 'Lost for Words', *Guardian*, 8 November, 37.

(2003b). 'Flashes of Wisdom in an Age of Chaos', *Guardian*, 4 October, 34.

(2003c). 'When Eriqui Hit Parati', *Guardian*, 16 August, http://books.guardian.co.uk/review/story/0,12084,1019433,00.html [Accessed 6 Ocober 2008].

(2003d). 'Hate and Hedonism', *New Yorker*, 7 July, http://www.newyorker.com/archive/2003/07/07/030707crbo_books [Accessed 5 July 2006].

(2003e). 'Worlds within Words', *Guardian*, 28 June.

(2003f). 'Puritan Pies and Decadent Dinners', *Guardian*, 14 June, http://www.guardian.co.uk/books/2003/jun/14/julianbarnes.houseandgarden [Accessed 7 July 2008].

(2003g). 'Bottom Drawer,' *Guardian*, 7 June, http://www.guardian.co.uk/books/2003/jun/07/julianbarnes.houseandgarden [Accessed 7 July 2008].

(2003h). 'Love One', *Guardian*, 31 May, http://www.guardian.co.uk/books/2003/may/31/julianbarnes.houseandgarden [Accessed 7 July 2008].

(2003i). 'How Beetroot Got Itself Out of a Pickle,' *Guardian*, 24 May, http://www.guardian.co.uk/books/2003/may/24/julianbarnes.houseandgarden. [Accessed 17 April 2010].

(2003j). 'Keep It Simple,' *Guardian*, 17 May, http://www.guardian.co.uk/books/2003/may/17/julianbarnes.houseandgarden [Accessed 7 October 2008].

(2003k). 'Now They Tell Me!,' *Guardian*, 10 May, http://www.guardian.co.uk/books/2003/may/10/julianbarnes.houseandgarden [Accessed 23 July 2009].

(2003l). 'When Once Is Enough,' *Guardian*, 3 May, 36. [Accessed 8 June 2008].

(2003m). 'Are You Being Served?', *Guardian*, 26 April, http://www.guardian.co.uk/books/2003/may/03/julianbarnes.houseandgarden [Accessed 7 July 2008].

REFERENCES

(2003n). 'Take a Green Leaf from These Books', *Guardian*, 19 April, 36.
(2003o). 'Union Blues', *New Yorker*, 79 (9), 21–28 April, 145.
(2003h). 'Picture Perfect', *Guardian*, 12 April, 36.
(2003p). 'Holy Hysteria', *New York Review of Books* 50 (6), 10 April, 32–34.
(2003q). 'Mrs Beeton to the Rescue', *Guardian*, 5 April, 37.
(2003r). 'The Seeds of Rebellion', *Guardian*, 29 March, 37.
(2003s). 'Secrets of the 10-Minute Maestro', *Guardian*, 22 March, 37.
(2003t). 'Size Counts', *Guardian*, 15 March, 37.
(2003u). 'Recipe for Success', *Guardian*, 8 March, 37.
(2003v). 'The Virtues of Precision', *Guardian*, 1 March, 37.
(2003w). 'Sentimental Journeys', *Guardian*, 11 January, 2.
(2005a). 'Always There', *London Review of Books* 27: 24, 15 December, http://www.lrb.co.uk/v27/n24/julian-barnes/always-there [Accessed 3 December 2010].
(2005b). 'Soul Brothers', *Guardian*, 5 November, http://www.guardian.co.uk/books/2005/nov/05/fiction.classics [Accessed 3 December 2010].
(2005c). 'The Road Not Taken', *Guardian*, 8 October, http://www.guardian.co.uk/books/2005/oct/08/julianbarnes.gustaveflaubert [Accessed 3 December 2010].
(2005c). 'Tales from the Confessional', *Guardian*, 2 July, http://www.guardian.co.uk/books/2005/jul/02/classics.julianbarnes [Accessed 3 December 2010].
(2005d). 'When Flaubert Took Wing', *Guardian*, 5 March, 30.
(2006a). 'An Inspector Calls', *Guardian*, 7 July, http://www.guardian.co.uk/books/2007/jul/07/architecture.art [Accessed 3 December 2010].
(2006b). 'Blood and Nerves', *Guardian*, 25 November, http://www.guardian.co.uk/stage/2006/nov/25/theatre.stage [Accessed 3 December 2010].
(2006c). 'The Rebuke', *Guardian*, 30 September, http://www.guardian.co.uk/books/2006/sep/30/fiction.julianbarnes [Accessed 3 December 2010].
(2006d). 'Sherlock Holmes and the Case of the Property Developers', *Guardian*, 8 July, http://www.guardian.co.uk/uk/2006/jul/08/arts.books [Accessed 3 December 2010].
(2006e). 'After the Ball', Times Literary Supplement 5366, 3 February, 3–4.
(2007a). 'An Inspector Calls', *Guardian* (Review), 7 July, 4–6.
(2007a). 'Behind the gas lamp', *London Review of Books*, Vol. 29, 4 October, 9–11.
(2007b) 'Better with their clothes on', *Guardian*, 3 November.
(2007c). 'Christmas books past, present and future: Part one', *Guardian* (Review), 24 November, http://www.guardian.co.uk/books/2007/nov/24/bestbooksoftheyear.bestbooks4 [Accessed 3 December 2010].
(2008a). 'The lost governess: and other gaps in Gustave Flaubert's letters on sex, art, bankruptcy, and the perfect layers of flint', *Times Literary Supplement*, 5476, 14 March, 3–5.
(2008b). ''Cold courtesies', *Times Literary Supplement*, 5588, 3–5, 7 May, 3–5.
(2008c). 'The saddest story', *Guardian* (Review), 7 June, 2–3.
(2008c). 'How did she do it?', *Guardian*, 26 July.
(2008d). 'Brits abroad', *Guardian* (Review), 18 October, 20–21.

(2009a). 'Such, Such Was Eric Blair', *New York Review of Books*, 56 (4), 12 March, http://www.nybooks.com/articles/archives/2009/mar/12/such-such-was-eric-blair/ [Accessed 6 September 2010].
(2009b). 'When in Rome', *Guardian*, 18 April, http://www.nybooks.com/articles/archives/2009/jun/11/flights/ [Accessed 6 September 2010].
(2009c). 'Flights', *New York Review of Books*, 11 June, http://www.nybooks.com/articles/archives/2009/jun/11/flights/ [Accessed 6 September 2010].
(2009d). 'Running Away', *Guardian*, 17 October 2009 http://www.guardian.co.uk/books/2009/oct/17/julian-barnes-john-updike-rabbit [Accessed 6 September 2010].
(2009e). 'On We Sail', *London Review of Books*, 31 (21), 5 November: 25–28 http://www.lrb.co.uk/v31/n21/julian-barnes/on-we-sail [Accessed 6 September 2010].
(2010a). 'A City of Sand and Puddles', *London Review of Books*, 32 (8), 22 April, 9–11.
(2010b). 'Ford Madox Ford's Passionate Affair with Provence', *Guardian*, 21 August, http://www.guardian.co.uk/books/2010/aug/21/ford-madox-ford-provence-julian-barnes [Accessed 6 September 2010].

II Critical Material

Book-length Studies
Childs, P. (2011), *Julian Barnes*. Manchester: Manchester University Press.
Groes, S. and V. Guignery. (2009), 'Worlds within Words: Twenty-first Century Visions on the Work of Julian Barnes', *American, British and Canadian Studies*, 13. Sibiu, Romania: The Academic Anglophone Society of Romania.
Guignery, V. (2006), *The Fiction of Julian Barnes*. London: Palgrave.
Guignery, V. and R. Roberts (eds). (2009), *Conversations with Julian Barnes*. Jackson: University Press of Mississippi.
Holmes, F. M. (2009), *Julian Barnes*. London: Palgrave.
Moseley, M. (1997), *Understanding Julian Barnes*. Columbia: South Carolina: University of South Carolina Press.
Pateman, M. (2002), *Julian Barnes*. Plymouth: Northcote House.
Sesto, B. (2001), *Language, History, and Metanarrative in the Fiction of Julian Barnes. Studies in Twentieth-Century British Literature*, Vol. 3. Amsterdam: Peter Lang.

Selected Books and Book Chapters
Bedggood, D. (2005) (Re)Constituted Pasts: Postmodern Historicism in the Novels of Graham Swift and Julian Barnes. Acheson, J. and Ross, S (eds), *The Contemporary British Novel*. Edinburgh: Edinburgh University Press, 203–16.
Finney, B. (2006), *English Fiction since 1984: Narrating a Nation*. Basingstoke: Palgrave Macmillan. 34–52.

Henstra, S. (2005), "The McReal thing: personal/national identity in Julian Barnes's England, England" in Bentley, N. (ed.) *British Fiction of the 1990s*. London: Routledge, 95–107.

Koenigsberger, K. (2007), *The Novel and the Menagerie: Totality, Englishness, and Empire*. Ohio: Ohio State University Press, 212–17.

Head, D. (2006), "Julian Barnes and a Case of English Identity" in Mengham, R. and P. Tew (eds) (2006), *British Fiction Today*. London: Continuum, 15–27.

Mosely, M. (2006), 'Julian Barnes's *Flaubert's Parrot*' in Shaffer, B. (ed.) *A Companion to the British and Irish Novel 1945–2000*. London: Blackwell, 481–92.

Journal Articles

Aldeheff, A. (2008), 'Julian Barnes and the Raft of Medusa', in *French Review*, 82 (2), 276–91.

Bentley, N. (2007), 'Re-writing Englishness: imagining the nation in Julian Barnes's *England, England* and Zadie Smith's *White Teeth*', in *Textual Practice*, 21 (3), September, 483–506.

Berlatsky, E. (2009), ' "Madame Bovary, c'est moi!": Julian Barnes's *Flaubert's Parrot* and Sexual 'Perversion', in *Twentieth-century Literature*, 55 (2), 175–208.

Bernard, C. (1997), 'A Certain Hermeneutic Slant: Sublime Allegories in Contemporary English Fiction', in Thomas Schaub (ed.), *Contemporary Literature*, 38 (1), Spring, 164–84.

Brooks, N. (2000), 'Interred textuality: *The Good Soldier* and *Flaubert's Parrot* (Ford Madox Ford, Julian Barnes)', in *Critique-Studies in Contemporary Fiction*, 41 (1), 45–51.

Buxton, J. (2000), 'Julian Barnes's theses on history (in 10½ Chapters)', in *Contemporary Literature*, 41 (1), Spring, 56–87.

Candel Bormann, D. (2001), 'Julian Barnes's A History of Science in 10½ Chapters', in *English Studies*, 82 (3), June, 253–61.

Candel Bormann, D. (1998), 'From Romanticism to Postmodernity: Two Different Conceptions of Nature in Julian Barnes' *A History of the World in 10½ Chapters*', in *Revista Canaria de Estudios Ingleses*, 36, 173–83.

Candel Bormann, D. (1999), 'Nature Feminised in Julian Barnes's *A History of the World in 10½ Chapters*', in *Atlantis: Revista de la Asociación Española de Estudios Anglo-Norteamericanos*, XXI, 1 (2), June–December, 43–58.

Cox, E. (2004), "Abstain, and Hide Your Life': The Hidden Narrator of *Flaubert's Parrot*', in *Critique*, 46 (1), Fall, 53–62.

Craps, S. (2006), 'Who lets a big question upset his small, safe world'? British postmodern realism and the question of ethics', in *Zeitschrift fur Anglistik und Amerikanistik*, 54 (3), 287–298.

Dannenberg, H. (2004), 'Obsessions with the past: History and memory in the narrative fiction of Julian Barnes', in *Anglia-Zeitschrift fur Englische Philologie*, 122 (1), 178–80.

Finney, B. (2003), 'A worm's eye view of history: Julian Barnes's *A History of the World in 10½ Chapters*' in *Papers on Language and Literature*, 39 (1), Winter, 49–70.

Forward, S. (1999), 'Chapters in history', in *English Review*, 9 (3), February, 34–37.
Ganteau, J. M. (2007), 'The fiction of Julian Barnes. A reader's guide to essential criticism', in *Etudes Anglaises*, 60 (1), 118.
Goode, M. (2005), 'Knowing seizures: Julian Barnes, Jean-Paul Sartre, and the erotics of the postmodern condition', in *Textual Practice*, 19 (1), September, 149–73.
Guignery, V. (1999), '"My wife . . . died': death by suggestion in Julian Barnes's *Flaubert's Parrot*', in *Etudes britanniques contemporaines*, 17, December, 57–68.
Guignery, V. (2001), '"Re-Vision' and revision of sacred history in the first chapter of Julian Barnes's *A History of the World*', in *Alizes*, 20, July, 67–86.
Guignery, V. (1998), 'Eccentricity and Interlinguism in Julian Barnes's *Metroland* and *Talking it Over*', in *Etudes britanniques contemporaines*, 15, December, 13–24.
Guignery, V. (2001), 'From repetition to emancipation? Flaubertian transtexuality in Julian Barnes's *Flaubert's Parrot*', in *Etudes britanniques contemporaines*, 20, June, 1–17.
Guignery, V. (1997), 'Generic pastiche and palimpsest in Julian Barnes', in *Etudes Anglaises*, 50 (1), 40–52.
Guignery, V. (2001), 'The narretee, or the reader through the looking glass in Julian Barnes's *Flaubert's Parrot*', in *QWERTY*, 11, October, 167–76.
Hamilton, C. (2004), 'Bakhtinian narration in Julian Barnes's *Talking It Over* and *Love, etc.*', in *Imaginaires*, University of Reims, 10, 177–92.
Hateley, E. (2001), 'Erotic Triangles in Amis and Barnes: Negotiations of Patriarchal Power', in *Lateral*, 3. http://www.eng.fju.edu.tw/iacd_2004S/modern_postmodern/reading/Erotic%20Triangles%20in%20Amis%20and%20Barnes.doc [Accessed 4 September 2010].
Hateley, E. (2001), '*Flaubert's Parrot* as Modernist Quest', in *QWERTY*, 11, October, 177–82.
Henke, C and Goer, C. (2000), 'Art and catastrophe. Theodore Gericault's painting 'Flossder Medusa' in Julian Barnes's novel *A history of the world in 10 and a half chapters*', in *Wiemarer Beitrage*, 46 (1), 129–36.
Humphries, Jefferson (1987), '*Flaubert's Parrot* and Huysman's Cricket: The Decadence of Realism and the Realism of Decadence', in *Stanford French Review*, 11 (3), Fall, 323–30.
Johnston, G. (2000), 'Textualising Ellen: the Patriarchal 'I' of *Flaubert's Parrot*', in *Philological Papers*, 46, 64–69.
Kelly, L. (1993), 'The Ocean, The Harbour, The City: Julian Barnes's *A History of the World in 10½ Chapters*', in *Etudes britanniques contemporaines*, 2, June, 1–10.
Kempton, A. (1996), 'A Barnes Eye View of France', in *Franco-British Studies*, 22, Autumn, 92–101.
Kenneth, C. P. (2008), 'Braithwaite's Rules and Barnes's Reversals', in *Notes and Queries*, 55 (4), 507–10.

Kotte, C. (1997), 'Random patterns? Orderly disorder in Julian Barnes's 'A History of the World in 10½ Chapters'', in *Arbeiten aus Anglistik und Amerikanistik*, 22 (1), 107–28.

Krasteva, Y. (2000), 'Julian Barnes' *The Porcupine*: Recent Balkan history under Western eyes', in *Zeitschrift fur Anglistik und Amerikanistik*, 48 (4), 343–53.

Lea, D. (2007), 'Parenthesis' and the unreliable author in Julian Barnes's *A History of the World in 10½ Chapters*', in *Zeitschrift für Anglistik und Amerikanistik*, 555 (4), 379–93.

Meyer, M. (2005), 'Obsessions with the past: History and commemoration in the narrative work of Julian Barnes', in *Zeitschrift fur Anglistik und Amerikanistik*, 53 (1), 99–101.

Miracky, J. J. (2004), 'Replicating a Dinosaur: Authenticity Run Amok in the 'Theme Parking' of Michael Crichton's *Jurassic Park* and Julian Barnes's *England, England*', in *Critique*, 45 (2), Winter, 163–71.

Nuenning, V. (2001), 'The invention of cultural traditions: The construction and deconstruction of Englishness and authenticity in Julian Barnes' *England, England*', in *Anglia-Zeitschrift fur Englische Philologie*, 119 (1), 58–76.

Pedot, R. (1998), 'A journey to the centre of a metaphor: Julian Barnes's *Staring at the Sun*', in *Etudes britanniques contemporaines*, 15, December, 1–11, 117.

Poree, M. (1990), 'Hidden facts since the foundation of the Ark', in *Critique*, 522, November, 900–10.

Raucq-Hoorickx, I. (1991), 'Julian Barnes' *History of the World in 10½ Chapters*: A Levinisian Deconstructionist Point of View', in *Le Langue et l'homme: Recherches pluridisciplinaires sur le langage*, 26 (1), 47–54.

Rubinson, G. J. (2000), 'History's Genres: Julian Barnes's *A History of the World in 10½ Chapters*', in *Modern Language Studies*, 30 (2), 159–79.

Salyer, G. (1991), 'One Good Story Leads to Another: Julian Barnes's *A History of the World in 10½ Chapters*', in *Journal of Literature & Theology*, 5, June, 220–33.

Semino, E. (2004), 'Representing Characters' Speech and Thought in Narrative Fiction: A Study of England, by Julian Barnes', in *Style*, 38 (4), Winter, 428–51.

Shepherd, T. (1997), 'Towards a Description of Atypical Narratives: a Study of the Underlying Organisation of *Flaubert's Parrot*', in *Language and Discourse*, 5, 71–95.

Shiner, L. (1990), '*Flaubert's Parrot*, Agee's *Swan*: From 'Reality Effect' to "Fiction Effect'", in *Journal of Narrative Technique*, 20 (2), 167–78.

Wilson, K. (2006) "Why aren't the books enough?' Authorial Pursuit in Julian Barnes's *Flaubert's Parrot* and *A History of the World in 10½ Chapters*', in *Critique*, 47 (4), Summer, 362–74.

Zwierlein, A. J. (2008), 'The gift of Seeing – "The eyes of faith": Visual evidence and supernatural in Julian Barnes's 'Arthur and George' and other neovictorian detective novels', in *Zeitschrift fur Anglistik und Amerikanistik*, 56 (1), 31–48.

Selected Reviews of Barnes's Work

Metroland
Bailey, P. (1980), 'Settling for Suburbia', in *Times Literary Supplement*, 28 March, 345.
Blishen, E. (1980), 'Growing Up,' in *Times Educational Supplement*, 2 May, 22.
Church, M. (1980), 'Untitled', in *Times* (London), 27 March, 11.
Levin, B. (1980), 'Metroland: Thanks for the Memories', in *Sunday Times* (London), 6 April, 42.
Naughton, J. (1980), 'Smirking', in *Listener*, 27 March, 419.
Parini, J. (1980), 'Two Clever Lads From London,' in *New York Times Book Review*, 92, 3 May, 26.
Sturgess, P. (1980), 'Metroland,' in *Literary Review*, 16–19 May, 10.

Before She Met Me
Abley, M. (1982), 'Watching Green-Eyed', in *Times Literary Supplement*, 23 April: 456.
Greenwell, B. (1982), 'Flashback', in *New Statesman*, 103, no. 2665, 16 April, 18–19.
Krist, G. (1982), 'She Oughtn't to Have Been in Pictures', in *New York Times Book Review*, 91, 28 December, 12.
Montrose, D. (1982), 'Unhappy Families', in *Books and Bookmen*, June, 14.
Reynolds, S. (1982), 'Great White Hopes', in *Punch*, 28 April, 708–09.
Waugh, H. (1982), 'Green-Eyed', in *Spectator* 248, 17 April, 22.

Flaubert's Parrot
Adams, P. (1985), 'Flaubert's Parrot,' in *Atlantic* (02769077), 255 (4), April, 140–42.
Anon. (1985), 'Flaubert's Parrot', in *Virginia Quarterly Review*, 61 (3), Summer, 92.
Bragg, M. (1984), 'In Fine Feather', in *Punch*, 287, October 17, 22–23.
Brooks, P. (1985), 'Obsessed With the Hermit of Croisset', in *New York Times Book Review*, 90, March 10, 7, 9.
Coward, D. (1984), 'The rare creature's human sounds', in *Times Literary Supplement*, 4253, 5 October, 1117.
Hope, M. (1984), 'Pretty Polly', in *Spectator*, 253, November 3, 26–27.
Kermode, F. (1985), 'Obsessed With Obsession', in *New York Review of Books*, 32, April 25, 15–16.
Taliaferro, F. (1985), 'A Flaubertian Flight of Fantasy', in *Wall Street Journal*, April 5, 15.
Updike, J. (1985), 'A Pair of Parrots', in *New Yorker*, 61 (22), July 22, 86–90.

Staring at the Sun
Anon. (1987), 'Staring at the Sun,' in *Virginia Quarterly Review*, 63 (4), Autumn, 131.
Duchêne, A. (1986), 'Chekhov's carrot and other questions', in *Times Literary Supplement*, 4355, 19 September, 1029.

Fuentes, C. (1987), 'The Enchanting Blue Yonder', in *New York Times Book Review*, 92, 12 April, 3, 43.
Hamilton, I. (1986), 'Real Questions,' in *London Review of Books*, 8 (19), 6 November, 7.
Lawson, M. (1986), 'The Genre-Bender Gets it Wrong,' in *Sunday Times*, 28 September, 53.
Lodge, D. (1987), 'The Home Front,' in *New York Review of Books*, 7 May, 21.
McGrath, P. (1987), 'Julian Barnes', in *Bomb*, 21, Fall, 20–23.

A History of the World in 10½ Chapters

Adams, R. (1989), 'Balancing act,' in *New York Review of Books*, 36 (16), 26 October, 7.
Anon. (1989), 'Notes on current books: Fiction', *Virginia Quarterly Review*, 66 (2), Spring, 59.
Kermode, F. (1989), 'Stowaway Woodworm', in *London Review of Books*, 11, 22 June, 20.
Oates, J. C. (1989), 'But Noah was not a nice man', *New York Times Book Review*, 139, 4796, 1 October, 12–14.
Taylor, D. J. (1989), 'A Newfangled and Funny Romp', *Spectator*, 24 June, 40–41.
Wood, M. (1989), 'In search of love and judgment,' *Times Literary Supplement*, 4500, 30 June, 713.
Woods, J. (1989), 'Blinded by the Might', *Times*, 24 June, 36–37.

Talking It Over

Anon. (1992), 'Books', *Antioch Review*, 50 (3), Summer, 599.
Anon. (1991), 'He gave up smoking and irony', *New York Times Book Review*, 141, 4875, 13 October, 9.
Bayley, J. (1991), 'Getting to know you,' *New York Review of Books*, 38 (20), 5 December, 25–27.
Imlah, M. (1991), 'Giving the Authorized Version,' *Times Literary Supplement*, 12 July, 19.
Nicholl, C. (1991), 'Oliver's Riffs', *London Review of Books*, 13, 25 July, 19.
Taylor, D. J. (1991), 'Fearful Symmetry', *New Statesman & Society*, 19 July, 35.
Theroux, A. (1991), 'Was It Something They Said?', *Washington Post Book World*, 21, 13 October, 5.

The Porcupine

Atlas, J. (1992), 'Courtroom Drama', *Vogue*, November, 188, 190.
Bayley, J. (1992), 'Time of indifference', *New York Review of Books*, 39 (21), 17 December, 30–33.
Bell, P. K. (1993), 'Fiction chronicle', in *Partisan Review*, 60 (1), Winter, 63–78.
Byrne, J. (1993), 'Book reviews', *Review of Contemporary Fiction*, 13 (2), Summer, 252–54.
Duplain, J. (1992), 'The Big Match', *New Statesman & Society*, 13 November, 34–35.

Flower, D. (1993), 'Politics and the novel', *Hudson Review*, 46 (2), Summer, 394–402.
Harris, R. (1992), 'Full of Prickles', *Literary Review*, November, 26.
Kemp, P. (1992), 'Show trial, new style,' *Times Literary Supplement*, 4674, 30 October, 19.
King, F. (1992), 'Not Deep, but Crisp and Even', *Spectator*, 7 November, 55–56.
Kord, C. (1993), 'Books: Book reviews,' *Antioch Review*, 51 (3), Summer, 458–60.
Maier, F. (1993), 'Book reviews,' *America*, 168 (21), 19–26 June, 22–24.
Puddington, A. (1993), 'After the fall', *Commentary*, 95 (5), May, 62–5.
Stone, R. (1992), 'The Cold Peace', *New York Times Book Review*, 142, 49–179, 13 December http://www.nytimes.com/1992/12/13/books/the-cold-peace.html?scp=1&sq=cold+peace+&st=nyt [Accessed 3 December 2010].

Letters from London

Buckley, D. (1995), 'Little England, Big Apple', *Observer*, 9 April, 18.
Buruma, I. (1996), 'Mrs. Thatcher's revenge,' *New York Review of Books*, 43 (5), 21 March, 22–28.
Cockburn, P. (1995), 'I-Spy things unravelling,' *Times Literary Supplement*, 4803, 21 April, 32.
Dyer, G. (1995), 'City of Schoolboys,' *Manchester Guardian Weekly*, 16 April, 28.
Lawson, M. (1995), 'Marmite for New Yorkers,' *Independent*, 8 April, 26.
Paxman, J. (1995), 'London Calling', *Sunday Times*, 9 April, 1–2. Cross Channel.
Anon. (1996), 'Notes on current books: Fiction,' *Virginia Quarterly Review*, 72 (4), Autumn, 132.
Arana-Ward, M. (1996), 'Julian Barnes', *Washington Post Book World*, 19 May, 10.
Furbank, P. N. (1996), 'If the French Were Shorter in Flaubert's Day, Did They Need to Be Less Fat in Order to Be Called 'Fat'?', *London Review of Books*, 18, 4 January, 22.
Hutchings, W. (1997), 'World literature in review: English', World Literature Today, 71 (1), Winter, 149–51.
Kakutani, M. (1996), 'Fictional Fiction Writer Demonstrates His Magic,' *New York Times*, 16 April, C-15.
Kempton, A. (1996), 'A Barnes Eye View of France', *Franco-British Studies*, 22, Autumn, 92–101.
Kennedy, J. (1997), 'Books: A Russian view of the Cold War,' *Antioch Review*, 55 (1), Winter, 110.
Mangan, G. (1996), 'Tres british', *Times Literary Supplement*, 4842, 19 January, 24.
Patten, J. (1996), 'Book reviews', *Country Life*, 190 (11), 14 March, 60.
Wood, M. (1996), 'Another country', *New York Times Book Review*, 145, 50404, 21 April, 12.

England, England

Anon. (1998), 'Exiles from history,' in *Economist*, 349 (8089), 10 October, 89–90.
Anon. (1999), 'Notes on Current Books: Fiction', *Virginia Quarterly Review*, 75 (4) Autumn, 129.

Bradshaw, P. (1998), 'England, England', *London Evening Standard*, 24 August.
Carey, J. (1998), 'Land of Make-Believe', *Sunday Times*, 23 August.
Cowley, J. (1998), 'England, your England', *New Statesman*, 127, 4402, 11 September, 44–46.
Cunningham, V. (1998), 'England, England,' *Independent*, 29 August.
Dening, P. (1998), 'Inventing England', *Irish Times*, 8 September. [Includes interview with Barnes].
Eder, R. (1999), 'Tomorrowland', in *New York Times Book Review*, 148, 51517, 9 May, 17.
Flower, D. (2000), 'Cynicism and its discontents', in *Hudson Review*, 52 (4), Winter, 657–65.
Hutchings, W. (2000), 'England, England', *World Literature Today*, 74 (1), Winter, 156.
Kakutani, M. (1999), "England, England': England as Theme Park,' *New York Times*, 11 May, B7.
Kennedy, J. 'Books', in *Antioch Review*, 58 (1), Winter, 117.
Lanchester, J. (1998), 'A Vision of England', *Electronic Telegraph*, 29 August. [Includes interview with Barnes].
Landon, P. (1999), 'Book Reviews,' in *Review of Contemporary Fiction*, 19 (3), Fall, 174.
Roberts, R. (1998), "England, England' (Reply to Tom Shippey's review of Julian Barnes's new novel)', in *Times Literary Supplement*, 4981, 19.
Shippey, T. (1998), 'A better bogus', in *Times Literary Supplement*, 4978, 28 August, 22.
Thwaite, A. (1998), 'Buying up Buck House', *Electronic Telegraph*, 29 August.
Veale, S. (2000), 'New & Noteworthy Paperbacks', *New York Times Book Review*, 149, 51367, 23 April, 24.
Wiegand, D. (1999), 'England Imagined as a Theme Park in Julian Barnes' Witty Satire', *San Francisco Chronicle*, 23 May, 3.
Wood, M. (1999), 'Tight little hand', *New York Review of Books*, 46, 11, 24 June, 56–60.

Love, etc.

Adams, T. (2000), 'The Eternal Triangle,' *Observer*, 23 July, http://www.guardian.co.uk/books/2000/jul/23/fiction.julianbarnes [Accessed 3 December 2010].
Anderson, J. (2001), "Love medicine,' Etc. (Response to Sven Birkerts' review of Julian Barnes's novel 'Love, etc.')', *New York Times Book Review* (2001), 4.
Annan, G. (2001), 'Act Two', in *New York Review of Books*, 48 (6), 12 April, 16.
Anon. (2001), 'And Bear In Mind,' in *New York Times Book Review*, 150, 51682, 4 March, 30.
Anon. (2000), 'The rest of it,' in *Economist*, 356, 8183, 12 August, 75.
Benfer, A. (2001), '"Love, etc." by Julian Barnes', *Salon.com*, 21 February, http://www.salon.com/books/review/2001/02/21/barnes [Accessed 9 July, 2010].
Birkerts, S. (2001), 'Talking It Over Some More,' in *New York Times Book Review*, 150, 51675, 25 February, 8.

Coldstream, J. (2000), "I'd be very jumpy if I wasn't writing", *Daily Telegraph*, 27 July.
Herbert, S. (2000), 'Hello! We've met before', *Daily Telegraph*, 22 July, 4.
Hutchings, W. (2001), 'Love, etc. (Book Review)', in *World Literature Today*, 75 (2), Spring, 329.
Imlah, M. (2000), 'Revenge of a tortoise', in *Times Literary Supplement*, 5078, 28 July, 19.
Kakutani, M. (2001), 'An Old Love Triangle Reassembled in a New Decade', *New York Times*, 9 February, E-45.
Landon, P. (2001), 'Love', in *Review of Contemporary Fiction*, 21 (2), Summer, 167.
Shilling, J. (2000), 'A trio for married voices', *Sunday Telegraph*, 23 July, 13.
Taylor, D. J. (2000), 'Not the end of the affair', *Sunday Times*, 30 July.
Veale, S. (2002), 'New & Noteworthy Paperbacks', *New York Times Book Review*, 151, 52186, 21 July, 20.
Wroe, N. (2000), 'Literature's Mister Cool', *Guardian*, 29 July, http://www.guardian.co.uk/books/2000/jul/29/fiction [Accessed 3 December 2010].

Something to Declare

Clarke, N. (2002), 'Le vrai Barnes', *New Statesman*, 131, 4570, 14 January, 53.
Cowley, J. (2002), 'New Gauls, Please', *Observer*, 6 January, 15. Reprinted in the *Manchester Guardian Weekly*, 29 January, 17.
De Botton, A. (2001), 'The French Master,' *Sunday Times*, 30 December.
Dyer, G. (2002), 'All aboard the Eurostar,' *Guardian*, 5 January, 8.
Heptonstall, G. (2002), 'A Francophile on France,' in *Contemporary Review*, 281, 1639, August, 116.
Hooper, B. (2002), 'Something to Declare: Essays on France', *Booklist*, 99 (2), 15 September, 202.
Messud, C. (2002), 'Tour de France', in *New York Times Book Review*, 152, 52263, 6 October, 25.
Strange, A. J., Koop, M. (2004), 'Something to Declare: Essays on France (Book)', in *French Review*, 77 (5), April, 1049–50.
Tindall, G. (2002), 'Monsieur Barnes crosses the Channel', *Times Literary Supplement*, 5157, 1 February, 36.

The Pedant in the Kitchen

Beachcomber. (2003), '86 Years Old and Still Cooking Up a Treat', *Express*, 22 October, 44.
Caplan, N. (2003), 'Barnes's Tasty New Recipe', *London Evening Standard*, 21 October.
Davidson, M. (2003), 'Flaubert's Carrots', *Sunday Telegraph*, 26 October, 15.
Fort, M. (2003), 'Too Much of a Good Thing', *Observer*, 2 November, 15.
Jakeman, J. (2003), 'The best possible taste', *Times Literary Supplement*, 5253, 5 December, 29.
Rumbold, J. (2003), 'What Jamie Could Teach Julian', *Guardian*, 15 October, 5.
Taylor, A. (2003), 'Simple Recipes Should Be Made to Measure', *Sunday Herald*, 19 October, 11.

The Lemon Table

Anon. (2004), 'And Bear In Mind', in *New York Times Book Review*, 153, 52907, 11 July, 22.

Clark, A. (2004), 'Age before Beauty.' *Sunday Times*, 7 March, 53.

Craig, A. (2004), 'Do not go gentle', *New Statesman*, 133 (4679), 15 March, 55.

Harding, J. (2004), 'New Fiction', *Daily Mail*, 12 March, 56.

Hore, R. (2004), 'To the Bitter End', *Literary Review*, March.

Johnson, D. (2004), 'Stiff Upper Lip', *New York Review of Books*, 51 (16), 21 October, 26.

Kermode, F. (2004), 'Age Has Not Withered Him', *Guardian*, 13 March, 26.

Mallon, T. (2004), 'As Young as You Feel', *New York Times Book Review*, 153, 52893, 27 June, 7.

Massie, A. (2004), 'Tremors at Twilight', *Scotsman*, 13 March, 9.

McFarlane, R. (2004), 'The greater and the lesser pain', *Times Literary Supplement*, 5267, 12 March, 19–20.

Merritt, S. (2004), 'Things Can Only Get Bitter', *Observer*, 14 March.

Moore, C. (2004), 'How to Pass the Acid Test'. *Sunday Telegraph*, 7 March, 16.

Seaman, D. (2004), 'The Lemon Table (Book)', *Booklist*, 100 (19/20), 15 June, 1697.

Tayler, C. (2004), 'Like choosing between bacon and egg and bacon and tomato', *London Review of Books*, 26 (8), 15 April, 17–18.

Taylor, A. (2004), 'Every Second Counts When the End Is Nigh', *Sunday Herald*, 21 March.

Wroe, A. (2004), 'Longing to be Noticed', *Daily Telegraph*, 13 March, 3.

Arthur and George

Anon. (2005), 'The law was blind, and Sir Valiant too' *Economist*, 376 (8434) 9 July, 74.

Barnes, J. (2005), 'The pig-chaser's tale', *Times Literary Supplement*, 5336, 8 July, 19.

Berger, J. (2007), 'Arthur & George', Psychiatric Services, 58 (12), 1613–14.

Bernard, A. (2007), 'The Casual Reader', *Kenyon Review*, 29 (2), Spring, 2–10.

Bernstein, S. (2006), 'Arthur & George', *Review of Contemporary Fiction*, 26 (1), Spring, 146.

Garner, D. (2006), 'TBR: Inside the List', *New York Times Book Review*, 155 (53481), 5 February, 22.

Hanks, R. (2005), 'Elementary, my dear Barnes', *Independent*, Arts & Books Review, 8 July, 20–21.

Lanchester, J. (2006), 'A Matter of English Justice', *New York Review of Books*, 53 (6) 6 April, 12–14.

Rafferty, T. (2006), 'The Game's Afoot' *New York Times Book Review*, 155 (53460), 15 January, 1–11.

Seaman, D. (2006), 'Arthur & George', *Booklist*, 102 (9/10), 1 January, 22.

Tait, T. (2005), 'Twinkly', *London Review of Books*, 27 (17), 1 September, 25–26.

Taylor, I. (2007), 'Paperback Row', *New York Times Book Review*, 156 (53824), 14 January, 24.

Winder, R. (2005), 'Bumps in the night', *New Statesman*, 134 (4748), 11 July, 49–50.

Nothing To Be Frightened Of
Barber, L. (2008), 'Julian Barnes Dances around Death', *Telegraph*, 5 March.
Beresford, L. (2008), 'Intimations of Mortality', *New Statesman*, 6 March.
Carey, J. (2008), 'Nothing to Be Frightened Of by Julian Barnes', *Sunday Times*, 2 March.
Dirda, M. (2008), 'Memento mori', *Washington Post*, 31 August, BW10.
Eder, R. (2008), 'Darkness visible', *Boston Globe*, 31 August, C5.
Hennessy, V. (2008), 'Sorry but dying's a dead cert', *Mail on Sunday*, 14 March.
Heinegg, P. (2009), 'Alas, Poor Julian', *America*, 200 (1), 32–34.
Keillor, G. (2008), 'Dying of the Light', *New York Times Book Review*, 3 October, 1.
Lalasz, R. (2009), 'Nothing To Be Frightened Of', *Virginia Quarterly Review*, Vol.85 (1), 245.
Miller, R. E. (2009), 'Nothing To Be Frightened Of, and: Final Exam: A Surgeon's Reflections on Mortality, and: Swimming in a Sea of Death: A Son's Memoir', *Literature and Medicine*, Spring, 28,1, 172–82.
Spurling, H. (2008), 'Colder but wiser', *Guardian*, 2 March.
Shilling, J. (2008), 'Julian Barnes: Nothing to be Frightened of' *Sunday Times*, 7 March.
Tayler, C. (2008), 'Into the Void', *Guardian Review*, 8 March.

Interviews and Profiles
Anon. (2006), 'An Interview With Julian Barnes', http://www.abebooks.co.uk, February.
Anon. 'Bibliofile: featuring Julian Barnes.' *Sunday Times*, 30 August 1998.
Anon. 'Shelf Life: Julian Barnes.' *Scotland on Sunday* (13 January 2002).
Anon. (2002), 'You ask the questions: Julian Barnes', *Independent*, 16 January.
Anon. (2005), 'Julian Barnes: Arthur & George,' *New Zealand Herald*, 21 August.
Anon. (1998), 'He's turned towards Python. (But not the dead Flaubert's Parrot sketch . . . ' *Observer (Review)*, 30 August, 15.
Anon. (1995), 'Windows on to the French', *Bookseller*, 27 October, 26–27.
Barnes, J. (2001), 'My Team Leicester City', *Observer Sport Monthly*, 5 August, 61.
Barnes, J. (2002), 'The Books Interview', *Observer*, 19 May, 17.
Baum, C. 'Shaken and Not Stirred', *Sydney Morning Herald*, 14 February, 9.
Behe, R. (2006), 'Reconstructing a Case', *Pittsburgh Tribune-Review*, 22 January.
David, L. (2008), 'We made up the Bible as a good novel', *Liverpool Daily Post*, 11 June, 18–19.
Denning, P. 'Inventing England', *Irish Times*, 8 September, 12.
Edwards, B. (1999), 'Julian Barnes on His New Novel *England, England*', *Morning Edition*, National Public Radio, 26 May.
Eichenberger, B. (2006), 'Q&A – Julian Barnes', *Columbus Dispatch*, 25 January, 4.
Freeman, J. (2006), 'Elementary Justice: Julian Barnes Discusses *Arthur & George*', *New City Chicago*, 31 January.

REFERENCES

Guppy, S. (2006), 'The art of fiction CLXV, An interview with Julian Barnes', in Paris *Review*, 157, 54–84.

Hawtree, C. (1996), 'Novel Escape', *Times*, 13 January, 18–19, 21–22.

Hayman, R. (1980), 'Julian Barnes in Interview', *Books & Bookmen*, May 1980, 36–37.

Hazleton, L. (1999), 'Julian Barnes Is Just a Normal Guy', *Seattle Times*, 12 April, E1.

Kastor, E. (1987), 'Julian Barnes' Big Questions: The British Novelist Tackling the Unknown', *Washington Post Book World*, 18 May, B1, B9.

Kellaway, K. (1996), 'The Grand Fromage Matures', *Observer Review*, 7 January, 7.

Lancaster, J. (1998), 'A Vision of England', *Daily Telegraph*, 29 August, 5.

Lanham, F. (2006), 'Fact and Fiction', *The Houston Chronicle*, 23 January, 1.

March, M. (1997), 'Into the Lion's Mouth: A Conversation with Julian Barnes', *New Presence*, December, http://www.new-presence.cz/article.php/?str=3 [Accessed 3 December 2010].

McCloskey, J. (2005), 'Julian Barnes in Conversation', *Brooklyn Rail*, September.

McMahon, R. (2002), 'There's something about France (Q & A: Julian Barnes)', San *Francisco Chronicle*, 6 October, 2.

O'Connell, John. (2008), 'Julian Barnes: Interview.' *Time Out*, 13 March, http://www.timeout.com/london/books/features/4416/Julian_Barnes-interview.html [Accessed 3 December 2010].

O'Hagan, S. (2002), 'Interview: Julian Barnes – I May Not Like It Much, But I Still Live Here', *Independent on Sunday* , 1 December.

O'Regan, N. (2003), 'Cool, Clean Man of Letters', *Sunday Business Post*, 29 June.

Poole, S. (1998), 'Why Don't We Make It All Up?', *Independent*, 30 August, 10.

Renzetti, E. (2005), 'Down at the Pub with Julian', *Globe and Mail*, 6 October.

Saunders, K. (1989), 'From Flaubert's Parrot to Noah's woodworm', *Sunday Times*, 18 June, G8–9.

Seiler, C. (2006), 'Sir Arthur Investigates', *Times Union* (Albany, NY), 29 January, J1.

Sinclair, M. (1986), 'Julian Barnes', *Zigzag*, 3 (5), February.

Smith, A. (1989), 'Julian Barnes', *Publisher's Weekly*, 236 (18), 3 November, 73–74.

Stoop. (2002), 'Interviews: Julian Barnes', http://www.bookmunch.co.uk, 3 June.

Stout, M. (1992), 'Chameleon Novelist', *New York Times Review of Books*, 22 November, 29, 68 – 72, 80.

Stuart, A. (1989), 'Endpapers: A Talk with Julian Barnes', *Los Angeles Times*, 15 October, 15.

Summerscale, K. (2008), 'Julian Barnes: Life as he knows it', *Telegraph*, 1 March.

Swanson, C. (1996), 'Old Fartery and Literary Dish', *Salon Magazine*, 13 May.

Thomas, R. (2006), 'A Long Way from Holmes', *Capital Times* (Madison, WI), 3 February.

Timberg, S. (2001), 'A Tip of the Hat to Kurosawa', *Hartford Courant*, 28 January.

Webb, A. (2002), 'Barnes and France: Love Requited', *BBC Online: Arts*, 18 January, http://news.bbc.co.uk/1/hi/entertainment/1766800.stm [Accessed 19 August 2009].

Websites

http://www.julianbarnes.com – Ryan Roberts's meticulously maintained official site.

http://www.facebook.com/pages/Julian-Barnes/27851631393 – Julian Barnes's Facebook page.

http://www.contemporarywriters.com/authors/?p=auth1 [Profile and Critical Overview].

http://www.litencyc.com/php/speople.php?rec=true&UID=267 [Critical Overview by Merritt Moseley].

Index

1960s 21–3
1968 (May) 16–18, 21
1970s 22

Ackroyd, Peter 50
adultery 78
afterlife 62
ambiguity 21, 24
Amis, Kingsley 43, 74
Amis, Martin 52
anglicism 41
anxiety of influence 47–8
art 20
Arthur & George (play) 2
atheism 8, 51–68
Augustine 65
  Confessions 65
authorial intention 33
authorship 26, 32, 34–5
autobiography 39, 63, 130

bad faith 19
Balzac, Honoré de 7
Bakhtin, Mikhail 45
Barnes, Djuna 118
Barnes, Jonathan 39
Barnes, Julian
  Arthur & George 2, 5, 6, 9, 10, 52, 62–5, 68, 104, 117–33
  Before She Met Me 6, 9
  'Candles for the Living' 83
  Cross Channel 8, 37, 42, 69, 70, 103
  Duffy Omnibus, The 1
  England, England 2, 6, 9, 46, 64, 92–102, 119
  Flaubert's Parrot 1, 2, 9, 12–13, 24–36, 37, 43, 45, 46, 49, 69, 82, 83, 93, 108, 117–18, 119, 129
  History of the World in 10 ½ Chapters, A 1, 5, 9, 13, 42, 43, 52, 58–62, 64, 66, 67, 82, 85, 103, 119
  In the Land of Pain (translator) 3, 43, 48

Lemon Table, The 8, 31–2, 55, 82, 103–10, 114
Letters from London 6, 70, 74
Love, etc 37, 41
Metroland 2, 4, 9, 11–23, 34, 35, 37, 40, 41, 42, 43, 46, 73, 74, 104, 118
Nothing To Be Frightened Of 8, 9, 10, 37, 41–2, 43, 44, 52, 65–8, 104, 106, 109–10, 119
Porcupine, The 4–5, 7, 9, 81–91
Pulse 8, 9, 81, 82, 103, 110–16
Something to Declare 37, 38, 40, 41, 43, 49, 72
Staring at the Sun 6, 9, 52–7, 58, 61, 66
Talking it Over 2, 4, 9, 37, 40, 41, 75–80
Truth about Dogs, The (translator) 3
Barstow, Stan 92
Barth, John 49
Battle of Britain 94
Baudelaire, Charles 4, 13, 39, 41, 43, 45, 118
  Les Fleurs du Mal 35
  'The Painter of Modern Life' 13
Baudrillard, Jean 46
Bayley, Peter 44
Benjamin, Walter 13, 14
Berberich, Christine 3, 5, 9, 117–28, 132, 133
Berlin Wall 82
Bible, The 8, 58–62
Bildungsroman 52
biography 9, 24–5, 29–32, 36, 121, 129–33
Blair, Tony 5
Blanch, Lesley 129
  The Wilder Shores of Love 129
Bloom, Harold 47
Bonnard, Pierre 45
Booker Prize 9
bourgeoisie 11–12, 16–17, 23

INDEX

Bowlby, Rachel 14
   Virginia Woolf 14
Bradford, Richard 3, 6, 8, 92–102, 119
Braine, John 92
Brassens, Georges 38
Brel, Jacques 38
Brown, Callum 51
Browning, Robert 28
Brezhnev, Leonid 85, 87
Broch, Hermann 7
Bulgaria 5, 7, 82, 83, 85, 87, 91
Byatt, A. S. 50

Camus, Albert 42, 43, 74
Carey, John 15, 19
   The Intellectuals and the Masses 15
Caroline, Sarah 93–7
Cavalié, Elsa 119
Cavazza, Boris 2
Ceausescu, Nicolae 87
Cervantes, Miguel de 6, 7
Chamfort, Nicolas 4, 79
Channel, The 69
Childs, Peter 3, 8, 62, 103–16
Christian tradition 55, 58, 66
cinema 40
   nouvelle vague 40
Cokan, Valerija 2
Cold War 4, 7, 82
Coleridge, Samuel Taylor 28
Colet, Louise 29
Collins, Wilkie 122
Communism 82
Conan Doyle, Arthur 9, 10, 63–6, 118–33
   Memories and Adventures 63
confession 66
connoisseur 108
consumerism 62
Cooke, Alistair 71
cosmopolitan 11
Courbet, Gustave 45
Cowan, Andrew 92
   Pig 92
Cowper Powys, John 6
   A Glastonbury Romance 6
Crosland, Tony 15

Daily Express, The 98
Daily Mail, The 98
Daily Telegraph, The 125

Darling, Julia 93
Daudet, Alphonse 3, 42, 43, 44, 48, 50
   La Doulou 50
   Letters From My Windmill 44
   Tartarin de Tarascon 44
Dawkins, Richard 8, 66
De Gaulle, Charles 72
death 44, 55, 103–5, 109–10
Debord, Guy 17, 46
Degas, Edgar 45
Dérive 17
detective fiction 65, 121
dialogism 45–8
Dickens, Charles 55, 74, 122
   Old Curiosity Shop, The 55
   Our Mutual Friend 74
Diderot, René 45
Drabble, Margaret 83
Dreyfus case 119
Durrell, Lawrence 20
   Mountolive 20
dystopia 63

Eagleton, Terry 51
East Anglia 96
Edalji, George 9, 63–6, 118–33
Edgar, David 2
Eliot, George 56
   Middlemarch 56
Eliot, T. S. 14, 25, 46
   'Burnt Norton' 106
   The Waste Land 14
   'Tradition and the Individual Talent' 46
Elizabeth II 90
Englishness 92–102, 124
ennui (boredom) 13
essayistic tradition 41–3
Europe 71–2
European tradition 7
Existentialism 17
experimentation 6

family 12, 19–20
fictional truth 24–36
Fielding, Henry 45
flâneur 4, 12, 13–15, 19, 23
Flaubert, Gustave 4, 7, 24–36, 37, 38, 42, 45, 46, 47, 50, 108
   Dictionary of Accepted Ideas 47

Madame Bovary 27, 31, 33–6, 48
Un Coeur simple 25, 108
Flint, Kate 20
Forster, E. M. 6, 15, 105
   Abinger Pageant 6
   England's Pleasant Land 6
Francophilia 6, 37, 41, 45, 69–80
Frankl, Georg 22
   The Failure of the Sexual Revolution 22
free choice 19, 106
French literature 3–4, 12, 37–50

Gautier, Théophile 13, 39
Genesis 58, 59
Géricault, Théodore 59
Gide, André 43
Godard, Jean-Luc 40
Golding, William 28
   The Lord of the Flies 28
Goncourt, Edmond and Jules de 42, 45
Gorbachov, Mikhail 85, 90
Greene, Graham 15
Gregory, Philippa 121
Griffiths, Niall 93
Grossmith, George and Weedon 18
   The Diary of a Nobody 18
Guignery, Vanessa 2, 3, 4, 24, 25, 33, 37–50, 78, 127

Harris, Robert 90
Hawes, James 92
   Speak for England 92
Hawkins, Louise (Touie) 125, 130
Hawthorne, Nathaniel 113
Head, Dominic 3, 51, 118
Hebrews (Bible) 65
hedonism 74
historical novel 5, 117–19, 123, 128
Hitler, Adolf 98
Hobsbawm, Eric 22
Hodges, Adrian 2
Holmes, Frederick 3, 6, 118, 126–7
Holocaust 59
Holroyd, Michael 84
Hornung, E. W. 130
Houellebecq, Michel 43
Hutcheon, Linda 49, 118

intertextuality 47–9, 132
irony 21, 46

Johnson, Samuel 73, 93
Jonah (Bible) 60
Joseph-Vilain, Mélanie 32
journalism 36
Joyce, James 7, 12, 56, 118
   Dubliners 56

Kafka, Franz 7
Kavanagh, Pat 82, 84, 129
Keats, John 56
Kermode, Frank 65
Kierkegaard, Søren 56, 57
Kondeva, Dimitrina 3, 4, 5, 7, 81–91
Kriegel, Volker 3
Kundera, Milan 7

La Rochefoucauld, François de 43
Larkin, Philip 74
Lawrence, D. H. 20
   Lady Chatterley's Lover 20
Leckie, Jean 125, 130, 131
Lee, Hermione 49
Levenson, Michael 76
London 11–23, 93
London Review of Books 25, 29
love 20, 61–2
Love, etc (film) 2
Lycett, Andrew 8–9, 129–33

Mallarmé, Stéphane 13, 19, 45
Manet, Edouard 45
Mann, Thomas 7
Mantel, Hilary 121
Mao Tse-Tung 111
marriage 12, 20–2, 61, 110–11, 125–6
materialism 51
Masterman, C. F. G. 15
Matisse, Henri 45
Maupassant, Guy de 43, 129
Mauriac, François 42, 43
Mayle, Peter 76
   Toujours Provence 76
McEwan, Ian 8, 52
metafiction 2
Metroland 15–16
Metroland (film) 2, 20

Meudal, Gérard 71
Michelangelo 61
modernism 46
Monnet, Jean 72
monogamy 21
Montaigne, Michel de 42, 43, 45
Moseley, Merritt 3, 4, 32, 69–80
Murray, John 93
music 104–5
Musil, Robert 7

Nabokov, Vladimir 27
Napoleon 14, 98
Nash, John 14
nationalism 63, 70, 96
Nazism 95
neo-Victorian novel 38, 46
Nerval, Gérard de 39
New Atheism 66
New Atheist Novel 52
New Labour 5, 100
New Statesman,The 28, 30
New York Times 30
New Yorker, The 110
Noach (Bible) 60, 61
nostalgia 70
novel of ideas 52

Orwell, George 16
  Coming Up for Air 16

pageant play 6
palimpsest 45, 46
Paris 11–23
Parsons, Deborah 14
  Streetwalking the Metropolis 14
pastiche 64
Pateman, Matthew 7, 32, 58
patriotism 96, 98
Pearsall, Simon 2
pedagogy 98–9
philistinism 15
postcolonial fiction 96
  postmodernism 2–3, 5, 6, 12–13, 32, 45, 117–18, 122
prayer 53
Princess Diana 98
Proust, Marcel 7
Psalms 53
Pushkin, Alexander 27

rationality 55, 57, 105
Reagan, Nancy 90
realism 5, 122, 125–6
Redon, Odilon 45
Reid, Mayne 130
religion 51–68
Renard, Jules 4, 42, 44, 45, 50, 67
  Journals 44
  Poil de Carotte 44
retro-Victorian novel 38, 46, 119
Revalation (Bible) 58, 62
revolutions (French) 16
Rhys, Jean 9
  Wide Sargasso Sea 9
Richardson, Samuel 6
Ricks, Christopher 28
Rimbaud, Arthur 4, 13, 39, 43, 73
Ritchie, June 73
Roberts, Ryan 2, 3, 24–36
Rushdie, Salman 118
Rutherfurd, Edward 121

St George 100
St Louis 59
Salyer, Gregory 60
Sand, George 45
Sartre, Jean-Paul 17, 29, 31, 43
  Being and Nothingness 17, 49
  The Family Idiot 29, 49
satire 18
Saville, Philip 2
Scanlon, Hugh 28
scepticism 64–5, 67
Schneider, Ana-Karina 123, 128
science 64
Sebald, W. G. 121
sex 20–1, 105–7, 115
sexual revolution 21–2
Shakespeare, William
  Henry V 97
short stories 103–16
Sibelius, Jean 105, 107, 110
Sillitoe, Alan 92
simulacrum 46
Sinatra, Frank 90
Situationist International 17
smoking 112
society of the spectacle 46
spiritualism 8–9
Stalin, Joseph 7, 86–7

INDEX

Starkie, Enid 32
Stefanova, Julia 88
Stein, Gertrude 12
Stendhal 42, 67
Sterne, Laurence 6, 45, 47
  Tristram Shandy 45, 47
Stevens, Wallace 67
Stevenson, Robert Louis 30
Stoppard, Tom 9
  Rosencrantz and Guildenstern are Dead 9
Storey, David 92
Stout, Mira 2, 6
Stravinsky, Igor 107
suburbia 11, 14–15, 20
Summerscale, Kate 122
Swinburne, C. A. 73, 96
Swift, Graham 93
  Waterland 96

Tate, Andrew 3, 8, 9, 51–68, 132
  The New Atheist Novel (with Arthur Bradley) 8, 52
Taunton, Matthew 3, 4, 5, 11–23, 118
  Fictions of the City 16
Tennyson, Lord Alfred 28
  'The Charge of the Light Brigade' 28
Thackeray, William 74
thanatophobia 55
Thatcher, Margaret 4, 23
Thatcherism 23
Thomas, Edward 100–1
  'Adlestrop' 100–1
Thorpe, Adam 96–7
  Ulverton 96–7
Times Literary Supplement 129
Tolstoy, Leo 7

tourist vision 93
Tournier, Michel 43
Trewin, Ion 129
Truffaut, François 40, 78, 79
  Jules et Jim 40, 78, 79
Turgenev, Ivan 106–7

Updike, John 57
  Roger's Version 57
unreliable narrator 27, 30

Verlaine, Paul 4, 39, 43
Vernoux, Marion 2
Victorians 16
Voltaire 41, 42, 43, 73
Vuillard, Édouard 45

Wain, John 28
Waterhouse, Keith 92
Watson, Emily 20
Welsh, Irvine 97
  Trainspotting 97
Werner, Oskar 78
Wilhelm II 98
Wilson, Keith 32
working-class fiction 92–3
Wood, James 52
Woolf, Virginia 6
  Between the Acts 6

Yeats, W. B. 28, 54
  'An Irish Airman Foresees his Death' 54
Yevtushenko, Yevgeny 27

Zhivkov, Todor 82, 84, 85, 89, 90, 91
Zola, Émile 13, 42